Passing Through the Eye of a Needle

By

Michael Hilliard Patterson

This book is a work of fiction. Places, events, and situations in this story are purely fictional. Any resemblance to actual persons, living or dead, is coincidental.

ISBN: 0-7596-6753-5 (electronic)
ISBN: 0-7596-6754-3 (softcover)

This book is printed on acid free paper.

1st Books - rev. 08/05/02

Chapter ONE

My name is John Fairfax. I am a recovering addict. I have chosen to recover in a twelve-step program. For several years a group of us (recovering addicts) have lived on a farm. We help others who are getting off drugs to start over. We live like we were a giant old fashion farm family, complete with old fashion values. We were good neighbors. The people in the surrounding area became very fond of us. They would come from all the near-by cities and towns to help us out and enjoy open house at the farm...we always had a great time. We still hold a flea market to raise money for expenses. We grow and can vegetables for sale and for our use at the farm during the off-season. We also sell other items and rent spaces to others so they can sell their wares. On those weekends the farm is a beehive of activity.

On a day a few years ago that had begun as uneventfully as any ordinary day. Somehow, took on an air of perfection as the hours passed and everything went exactly as we planned. Ordinarily, that would have been a warning of impending doom for me but not this time. I guess my outlook was getting better. We had more people show up than ever before. The weather was as beautiful as any spring day I had ever seen... and I really love springtime. There was a beauty in that spring day that surpassed the warm feeling of the sun as it caressed the skin on the back of my neck. It ran deeper than the loveliness of nature with all of the newly blooming greenery. Everything around us held so many possibilities, another chance to enjoy life after a harsh winter. I think that the men at the farm could see a parallel between their lives just by looking around them in the spring. God starts His world anew, through some magical process, all of nature comes back to life. Everything on God's earth is resurrected. His power to renew life seems so apparent in the springtime. There should be no atheists on a spring day.

I could smell spring flowers in the brisk Washington air. I delighted at the sound of children laughing. People were all over the place buying, selling, bartering and trading. It seemed like one of those Middle-Eastern bazaars. Somebody even had some oriental rugs for sale. We had everything there except belly dancers. I was very pleased. You see, I'm an accountant and we were raising lots of money. Who could ask for more? My only worry was that the wind might change and the scent of the flowers would blow the other way.

On a beautiful day like that I have to pause and thank God. To me it's like God has taken His world back and turned it into a natural cathedral. New flowers blooming, birds returning to their summer homes, tress sprouting new leaves and the smell of all those flowers in the air all around me. In the distance I could see snow capped mountains kissing the clouds. The sheer beauty of His handy work was awe-inspiring. That was exactly what I was feeling as I sauntered carefree as could be toward the small cottage where I lived. Life in the country suited me. I was sure that when I recalled this day, sometime in the future it would bring me a great deal of joy. I had never felt more content.

George Tillman, my good friend, had donated the land. He also endowed the money to keep us open. But if we wanted any, and I mean any frills, we had to raise the money through one of our enterprises. We had several. Though the flea market wasn't our most profitable, we all enjoyed it. By raising our own money, it gave the new people on the farm a sense of being productive. Some of the guys had never worked before unless they were on work release or in prison.

George was also my first sponsor (that's someone who directs you on how to incorporate the twelve steps into your life). He and I came to be very close. He became my role model… you might even say a father figure to me. I had lost my father at an early age. George was in his forties, and he had traveled the world doing fascinating things. Most of the things he had done seemed like fantasies to someone like me. I was maybe twenty-six or twenty-seven. I hadn't lived a very adventurous life. I had only left my home state (Washington) to play college football. I had visited relatives in South Central L.A. a couple of times. I guess just walking down the street in South Central can be an adventure…at least it was for me.

The friendship between George and I had begun as hero worship on my part. Well, I guess he was flattered by being looked up to. But as time passed our bond of friendship grew… without doubt became very meaningful to both of us. I am confident in saying that we loved each other and we depended on each other for emotional support. Never in my life had I met someone as easy to talk with about any subject. At the time, I thought that I was having a lot of problems. I could talk to him about any of them. He had a way of making anybody feel at ease, open up and talk about intimate details of their lives. He seemed to have some kind of power that made you relax. I would say more like he had some mystical aura. You knew that you could trust him even if you had never trusted anybody before in your life. I can't remember him ever having betrayed anybody's trust.

We would talk for hours about everything from football, to recovery, to solving the world's problems and, naturally, women. We were both ex-jocks and I think we considered ourselves intellectuals of a sort. Most of the people I have met in recovery think they have great intellectual capabilities. We can solve the problems of the world but not our own. Some of the stories George told me about the women he had known were hard to believe. Some of the exotic places he had been made me long to travel to far away places. I guess I'm a country boy really, but; I became a lot more sophisticated just listening to him.

Looking back on it, George would allow me to do most of the talking about personal things. He would listen with an interest that was real. It was obvious that he cared and wanted to help. I have seen him talk to the most hard-hearted men in prison and get through to the human side of them. They talked to him about things that had been hidden for years from everybody. He helped so many people that way.

George understood his addiction problem better than most of us at the farm. He wasn't afraid to look at himself and face the imperfections he found. "Drugs ain't your problem, homeboy" he would say over and over again when we talked about addiction. "Keep it in today" Was another of his favorite clichés. At the time it seemed to me that he was a person that made it a point not to look back or carry around useless baggage, grudges or hidden agendas. He would talk about his feelings like being lonely but only in a way that wasn't self-pitying or self-serving. Never blaming others for his actions or for causing his feelings. We never talked about why he felt the way he felt; only what he was going to do to feel better. One never got the impression that George was being superficial or less than honest. He was just taking responsibility for his recovery. The fact that he rarely talked about himself made him very unusual for a recovering person. We are always whining about something or another. He seemed to be more concerned about the problems of others than his own "situations." He often said he had situations not problems.

George was more than willing to make an effort to change any negative aspect of his own personality. He was a very giving man, both of his time and worldly possessions. He always had a positive outlook and tried to make our outlooks more positive. Just trying to do that with someone like me was a full time job. I could make a problem of getting up in the morning. My glass was always half empty.

George always attempted to see the good in every situation and everybody. No matter what the circumstance,"There's some good in it for somebody; look for the good. Everything is either a lesson or a blessing. It's up to you to choose." At the time I thought he was a little crazy because he meant that literally. I'm not so sure he was the crazy one after all. I have spent a lot of time being depressed and lonely. I can truly say George never spent much time wallowing in self-pity.

George always went with me when I went places to tell my story. Telling our stories is something we do in recovery. We share our life's story as honestly as we can. We talk about ourselves, not so much about the drugs we used but the feelings we had and are still having. It takes most recovering people quite a while to understand this, however. George taught me that I needed help and drugs had little to do with the help I needed. When he told his story he concentrated on his selfishness (lack of concern for others) and self-centeredness (feeling that he was the center of the universe) the drugs being a symptom of that greater problem. This was different from the way that a lot of the rest of us in recovery told our stories or thought about our problem. We blamed drugs as if the drugs didn't need our help to enter our systems. His story was never a chronology of his drug use. His was an examination of his feelings and how he goes about dealing with them today.

Once I asked him why he never mentioned details of the places he had been and the people he had known. It seemed that he knew a little about everything. Our private conversations were a lot more interesting than his public sharing of his experiences. He simply told me, "I can't and please don't ask me why. One of these days I'll tell you all about me but you already know everything that is important about me now. I am an addict and I need your help." I knew George well enough to respect his wishes. He taught me the importance of keeping my thoughts in the present. I learned to let go of much of my past by watching him. George felt that the art of enjoying the moment was a skill that everyone needed to learn.

At about three or four in the afternoon, George was sitting on the back porch of his freshly painted cottage, admiring his neatly manicured lawn. (Boy, I sure have a green thumb), he most likely whispered to himself with a great deal of satisfaction as he glanced at his brightly colored flower garden. He was always saying that he had a green thumb. His flowers were the only things he was vain about. The months of dedication and hard work had paid off. It seemed that every color in the rainbow lay there looking back at him. George had gotten flowers from all over the United States. He imported others from all over the world. He had painstakingly planted them in the greenhouse and later transferred the tiny plants to the garden. Now he had azaleas, tulips, African and Asian flowers with names I'll never be able to pronounce growing and thriving in the Northwest thousands of miles from their natural habitats.

A shadow of a man with a shiny object in his hand appeared behind George. Without warning, I saw a flash of light and heard the faint sound of a muffled explosion. I saw George's body contort and fall forward. Then everything went into slow motion as I ran toward George in a vain attempt to save him. I was too late. When I got to the porch my friend lay dying on the floor in front of me. I must have blacked out because the next thing I remembered is the police questioning me an hour later. I couldn't provide them with many details of what happened. They told me that when they got there I was standing there with a glazed look in my eyes, starring down at the headless body of George's killer. I imagine I was, they had no reason to lie. But, I don't remember.

The phrase "it was the best of times, it was the worst of times" was burned into my memory forever that afternoon. That horrible tragedy nearly robbed me of enjoying the simple pleasures of a beautiful day. And for the second time in my life I had lost a father. For nearly two years I relived the events of that day. Searching, I guess for a way to change them. But the fact remains that on a day that seemed excessive in its beauty, a day when I felt the love of my closest friends so intensely that I prayed that the day would never end. My whole world seemed to crash around me.

I had witnessed the murder of the best friend I had ever known. His life was snuffed out by a series of circumstances begun more than forty years earlier and half a world away. I had never seen anybody killed before. I try not to even go to wakes to view dead relatives. I try not to attend funerals. I had no idea how to process the things I had just seen even though I couldn't remember very much of the things that others said they saw. Until then I never thought much about fate or destiny but I believe that, in his case, the events of that day were destined to happen. Maybe I had to tell myself that at first just to accept what happened. I made an honest effort to put this tragedy behind me but I really wasn't too successful. I loved George, as did the rest of us at the farm. Imagine our surprise when we found out that George wasn't even his real name. We all needed closure. After his death we couldn't find out anything about George. It seemed like he had never existed.

I am not exactly in touch with the spirit world. I would never have believed that I could have been a part of some super-natural phenomenon. However, the facts state positively that I was… maybe I'm still a part of it. I'm not a mystic that's for sure. I only know that there is a God and I'm not it. Skepticism has become a way of life for me. Though my belief in God is important to me. I have a built in dubiousness of any one who has had direct contact with the almighty. If there were no God, it would be certain that nothing would have meaning. Our existence would not have a purpose. But just how He manifests Himself in our daily lives is anybody's guess. That is God's choice. Its up to me to learn to live with whatever He does. Anyway, that is my belief. The events I am about to describe. I know happened but at times I don't believe them myself.

I had what I'm going to call a series of sessions with a dead man. No, I would say an invasion of my soul and mind like the downloading of a computer. George's thoughts, emotions, and spirit were downloaded into my mind and soul. I have more than knowledge of past events in George's life. I have the feeling that I had experienced those things. George's perceptions have become my own… while I still retain my own identity. These events did happen in the life of my close friend. He told me how to locate people I didn't know at the time and have them verify many of the things he passed on to me. He led me to these people just to make me feel at ease. I even recognized most of these people without ever having seen them. I just didn't quite know what to say to them at first. Subsequently, I have come to know these people. Some of them have become the most important people in my life… some I would even trust with my life.

On an unseasonably warm spring night, a couple of years after the murder, I was very restless. I couldn't fall asleep, so; I decided to take a walk along the lake. George and I had walked there many times, and I always felt his presence whenever I walked there alone. Sometimes I would talk to him. Maybe I should say talk to myself. I don't know, but I think that sort of thing is pretty normal, though I don't really know what normal is anymore. His presence was there, okay… I could feel it. Mind you, I had never expected him to talk back. Until that night I hadn't even thought that he might answer me. I can't really say whether I saw him or not, but I'm sure he was there. I think I heard him call me, maybe he tapped me on the shoulder. Somehow he got my attention. Anyway, he told me all the things I didn't know about both his death and his life. Up until that time, I didn't know why he had been killed. Nobody else at the farm knew either. All of us wanted and (I think) needed to know something. George said he choose to tell me because I was having the most difficulty getting pass what happened and I had a destiny to fulfill.

George began by telling me about what happened that last afternoon. He said he felt no pain at being shot. He simply drifted into a different and strange new level of consciousness. He was aware only of his being. The sheer newness of this consciousness frightened him for a while. It was so different. Then after a moment or some immeasurable passage of time, he lost all fear. Every fear he had ever experienced in his life.

George's soul was all he had left. All of his sins, guilt, fear and human contradictions were laid out before him in a way he had never seen them before. A presence was with him. It did make him feel safe but not at peace, not exactly. It seemed to surround him with a dull light that generated no heat. He could touch the light but he could not get to the outside of it. The light brought him comfort it seemed to free him, not imprison him. He couldn't perceive of anything hurting him as long as the light was around him. Nothing seemed to be able to get through the light to harm him. This feeling of safety gave him the courage to look at everything that lay there before him.

He seemed to know things, but; it was not through the usual thinking or sensory processes. This extra-sensory awareness was much deeper than the five senses and completely different. The concept of time had a different meaning. There was nothing physical, nothing that he could touch, not even the light. It only seemed to be there because George needed it to comprehend what was happening to him. Things were moving faster than his ability to understand. It seemed that he felt the essence of his being without his physical body being there. He felt a freedom he had never known. It was like he had been imprisoned inside his body, especially his brain. He was now unencumbered by the limits of the physical. He was not trapped in time or space. He could see things happening at different places before the things happened. He could see choices that others were yet to make and the results of each of their possible choices. He could predict things that had not yet happened.

George's strange level of contact with himself, or awareness of his being, or non-being continues to grow. I would try to explain, but; I don't quite understand it myself. Let's call it purgatory but not really, not in the way that religions think about it. It seemed like his purgatory wasn't being forced on him. Although I had a limited understanding of the situation, I got the feeling that he wanted or needed to have something to justify the grace he was receiving… justify it to himself that is. He somehow downloaded much of what he saw about himself into me. The downloading began with the circumstances of his birth and of course his real name. Even a name was not a simple thing to figure out with George.

Chapter 2

James Marco Tillman was born June 17, 1947 to Elaine Margaret Posey and Boyd Edward Tillman. This announcement would never be printed. The name that George's mother planned for him would never be. Willie Posey, Elaine's father, would not allow it. No one in Savannah would know that his 13-year-old daughter was having a baby. Proud, self-righteous, Willie attended church every Sunday. He brought his Bible, hymnal, and tambourine, everything except his mind. Willie had retranslated the Gospels to suit his own brand of piety. He shunned the ungodly (that was anyone who disagreed with him) and their wicked ways. He never missed an opportunity to let anyone who would listen know of his saintly perfection.

Willie's life had been difficult from birth. His family had little in the way of material things. They had less in love and kindness. Willie's mother had abused him. She would beat him with ropes or leather straps from the harness used on mules. She would even lock him in a dark closet for hours. Once he laughed out loud in church, his mother slapped him in the face in the middle of the service. When he got home she tied the ten-year-old boy to a tree in the backyard and beat him severely. He was forced to sleep tied to that tree and sent to school the next day without eating. She didn't let him eat again for two days. In those days you got no free lunch at school.

Willie left home at fifteen, he worked hard. He was too proud to ask anybody for anything. For a while he seemed to have escaped the horrors of his childhood. Willie had moved from Augusta to Savannah to get some freedom and quiescence. He knew that he would have to cut all ties with his mother. His mom had dominated his thinking before he married. She thought that any kind of fun was a sin. Her bitterness infected everyone around her. Willie had struggled for years to free his soul from her influence. Laura, his wife, remembered when they first met; Willie loved her more than she thought was possible for a man to love a woman. Both Willie and Laura were in their teens when they got married. Willie was completely devoted to her. They agreed that they had a marriage made in heaven. Laura had never met someone who was as exciting as Willie and at the same time as kind and loving. Willie really worked at doing little things that made Laura smile… her sweet shy childlike smile. As a young woman, Laura would hide her face and giggle. Willie would get her to laugh at least once every day. Her laughter would send chills through him. Laura was completely dependent on Willie and he loved it. Willie loved life. Everything about him seemed to reflect rays of happiness that landed on everyone around him. Just his presence helped everyone around him to lift their spirits if they were down. Willie tried to remove any obstacle that might be on Laura and his path to happiness. Laura was so fragile that his mother would rob them both of any chance that they might have at having a happy life. Willie was able to cut his ties for a while.

.

Willie loved to dance. He even claimed that he invented the Charleston. He won contests all over town. The happy couple went dancing every weekend. All Willie had to do was see a dance step once. He even learned tap dancing and picked up a little extra money on weekends dancing in local clubs. Secretly, he really wanted to be the next Bill (Bojangles) Robinson. He had enough talent to make a living as a showman. Willie was a born entertainer who loved to see people have a good time.

A few months into their marriage Laura became pregnant. Cornelius was the baby's name. He was named after Laura's father though he looked more like Laura's mother but with Willie's eyes. Sometimes Willie would just stand by the baby's crib and stare at his son with tears of joy welling up in his eyes. The month that the baby lived was the happiest time of his life. Willie had everything he ever wanted… he thought. Willie and Elaine had never experienced more joy in their lives. The infant looked perfect and had an infectious toothless grin. Seemingly, the baby was born with the laughter of a grown man; Willie would say, years later that was because he didn't get to stay here long. The child seemed to enjoy his short life. The grief and pain that Willie felt when he found the infant lying there dead for no apparent reason was indescribable. It seemed to crush his soul and distort his faith. Willie became bitter and cruel. He had never experienced that kind of grief; the desperation Willie felt at the lost of the child compelled him to seek a way out of his pain. Willie ran to the twisted theology of his mother. He probably was feeling guilty and afraid about his anger toward God, the Power that he claimed to love so much. Willie never thought of the inherit contradiction of a vengeful, punishing God who tortured you constantly, yet was supposed to bring you peace but only if you were perfect. So; like his mother, he tried to fool God with a grand show of piety. He had gotten away from her geographically, but he couldn't get away emotionally; his mother had seen to that a long time ago.

Willie prayed all night for the child to be resurrected. All his prayers were to no avail, convincing Willie that God was out to get him for past wrongs. When he finally accepted the baby's death or maybe he only accepted that the baby wasn't coming back. Each day for a month he prayed for peace, but he got no absolution from his suffering, as time passed he talked more about the wrath of God. Willie was so afraid of his feelings that he never talked about his anger with the Almighty. God was punishing him too much for his transgressions he thought; each new day that passed without relief reinforced that to his twisted way of thinking. I guess what Willie's grandmother told him applies in this case, "When you don't know much your can't do much." Willie sure didn't know much.

Laura had nearly died from a childhood illness. She was not capable of dealing with the harsh life of rural Georgia. Life in Savannah was less difficult for Laura. She thought she had escaped the fate that would have been in store for her if she had not met Willie. The emotional presence of an over bearing mother-in-law would prove to be Laura's undoing. Deep down she always thought that she would have been doomed to a very short painful life. She loved Willie and he was a way out of the cotton fields. That is probably what accounted for her staying with him even after Willie lost it. His mother and his own negative perceptions had crippled him spiritually and limited his ability to love. But; Laura was so tied to him. She didn't know where she ended and Willie began. The love Laura had for Willie gave him strength and validation for a time. But in the end would not be enough to stop him from drowning in a sea of self-pity and distorted beliefs. Nobody could have saved Willie from Willie. He couldn't free himself of the selfishness inside him. This made the wrathful foundation to his spiritual life all the more appealing to him.

Willie was angry with God for taking his infant son and leaving him all this pain. He was angry with himself for being powerless to do anything about it. It seemed that he was caught in the middle of an irreconcilable dilemma. He was truly between a rock and a hard place. He needed God but his fear and anger drove him deeper into a state of spiritual confusion. Willie was the ultimate contradiction. Though he was a man with unshakable all be it-distorted faith. His views brought him no comforting assurance that a strong belief probably should bring. God was always there in Willie's mind frightening the hell out of him. Willie couldn't see the truth; God always loved him and always showed him mercy. The problem was his perceptions. I think that if Willie hadn't believed absolutely that God existed, he would have been totally abandoned and isolated from God's grace. Willie feared God too much to leave any room for love and honesty in his relationship with Him. Willie lied to himself and God about his inner desires and feelings. After a while, Willie's anger passed but not his self-loathing.

Willie had tasted liquor but didn't like it. Gambled a little, lost five dollars once and of course his dancing. Willie spent a lot of time trying to figure out why God was so unfair to him. He couldn't admit to himself that he was questioning God. So Willie decided that he must be a special case, a man who had to live above sin to be worthy of God's love. Laura saw everything that was kind and loving about Willie buried with their month old son. Laura was left to grieve alone and deal with Willie. He felt cursed. Willie drove everyone close to him away. He lost the capacity to love and even the will to try to love others. He refused every blessing that God ever offered him. God gave him chance after chance to love his fellow man. It took Willie many years to realize that loving your fellow man is the greatest gift God can give any of us.

After a few years Laura had another son. She was very happy because the baby looked so much like Willie. As he grew up he acted so much like Willie had acted in his happy times. Laura named the baby James after the brother of Jesus, but; by the time James came along Willie's soul had too much fear in it. It seemed that there was no love left in his heart. Willie had no outward delight at James' birth but somewhere in his heart Willie must have loved his son. Sadly the boy's birth seemed to make Willie more fearful and grievous. He sunk deeper into his distorted Biblical interpretations further from the people that loved him.

Willie imagined he had been cursed to have a son who was so like he had been before the tragedy. James was cheerful he had a way of seeing how ludicrous life could be. James had the ability to laugh at life and his own shortcomings. But the thing that really bothered Willie most was the youngster's love of dancing. James was the best dancer at his school. He would say that he invented the "Lindy Hop". Willie would go into a rage every time James' dancing was brought to his attention. Sadly, there was nothing James could do to please his father. But try as he might, Willie could not do anything that would break James' spirit either. Willie, on the other hand, was worse off than his son was; he felt that he could do nothing to please God. He believed God used senseless pain to purify our souls. Unearned suffering can touch the heart of God...but Willie felt that he didn't deserved to be punished this severely.

James constantly struggled to make his father happy but he could never get the love he wanted and needed from Willie. James used his teachers in school and some of the men at church as role models or just as someone to talk to. James fortunately was incapable of prolonged anger. His forgiving spirit prevented him from ever hating his father. James kept that longing to be close to his father throughout his life.

Elaine was born 10 years later. For some reason, Willie didn't fear the birth of a daughter as intensely. However, he still didn't know how to love her. To make bad matters, worse between James and Willie. James loved his sister and mother and he wasn't afraid to express it. Willie didn't know how to express his love for his family. The unfortunate fact was, they all thought he didn't care about them. James spent time with Elaine, made her laugh. He also always had time for whatever his mother wanted. Elaine truly loved her big brother and that greatly annoyed Willie. He was just plain jealous. Elaine was devastated when Willie put James out when she was eight years old.

It seems that James and a few friends celebrated a little too much after graduation. James had been the first in his family to finish high school. Laura was very proud, but; again Willie felt left out. James and his friends had a drink or two. Willie found out about it. James had been warned. "Nobody under my roof would touch that devil's brew." James' simple response was, "I wasn't under your roof when I drank." To which Willie retorted. "That's right and you will never sleep under it again." The two of them would not talk to each other again for 40 years.

Chapter 3

Boyd Tillman had as unfortunate a beginning to his life as you could have imagined. When he was twelve years old his parents were killed in an accident. He had a grown sister but she had lost contact with them. As a thirteen-year old she had run away from home with a man twice her age. They lived in New York for a brief time however he was killed leaving her alone all she knew was how to let someone take care of her. Vinnie (that was her name) migrated south. The Tillmans were good people and would have welcomed her back. But, when she got as far as Savannah she met and married a man from there.

Her husband was a very possessive man and allowed her no interaction with her family. Her mother and father had not heard from her since she moved back to the south. Even if Boyd knew where to write his sister she would have never received it because her husband kept an eye on all of her incoming mail. In fact he got a post office box and didn't allow her to have a key…in those days very few people had telephones. When her parents were killed the news of their deaths didn't get to her until months after the funeral. A friend of her husband had been to Brunswick and heard about the accident through a mutual friend. A lawyer had been trying contacted her about her parent's property but nobody knew where she was. The only reason Vinnie's husband let her see the lawyer was he thought that she might be coming into a little money. She did inherit a house that he quickly sold…the lawyer also gave her some personal papers from her parents. Vinnie inquired about Boyd but he had disappeared.

Boyd was left on his own. The youngest was frightened and confused. The Tillman's had no relatives other than their daughter. Boyd didn't like the idea of moving in with the people who were keeping him when his parents were killed; they were too old he thought. He ran away. Boyd didn't have a way of getting in touch with his sister and he figured that she didn't care anyway. When Boyd ran away from Brunswick he had no destination in mind. Anyplace but Brunswick was all right with him. He came to Savannah and ran straight into trouble. For a while it seems that trouble was the only thing he could count on having.

Boyd was strong for his age and even at twelve could do the work of a grown man. He got a job on the docks unloading cargo. He rented a room at a boarding house in a run-down section of town. He was taking care of himself pretty well at least on the surface. His physical needs were being met anyway. Though he had little education he could manage money. He could cook well enough to feed himself. He had no one to talk to and he kept the grief over the lost of his parents inside. He spent many nights crying longing to have his parents back, someone that cared about him.

One day at work Jim Carstairs, a white man of thirty, six feet tall and 180 pounds slapped Boyd because the youngster didn't get a requested item fast enough. It was Jim's custom to pick on blacks that he thought to be unwilling or unable to defend themselves. The quiet boy who had never talked back unleashed an attack on the surprised bully with such viciousness that before onlookers could stop it Corsairs had a broken nose and three cracked ribs.

Police were called. Boyd's age was determined and no family could be found. Boyd provided the authorities with no information beyond his parents were dead. He was put in reform school because they had no other place for him to go. Boyd went to school in the reformatory he liked to read but his reading materials were limited mostly to the Bible and his outdated schoolbooks… he read what ever he got his hands on. Boyd was released at the age of sixteen when Willie's preacher promised to take care of Boyd and some other boys. What the minister really had in mind was renting the youngsters a room and pocketing most of the money that the kids would earn.

Boyd was again working and pretty much on his own when he met Elaine. He kept the preacher paid and caused no trouble. Boyd had never had a girlfriend when he saw Elaine he knew she was the one for him. This shy overprotected girl gravitated to Boyd immediately as well. For the first time since his parent's death Boyd felt something for another human being…and had those feelings returned. Elaine had been sure for some time that her father had crossed the line of religion into insanity. She was just as lonely as Boyd. The two youngsters would meet everyday after school and each Sunday after church. Elaine convinced the preacher to let her help Boyd improve his reading skills…the two them really did do a lot of reading. She had access to a lot of books. Boyd and Elaine were drawn together out of loneliness but they bonded with a spiritual connection that few people ever find. Even that young both of them seemed to know that they were right for each other.

Most of men in the church shunned Boyd and the three other kids that had been in reform school. The young minister's attempts at being a savior to these boys were not at all well received by many of the church members. The church itself profited nothing from the kids paying rent to the minister.

The boys might have been better received if the church had been paid rent. The boys caused no trouble but most of the men were careful not to let their families come in contact with the boys.

The news of Elaine's pregnancy spread throughout the church. (Despite Willie's best attempts at preventing it.) I guess bad news travels. No one dared talk to Willie about it but everyone knew about Elaine's misfortune. Willie was still too ashamed to admit it to them. He didn't want any of his narrow-minded so-called Christian friends to know for sure. He was extremely angry with Elaine for disgracing him. So he decided to send Elaine to his sister's home in Augusta.

Chapter 4

Willie and his sister's employers were extremely fond of them. Both of their bosses would let them receive and make emergency phone calls. When their mother died, (Rosetta) his sister's employers let her call Willie's boss's office and notify him. This time it was Willie that made the call. He knew that his sister went to work at seven in the morning and stayed till six in the evening. His sister (Rosetta) would answer the phone when she was there alone usually at about three o'clock...the lady of the house would be out at that time...picking the kids up from school. Willie got permission to call and sure enough Rosetta answered.

Willie said "Hay Rosetta, "dis Willie I need you to let Laine stay with you. She's gone and got herself in trouble." Rosetta, Willie's half sister lived alone. Rosetta was a lonely ridged spinster who had few friends. Their mother had done a job on Rosetta too. The mom from hell had very nearly destroyed any trust she might have had in anyone especially those who didn't attend their church. She was ten years younger than he, Rosetta too was sinking down into a pit of religious gloom and doom. Rosetta had been the result of an affair her mother had with a minister who passed through Augusta leaving several children in his wake. Willie's mother had viewed Rosetta's birth as her punishment for not being celibate.

Willie left Augusta when Rosetta was only seven years old... the two siblings were not close. Her mother smothered Rosetta with her philosophy of everything is a sin including her life itself. She forced her to quite school at twelve and go to work as a housekeeper. Then right after Rosetta turned eighteen the hateful old woman had a stroke. Rosetta was then left with the responsibility of taking care of her and Willie's mother. Willie sent money to help the two women survive but he seldom visited. The family that Rosetta worked for bought the house where they lived and paid for the house to be brought up to the newly enacted city codes...to keep it from being condemned. If Rosetta's mother hadn't been there they would have asked her to come live with them.

Willie and Rosetta's mother was an ill-tempered and unkind woman whose physical condition didn't change her evil ways. She remained an invalid until she expired in 1945. Rosetta now nearly forty still a virgin, all alone and in all truth welcomed Elaine's company. All she had in her life was her job but she loved the people she worked for. Battling not to scream for joy at the prospect of having company she said. " I'll keep her, keep her in the house except for church and find a good home for the baby." Rosetta assured Willie. "Some God fearing folks."

Rosetta worked for Furman White, a prominent attorney. He was the senior partner of the largest law firm in Augusta. Furman was respected through out the area for his ability as a barrister. The whole family thought of Rosetta as a member of the White family. Rosetta was a great cook and was indispensable when the family needed someone to be there for the kids. Rosetta always talked to "Mr. White" about anything of importance to her. Rosetta always said, "White folks knows things niggers don't." She felt Furman White was smarter than most whites. The only other people Rosetta associated with were the people at her church. The White family was the closest to a family she had...she had no idea how to contact her father and didn't want to contact him anyway.

The only other blacks Furman knew personally were Redmond and Wilma Perry. His firm had handled some real estate for the Perry's. Redmond also worked on Furman and other wealthy white folk's cars. Redmond Perry was an honest, hard-working man who always kept his word. He was a genius at fixing motors and getting along with people. The Perry Mechanic shop was thriving, he even had a contract fixing city vehicles. Wilma, a petite woman of barely five feet tall, she had more energy than any two Amazon women did on stimulants. Wilma was not exactly pretty by the conventional standards, but she made herself one of the more attractive women in Augusta. Wilma knew how to care for her skin; her hair was always in place. Though her wardrobe wasn't extravagant she knew how to wear her clothes in a way that enhanced both her figure and her clothing. Her make-up was flawless and her personality as captivating as any woman's in Augusta. She cast a spell that won the hearts of everyone she met, people loved her immediately.

Wilma didn't have to work in fact her husband didn't want her to work but she hated housework, cooking especially. She loved having something productive to do and she felt obligated to help others. She ran a beauty shop, beauty school and was the president of the local chapter of the cosmetology association. Wilma was responsible for getting countless young women started in business. While she wasn't the greatest hairdresser technically she was a very clever businesswoman and splendid teacher...Wilma valued education. She also was a well-respected church and community leader. Wilma was an incredible human being. The only thing missing was that they had no children of their own.

Furman asked Rosetta what she thought about him talking with the Perry's. Rosetta asked. "Does they go to church?" "Yes, the lawyer replied. Saint James Methodist Church is where they attend every Sunday. Wilma sings in the choir, heads a few committees. Redmond is on the Steward Board and people say he tithes." Rosetta really didn't think much of Methodist but one who tithes might be all right. Rosetta really wanted to keep the child herself but on her small income she could barely take care of herself...She never told Furman about wanting to keep the child. Furman told Rosetta that he would talk to the Perrys and get back to her.

"Come on in Mr. White," Redmond said welcoming the unexpected visitor to Perry home. "What can I help you with? Is your wife's car broken or is yours in need of repair?" "Oh no, nothing like that," White said. "Well my housekeeper, Rosetta's brother's daughter is in trouble and she asked me if" Wilma stopped him. Mr. White, she said in bewilderment, "I'm almost 45 (she was really forty-seven) and Redmond's 50 we might not be able to properly take care of a child, me working and all". Then to her complete surprise, Redmond said, "I've been wanting you to stop working so much for quite some time now I've always wanted a child and we can afford it". "We can do things for a child we couldn't do when we were younger". Wilma was as good a wife as any man could want and she knew it but she always thought her not having children was a disappointment to them both. They were both in good health and seemed younger than they were. Wilma knew without a doubt that she was loved. No man could have been more supportive and caring than her husband. However, she had never completely understood the depth of her husband's feelings or his devotion to her until that very moment. It was as if Redmond could read what was in her soul. Redmond knew that Wilma loved and wanted children. Redmond always tried to give Wilma anything she wanted. Though somewhat overwhelmed he was delighted at the possibility of giving her the thing she wanted most. The happiness showed on his face and in his eyes. Redmond seldom showed emotion and never cried in front of anyone. The tears in his eyes were evidence that his marriage was now complete. They were blessed to be able to have the child that the two of them had always wanted but had given up on having long ago.

Elaine left for Augusta the day after Christmas. Laura had insisted that Elaine be home for Christmas. Elaine cried silently the whole way down there. She made no attempt to talk to Willie...the ride was like being locked in a closet. When she got to her aunt's house she walked slowly toward the front door. The walk seemed endless. Elaine was feeling more emotions than she had ever felt in her life. She couldn't bear to look at anyone. Elaine was terrified. She looked down so not to make eye contact with her aunt. As she mumbled nearly inaudibly "Hey, Aunt Rosetta," entering Rosetta's small meticulously clean living room, "Speak up girl." Rosetta insisted as she hugged Elaine and said "girl you sho done growed, come here and let me look at you." Willie asked "Where do you want these bags?" pushing his way into the house. Rosetta replied "in the room where I used to sleep before Mama passed." Willie then said "She ain't gonna give you no trouble. That boy made a fool out of her, he ain't no good, always in trouble." " But Daddy", Elaine tried to explain. Willie scolded, "Don't interrupt. Grown up people is talking go unpack your clothes while me and Rosetta is talking."

Elaine went to the room and did as she was told. She knew that she wasn't going to see Boyd again at least for a long time. She wondered what she was going to do... what was going to happen to her and the baby? She cried as she unpacked and promised herself that she would somehow be a part of her baby's life. Elaine overheard voices emanating from the living room in the small house. She could hear Willie ranting about how she had hurt him. He declared he had a broken heart... ungrateful child was trying him like Job; sharper than a serpent's tooth the anguish caused by her ingratitude. Rosetta said nothing; she knew she couldn't get a word in anyway. Willie was just like their mother self-righteous to the core she thought as she sat trying not to hear a word he was saying, and suppressing a strong desire to smack Willie in the mouth. Willie gave Rosetta $50.00 and said, "I will send you some money every month." Rosetta thanked him and said, "Help out on the food... Is she been to a doctor yet?" Willie said, "No. Why she just having a baby. She healthy." Rosetta interjected "Mr. White said that she ought to go since she so young." "White folks" Willie said, "They got money for that." Willie ranted a little more then left with out saying good-bye to Elaine.

Rosetta walked slowly down the hall to the room where Elaine lay crying. "Child how you feeling" she asked with tenderness in her voice that let Elaine know Rosetta loved her. Elaine still sobbing hugged her aunt with all with all her strength and said, "I'm sorry I didn't mean for this to happen" Rosetta assured her trembling niece "I know baby I know... everything is gonna be all right."

The first night in Augusta was the longest loneliest night of Elaine's life. What little sleep she got was interrupted by dreams of gypsies. She saw visions of her chasing wagons full of wild-eyed gypsies. She would sit up, start to cry as she lay back down...cry herself to sleep only to dream again.

She asked herself over and over where is Boyd. Why doesn't he rescue me? She would get very angry then start to cry again...she knew that there was nothing Boyd could do. She had to go to see these awful people in the morning

The next morning Furman drove Rosetta and Elaine over to the Perry's house. As Furman drove, Elaine imagined the Perry's to be monsters. Maybe they would somehow steal her baby. They might be gypsies and run away with both her and the baby. She had read about things like that in books at school. She saw how scared people got when gypsies came to town. Even white people were scared of them; yeah they must be gypsies she thought why else would they want to steal other peoples' children?

Though the trip to the Perry house took nearly twenty minutes to Elaine it seemed to take only a few seconds. She thought everyone could hear her heart pounding as they pulled up to the curb in front of the Perry's home. Well at least these gypsies live in a house not in one of those wagons like the ones that come to Savannah; Elaine thought as they walked to the door. Elaine had to summon all of her courage not to run away. Elaine somehow looked fairly calm when Furman knocked on the door.

"Hello everybody it's so nice of you to come" said a smiling Wilma as she opened the door. Rosetta mumbled to herself "she talk like a school teacher." Elaine was surprised she had never seen a black gypsy before... that made her feel a little better. Those white ones were scary with all those funny clothes. Then Wilma turned to Furman and said; "Us girls have some girl talk no men allowed, I'll see to it that they get home all right".

Elaine had never seen a black woman handle herself with the poise and confidence of Wilma; she was impressed maybe these gypsies weren't all bad. Rosetta and Elaine could both see that Wilma thought she was as good as the white man that Rosetta revered so much. The young girl had to admit that her baby would be better off with this confident woman. She really wished she could be more like Wilma herself. Elaine was greatly relieved; she knew that her baby was going to be all right.

Wilma suggested Elaine be examined by the doctor... to insure that both mother and child were all right. Elaine had been to the doctor only once in her life when she had the mumps. Willie's boss had sent her and Willie both to the doctor. The childhood disease had kept Willie out of work for two weeks. Willie stayed in bed for the entire time. Elaine thought her father was going to die. Even after the young girl was back at school her father was still moaning in bed.

Redmond was a close friend of Dr. Martin, the most successful of the three Negro doctors in Augusta. Also he worked on the car of Dr. Abraham Fine, a young Jewish doctor from New York doing his residency in Augusta. The young doctor treated many blacks despite the fact that most white doctors refused to. Redmond made arrangements for Elaine to be examined by Dr. Martin at the colored hospital. Dr. Abe (that's what Doctor Fine wanted to be called) asked to examine Elaine; he wanted to see how being pregnant effected someone that young. Elaine was nervous about taking her clothes of in front of a white man but Dr. Abe made her feel comfortable fairly quickly. Both doctors were very pleased to find that she was healthy, especially for a girl her age. The two physicians worked together so well that they consulted each other on difficult pregnancies…until Doctor Fine returned to New York.

Wilma also made arrangements with Martha Williams (her cousin), an eighth grade teacher, to help Elaine with her schoolwork. Wilma had a large extended family...she had lost her mother and father during a flu epidemic when she was a child. She had no brothers or sisters. However, the Williams family was very large and had a great deal of influence in the colored community. Elaine was enrolled in a school where Grady Williams (Wilma's cousin) was the principal. Elaine was smart and Martha was an excellent teacher so Elaine was one of the top students in her class… even though she was not there after she started "showing." Elaine met the requirements to move on to the next grade.

Elaine enjoyed her stay in Augusta and learned to really admire her Aunt Rosetta and Miss Wilma. But it was Wilma's 95-year-old great-grandmother Lillie Williams that Elaine adopted as the grandmother she never had. The feisty old lady lived on the Williams' home place, a sixty-acre farm about 10 miles south of Augusta. Grandma Lillie, as everyone called her, was a bundle of energy. She loved to work in her garden or sweep her yard with an old fashion yard broom. Grandma Lillie would tell Elaine stories about slavery time. She knew old "African" stories her grandmother had told her and others she made up. Elaine would follow the Williams family matriarch around. She loved to help Grandma Lillie do work around the farm…more than anything she just like being around the old woman.

Elaine watched Grandma Lillie as the old woman cooked each day. Elaine quickly learned to cook, she loved it. She learned so fast she became as good a cook as her mother in only a couple of months. Quite an accomplishment; Laura was a pretty good cook. Wilma encouraged Elaine and let her cook anytime she was at the Perry home. Wilma hated cooking and was generally considered the worst cook in her family. Really, she was considered the worst cook in the state of Georgia. Everyone knew Redmond really loved Wilma when he ate her cooking and married her anyway. He even ate some biscuits she cooked... an act of real love. At the family reunion each year Wilma was allowed to make ice tea only...and that is allowed after tea bags were invented.

Elaine loved to listen to Grandma Lillie's stories and the old woman had one for almost every occasion. Elaine asked, "Why do cats and dogs fight so much?" Grandma Lillie said, "Well a long time ago in Africa the lion and mouse tried to trick the elephant. You see the elephant loved birds. Small birds landed on him and kept the insects off his back. The lion was lazy and hated to chase the faster animals. Antelopes, zebras, giraffes all could run faster than the lion so he told the mouse about it. The mouse told the lion that the elephant could knock down some trees and rocks and block a pass where the animals ran to get away from Lions. The lion could catch them if the pass was blocked. So the lion told the elephant if he blocked the pass give him all the birds. The elephant loved birds especially the ones that made nests behind his ears; the birds tickled him when they pecked the bugs out of his ears; just as they had convinced the elephant, the hyena laughed. The elephant love birds so much he forgot the lion couldn't fly." The lion and the hyena have been enemies ever since. The lion told all the other cats about it and all of them think any dog is a hyena. Wilma didn't like Grandma Lillies' stories. Wilma felt the stories were just wives tales that perpetuated ignorance. A hyena isn't even a dog Wilma would say. Grandma Lillie would always tell Wilma "maybe the loins didn't read that book you read"... "white folks don't know everything."

"Grandma Lillie, who is this?" Elaine said looking at a faded photograph. "This looks like Boyd, my boyfriend only darker and shorter." Grandma Lillie talked as rapidly as a machine gun seemingly the old woman didn't even catch her breath between words...a sentence might have a hundred words and no breaks for air. "Well child that's my youngest brother, Charles. He's been gone a long time. Had some trouble, went to Florida. We lost contact with him. His wife was an Indian. She was over six feet tall and he was just a little taller than I am." Pausing to chuckle, she slapped her thighs...she seemed to be thinking about something else. Then she continued. "They was a funny couple. You know... her being so tall and him so short. He was strong though. Strongest man I ever seen for his size. Would work all day long, plowing then built on a house at night. White folks burned it down thou; thought Clara was a white woman. You know Charles didn't take no mess." Again chuckling this time with a slight air of pride. "Well Clara was pregnant so they went to Florida and lived with Indians. I stopped hearing from them after about two years. They moved around a lots. But something must have happened to him for us not to hear from him." Now with sadness in her voice and a tear in her eye she concedes that Charles was probably dead...along time ago. The old lady prided herself in staying in touch with her relatives. Charles was the only one she couldn't find.

Grandma Lillie had a list of things a mile long Elaine could not do while she was pregnant. Grandma loved children and seemed to take a special interest in Elaine and her unborn child. "Don't wash your hair baby," she warned. "Get out of the night air." Said you gonna have a boy can tell by you carrying him low. Don't scare that child; the baby will be born popeyed. More wives tales and superstitions Wilma would counsel Elaine but Grandma Lillie would come up with more everyday it seemed. Elaine cherished Grandma Lillie and pretended to listen.

Even though Elaine was young, the birth of her baby went well, both mother and child came through the ordeal in good health. But it was the most difficult thing Elaine had ever done leaving the baby and returning home. After the Redmond Jr. was born, Grandma Lillie would go to visit Wilma everyday. Wilma was treated like she gave birth... the old woman wouldn't let Wilma do anything. Grandma Lillie and Rosetta doted over the child and one or the other jumped every time the baby cried. When Wilma protested the two doting segregate mothers would say that the baby couldn't stand Wilma's cooking. I think that they all missed Elaine...they wanted to comfort each other.

Furman White advised the Perry's to formally adopt Redmond Jr.... Wilma had grown so fond of Elaine and really wanted to adopt her and the baby. Wilma didn't want to lose contact with neither Elaine nor Rosetta. The two women had become friends and their bond grew after Redmond Jr. was born. The two of them so different on the outside yet so much alike on the inside especially when it came to the love they had for Elaine and the baby... Rosetta even went to church with Wilma. The first time she had ever been to a non-Holiness Church. The two women missed Elaine...they wished she could have stayed.

Chapter 5

The drive back from Augusta seemed to Elaine an endless desent into aloneness. That feeling of being alone worsened by the company of others that she could not understand. She had just come from a different world. A place, where a woman, like Wilma was free to speak her mind without the domination of men. " Glad to be getting out from round them peoples in Augusta," Willie said showing both relief and disgust...the same disgust he had for everybody that thought differently from him. Laura agreed, "Them folks that got the baby thinks they is white." She always agrees, Elaine thought. I wonder if mama knows daddy is a nut? Elaine silently asked herself. She chuckled out loud...both Willie and Laura thought she was agreeing with them.

Laura, while not unattractive looked to be 60 or 65 but had not yet reached 50. She dressed in long dresses, had her hair pulled back and of course no makeup. Her skin hard and wrinkled; life seemed to be oozing out of her with each passing day with Willie. Laura could barely read and hadn't worked since she was a child working as a sharecropper, she felt trapped. She had worked in a cotton field and peanut farming before coming to Augusta to look for work as a maid. But she met and married Willie before she got steady work. Willie always bragged, "No wife of mine would have to work" as was Willie's way he kept his word.

Laura knew she couldn't handle the farm life and she felt too intimidated by whites to work in their homes. Laura lived for many years on faith in God and hope that Willie would change. She was losing hope of Willie changing and her faith was bringing her less comfort as the years passed. The impoverished life or rural Georgia was the only alternative to Willie's religious haranguing. She had given up on life at least at being happy. What could she do? Where could she go? Laura asked herself a thousand times. The answer was always the same...nowhere.

Laura only insisted that her children go to school. Somewhere down deep inside she knew that if it was too late for her. The children had to have a chance at a better life than hers. James had finished high school, now if her baby girl could do as well. Laura even dreamed of Elaine going to college. She thought of that as a dream. She knew Willie would not encourage his daughter to go on to college. She doubted that he would pay for college unless it brought him sort of attention by people he wanted to impress. Maybe if Willie's boss or the preacher found out how smart Elaine was. Laura knew that Elaine wanted to be a nurse.

The helplessness that Laura felt at not being able to read tied her to Willie and gave her a fatalistic view of life. From the time James left home each day Laura seemed to withdraw back into herself. Acquiescing to all of Willie's twisted views and cowing down to his cruelty. Withdrawing further into almost a fantasy place. A place where she used to keep her hopes and dreams but now that place was empty. Now she was alone especially whenever Willie was around. Laura was an empty shell of a wife agreeing with a man that she knew was a fanatic. Fear griped her with an inescapable vise-like hold that shrunk her world, controlled her movements and crippled her thinking. Laura had no identity of her own; she had become a non-person agreeing.

"We is moving to Jacksonville," Willie announced one week after Elaine returned to Savannah. "Mr. Coleman want me to lead a crew of mens down there. I'll be making $50.00 a week," Willie said proudly. "They is got a house for us and everything. Praise the Lord." Laura agreed, "Praise the Lord." By the way I had that no good Tillman boy sent away. "I'll learn him a lesson. Don't mess with my daughter. I told yawl I'd get him." Willie boasted. Laura agreed, "You sho told us you sho did." Willie had lost the capacity to be kind, it didn't matter what happened to a helpless teenager. The boy had embarrassed him that was all that mattered.

Chapter 6

Willie had charged Boyd with taking advantage of a minor... again Boyd would take a trip to reform school. This time it would turn into Boyd's first trip to the chain gang. It seemed that the world was conspiring against him. I think that George's (now Redmond) destiny had begun and all the bad things that happened to his father were a part of that destiny. Sometimes we have to take the long way to get where we're going.

Superintendent of this reform school was a man named Martin Wilcox. He believed in the value of hard work. Wilcox cared about the young black boys in his charge. Stuck his neck out quite a bit, stretched the rules; he did whatever he could to help...most of the boys he took a special interest in never returned to jail. He had gotten several people in town to let the boys work in stores, on farms and various safe jobs at the local sawmill. Wilcox Feed Store was the largest store in town. Bob Wilcox (the superintendent's older brother) ran the family business that their father had started in 1911. The Wilcox family had a history of bad relations with the local Klan because they extended credit to black farmers.

Boyd was the largest and strongest boy at the school. This formally gangly string bean, already six foot four in height, now added a forty pounds to his muscular frame. Boyd could read as well as most high school graduates. Wilcox recognized that Boyd had potentials. Boyd struggled to believe that the concern shown by Mr. Wilcox was genuine...the youngster was starting to see a future for himself. He made a real commitment to change his life...but just beneath the surface Boyd had a lot of rage and fear. He had no idea of his potential academically and no clue of his physical strength...really he was a mystery to himself. Boyd had grown into a huge man-child. His boyish face, unsure adolescent manner barely covered a seething rage within him at times. Boyd feared that the world was against him, he slowly allowed himself to trust the Wilcox brothers.

When Martin Wilcox took Boyd to the store to go to work for his brother he had high hopes for the boy. Bob Wilcox took a personal interest in Boyd as well. He saw great deal of potential in the youngster also. Boyd was a hard worker he learned quickly and followed directions. The storekeeper would not have minded if the youngster came to work there when he was released...since Boyd had no family. Wilcox had plans for Boyd. He wanted to be a father figure to Boyd. Though given the state of the racial situation nether would have described it that way. One of the boys at the school had gone on to college after he got out of the school. Wilcox was about to speak with the principal of the local Colored High School for Boyd to attend. But just as he was all set to get Boyd enrolled trouble reared its ugly head, again.

Tom Godwin had worked for the Wilcox's for five years. He was a good worker but had no education beyond writing his name and a crude system he used to count inventory. He watched Bob Wilcox's attention to the young prisoner and when it seemed that Boyd was given greater responsibility. Tom became angry and consumed with fear, he had a wife and two children. Tom had overheard a conversation between Bob and his wife. They were talking about Boyd going to High School then maybe coming to work at the store…he didn't hear the part about Boyd going on to college then maybe going up north.

Ned and Billy Grantham were Tom's best friends. They decided that they would "Teach that Nigger a lesson." They recruited Wesley Baker, a massive man known for his toughness. Baker, a Klan member, had beaten a black man to death…enjoyed hurting people of all colors. He jumped at the chance "to set that boy straight." "Bob wants to give that nigger my job." Tom complained. Baker laughed. "When I get done with that boy he won't be taking no white man's job. He will take his black ass back to the cotton field if he can walk." The Grantham brothers said in unison. "We don't want to kill anybody, not even a nigger." Baker said. "You can't get a fight out of most of them no way." Laughing his frightening eyes shining with a murderous glow. Baker said, "I don't think I'll need you two. If the boy sees three or four white men are mad at him he will get the message. I might kick his ass for the fun of it. Just come and look mean. Yawl ain't scared to do that are you?"

The three men sheepishly agreed to let Baker beat Boyd up. They begged Baker not to kill him just scare him, teach him a lesson. They were scared of the law but Baker was more frightening than any trouble that they might face. They regretted involving Baker now but there was nothing they could do. They thought that they could more than handle one teenage nigger. Boyd was so shy and seldom talked he seemed to be afraid of people but in truth he just didn't know what to say to them. Blacks and whites communicated very little and trust was non-existent. Boyd was uncomfortable in the company of whites. He had no reason to be around white people other than work. So at work he kept quiet and did as he was told and tried to earn all the money he could.

The four men cornered Boyd in the back of the warehouse. Tom spoke first, "Hey boy, when you get your black ass out of that school, go back to

Savannah." Boyd said nothing. He looked around to see if he could find anything that he could use on the Good OLE boys. Baker spoke up. "Nigger can't you talk. You hear us white men talking to you black boy?" Boyd saw fear in Billy Grantham's eyes as Baker was talking. Without warning or any unnecessary movement Boyd grabbed him throwing Billy in the direction of the open window. Seemingly at the same instant, he smashed Tom in the face with a left hook as he kicked Ned in the testicles. Within seconds he smashed the surprised Baker with his right hand to the chin, then with cat like quickness Boyd was all over Baker beating him to his fat body. Then just as the Klansman struggled to breathe, Boyd caught Baker under the chin with an uppercut. Boyd then kicked him in his chest as Baker fell down near the window. Then Boyd turn his attention to Ned who was cowering in the corner doubled over in pain begging for mercy. Boyd threw him out of the window on top of his brother. Bob Wilcox and his wife ran from the front of the store just as Boyd deposited Baker's massive frame on top of the Grantham boys.

"Boyd what the hell going on?" Wilcox demanded. Boyd sat down and said. "I thought they were trying to lynch me." Tom now barely regaining consciousness said, "He just went crazy, we weren't doing nothing". Wilcox knew Tom was lying. Bob told Boyd to get in his pick up. We better get you back to school before there is any more trouble. Edna (Wilcox's wife) drove the now frightened boy back to school. Wilcox feared that the Klan might get involved since Baker was a member.

The local Klan leader, Ed Johnson had been unhappy with Baker. OLE WES had beat up one of his best farm hands breaking two of his ribs causing him to be unable to work. Baker also bullied his fellow Klan members. Johnson felt Wesley needed a lesson but not from a black teenager. The Wilcox brothers convinced Johnson that it would be best to keep this whole thing quiet. Boyd had to be punished they agreed. He was given an additional five years for assault on Tom Godwin. Then he was transferred to an adult prison. Boyd never held it against the Wilcox's. They had saved his life and he knew it.

Chapter 7

Boyd was sent to the county farm near Columbus. Chain gang life was harsh and this camp was one of the worst. The camp was segregated. The white inmates were housed in buildings that were kept in comparatively good repair. The colored barracks were kept clean but no money was spent on its upkeep. Both black and white inmate's labors were used to keep up the standards set by the state of white prisoner housing. There were no standards for housing for black prisoners.

"Yawl can make this easy time or hard. It's up to you." Captain Frank said. Boyd was shackled to three other men when they entered the camp. Frank Anderson the overseer of the camp greeted them. He set down the rules, which were "do as I say". Captain Frank was what he insisted on being called, a fat, cigar smoking, loud mouthed, corrupt man who was the living embodiment of the words red neck. "I'm Captain Frank. You'll call me Captain Frank not Mister Frank and sure as hell not just plain Frank. Ask one of the guards for permission to speak to me, don't just walk up to me and start talking. If they don't want to talk to you or for you to talk to me, don't talk back to the guards about it and don't try to come crying to me. Yawl hear me." Yes sir, the other three said. Boyd didn't say anything. Captain Frank said to Boyd, "Is something wrong with you black boy?" "No sir." Boyd said. "I didn't know if I should say something or not say anything you just said not to say anything to you." "Put this smart ass nigger in the hole. Boy you might not see the sun the whole time you are here." Captain Frank ordered. Captain Frank always put a new prisoner in the hole if three or four came in at one time... especially if the man hadn't been there before. He'd let you out the next day. He just wanted to put a little fear in your heart. You might not be overcome with fear but you had a pretty good idea you didn't want to go back to the hole not at this camp. There were no facilities and if you needed to go you had to go in the corner of the cell in a hold in the ground...the cell had a dirt floor. The tiny cubical was never disinfected, the feces was just covered up once a moth, the smell was unbearable. You were fed half rations but the smell stopped you from eating anyway for the first few days. Boyd was a very happy man when they let him out that next morning.

Boyd was considered dangerous because he was convicted of a violent crime. His legs were shackled. He was let out of the hole and a fifty-pound ball was attached to the leg chains. After Boyd was there a few weeks the ball was removed they kept him in shackles, however. Captain Frank knew of Baker's reputation so he wasn't going to take any chances with Boyd. Any man that could beat up Baker and three other men had to be dangerous.

Boyd kept to himself and stayed out of trouble. The shackles were taken off after two more weeks. Captain Frank told Boyd that if he caused any problems he would stay in the hole for the entire five-year sentence. Boyd saw no way that he or any man could survive that. He already knew that the best way to stay out of trouble in jail is to keep to quiet. His imposing size kept most of his fellow inmates at bay. But the truth was he was lonely. He had made friends at the boy's school and he missed their companionship. But he knew that he would have to adjust and do what ever he had to do to stay alive here. Most of the inmates here were older than he and looked like trouble.

My name is Billy Slick Robinson; a new inmate introduced himself to all in the room a few months after Boyd's arrival. "If any of you country boys play cards, I'm your man." Boyd said nothing. He didn't play cards. Willie James Pearson, Marvel Watson and John Henry Jackson didn't like the loud mouth youngster. These three would be tough guys who picked on new prisoners and bullied them out of whatever they could get from them. All three seemed to be fighting homosexual desires without much success. At least that was what Boyd thought of the three troublemakers.

"Who you calling country boys?" Pearson said. "Just a figure of speech, just my way of trying to get a game going." Slick apologized. "Fuck you" Marvel shouted and "that ain't no figure of speech". Slick sat down on his bunk. The three walked over toward him. "I don't like loud mouth ugly ass niggers like you. I might make you suck my dick for waking me up." Willie James declared laughing as he inched closer. Slick smiled with confidence at the three bullies. "What the matter pussy boy?" Pearson inquired sardonically. Slick stood up. "What you gonna do?" Watson asked. Boyd was lying on the bunk next to Slick. He looked the three over carefully and said "None of you going to do nothing cause I'm trying to get some sleep. "Fuck you." Jackson said flashing a home made shank. Boyd took a deep breath and stood up. "I'm sorry. Didn't mean no harm." Boyd said inching closer to Jackson. Jackson started to laugh. Just then Boyd unleashed a right hand that landed flush on Jackson's jaw, knocking him out and clear over to the other side of a nearby bunk. Pearson stepped back with a startled look on his face. Slick produced a club from somewhere and started hitting Watson with it. Boyd grabbed Pearson before he could run away slapping him in the face and made him carry Jackson to his bunk and put him in it. Boyd kept Jackson's shank and let him know he could get it all he had to do was take it back. “Thanks” Slick told Boyd. “I owe you” “Those niggers started to get on my nerves. It wasn’t going to be long before they fucked with me. I wanted it to be on my terms.” Boyd answered. “Slick don’t forget a favor.” The young con player said. Slick wondered why Boyd had helped him… hoped after seeing Boyd knock Jackson out with one punch that Boyd was not a big dangerous homo.

Odfus Muse was Slick’s given name. He confided in Boyd some years later. “Nobody knows who gave it to me so I gave myself the name Billy “Slick” Robinson. A combination of Billy Eckstien the singer and Sugar Ray Robinson the boxer, just the way Slick saw himself… a lethal combination smooth as silk with the power of dynamite. Billy “Slick” fancied his-self a born con man a natural for the “game”. He could find a weak spot and prey on you before you could blink an eye. He would trick anyone, he called that being true to the game. Billy had few friends…and for good reason.

Billy had worked his way to Pittsburgh and met Red Allen, a master con artist who became sort of a surrogate father to the eleven-year-old boy. Slick had run away from home at seven and “took up with” a minstrel show. The resourceful child survived somehow for four years before the aging crook took him in. Allen regretted the path he had taken with his own life so he taught Slick to read, encourage him to read books. Something Allen did on his frequent visits to jail. Despite Slick’s many faults he loved to read and did so with a veracious appetite. Slick, unfortunately misunderstood or misinterpreted much of what he read… mostly because this born con man’s views on life itself were twisted.

Allen had somehow gotten Slick into Paine College in Augusta, Georgia. Slick assumed the name Casper Whitlock and was doing quite well until a friend of the College President recognized Slick as the boy that had sold him a bogus treasure map when Slick and Allen played con in Alabama a few years before. Despite his “B” average there was no record of Odfus Muse ever having attended school anywhere. The embarrassed school officials hastily and quietly removed him from school…along with any record of him having been there. That was the first and for many years the only attempt that Billy Slick made at being a part of the “square life.”

The world was full of suckers Slick thought. Anybody who worked for a living was a sucker. Slick would shake his head in disgusted disbelief at the folly of hard work…”only thing it got you was more work.” He was grateful for the suckers though. After all where would a smart guy like him be without them?

Slick's philosophy was that it was just twelve types of "motherfuckers." Slick was grateful to Boyd for his help and eagerly shared his distorted ideas of wisdom with the impressionable less experienced convict. Billy really felt he had some important information and Boyd should listen. Boyd did and learned the "game" quickly. Number one the honest motherfucker. Willing to work pay for what he gets. That's what Slick thought he was. I know anything can happen out here and try to be ready for it. You can't play him because he doesn't want an easy way out. Suckers ought to know I can't do a damn thing for them. Think about it I tell this fool that if he reads this Bible verse with water in it. Give him a certain time to nail something to a tree and throw salt over his shoulder. That's going to make his wife stop fucking around or make it rain. A dishonest motherfucker is the second type of motherfucker. Thinks he is God, wants everything, don't want to pay for nothing. That's the always looking for something for nothing motherfucker. The insecure motherfucker he's scared of everything, wants to control shit. Number three you can sell him a piece of a rag call it a prayer cloth or sell him a catfish bone, or some graveyard dirt. You are really helping this fool you are giving him something to believe in. Number four the greedy motherfucker he trying to find a way to get your shit. You can show him something about riches in the Word, he's trying to control shit too.

Number five the phony motherfucker this one is out to fool everybody. You can get him with jewelry, stocks, and shit to keep him young… you know shit like that.

Number six the selfish motherfucker he wants to hold on to shit. Make that bitch he married behave, keep his money you know that type of thing.

Number seven the lonely motherfucker sell him something to get a bitch or a friend. This sucker really need help CHARGE him.

Number eight is the smart motherfucker. Know it all motherfucker. Thinks he knows shit you should know. Sell this fool some kind of information that will make him win an argument. Some shit like the meaning of numbers you know what seven really means in the Bible… this stupid ass don't know seven is the number after six and the number before eight and that's all.

Common sense motherfucker is number nine. You can't con him, he might move something if he can get away with it. But he got enough sense to know that some dirt or a Bible verse is not going to help him get rich.

Neurotic motherfucker is number ten. This is an unpredictable motherfucker just leave his ass alone…this motherfucker is damn near crazy

The crazy motherfucker is that motherfucker that crackers keep locked up in the crazy house or chain gang. The psychologists call this mother psychotic.

Whorish motherfucker you see that's what got me here. I should have left town after I played that cracker. But I didn't know that this bitch I was fucking; was fucking that same cracker. She gets me to go to his house well. If I hadn't let my dick control me I wouldn't be here. He lamented sadly. "Thank God for all the suckers I'm just glad I'm not usually one of them…I'll learn from this mistake, believe me." In Slick's mind that was more proof that you should never be weak and care about somebody.

Slick was a near expert on the Bible and frequently used it in cons. Allen had taught him well. Red would say that to be a good con player you had to be an expert on human nature. The Bible tells you all about human nature. "As long as there is niggers, something you can call graveyard dirt, good luck charms or hexes you will never be broke. They claiming Jesus but living voodoo."

Allen believed the old saying you can't con an honest man. Allen taught Slick to study people and find what you can use against them. Slick studied the warden very carefully he recognized that the warden was greedy and cared little about how he got his money. The two crooks, (Slick and Captain Frank) developed a strange bond. Slick helped Captain Frank with his boot legging. Slick's experience in that minstrel show was extremely helpful. While there he met a man who had a very efficient way to make liquor out of things other than corn. Potatoes were supplied by the state. This would make the warden more profit. Captain Frank loved money Slick put money in his pocket so he developed a fondness for Slick. Slick asked if he could fix the roof on the colored building and Captain Frank complied…making Slick somewhat of a hero among the other convicts. Slick really enjoyed that because that made the other convict, vulnerable to him.

Slick was doing quite well for himself. He wanted to repay Boyd and he liked the big "country boy". Boyd was somewhat of a babe in the woods but he was a lot brighter that OLE Slick thought. Slick had selfish motives in mind for wanting Boyd on his side. First because he did appreciate Boyd's help. Slick's ego wouldn't allow him to believe that he needed anybody though. Second he didn't like owing anyone anything in jail…that made him vulnerable. Third he needed an enforcer…like most con artist OLE Slick didn't like to fight. Most of the other inmates were afraid of Boyd…after that one punch knockout.

The camp Captain and his family owned most of the farmland around the camp. Though they used the free labor of the black prisoners many more farm workers lived in the area. A framer needed a lot of laborers to pick cotton. The system had been built on slave labor. The advent of farm machinery displaced farm workers one machine could do the work of many of them.

Red Allen once told Slick to always have something a cracker wants when you deal with them or you are just another nigger to them. Slick loved to cook he learned how at the minstrel show. He could make pork skins (cracklings as they were called then) with a very different flavor sweet smoked taste. He also had an unbelievable recipe for Bar B Q...Captain Frank liked food almost as much as money. Slick let the warden sample the combination. The warden loved it and saw the money he could make selling the stuff. The captain and Billy bagged up the skins in simple brown bags and put the sauce in small mason jars for the white folks in the area. Slick suggested that Captain Frank make a juke joint out of an empty house he had on his farm for the black folks. "Well, Captain Frank you can sell more liquor if they're eating and dancing. " "I know, don't no white man want to be bothered with a bunch of drunk niggers on a Saturday night. I would just need one more man to keep an eye on things in case someone acted a fool." Slick knew he couldn't suggest anyone the warden would get suspicious. Frank Anderson listened and liked the idea. "Who do you want to go with you?" Frank inquired. " Well" Slick said, "I know a guard will have to go with us."

Slick had not let Boyd into his plan. He wanted to develop a "natural bond" with Boyd. Slick didn't mind telling Boyd his crazy ideas but he didn't want Boyd to think that he was weak...liking someone in prison is a weakness. Captain Frank was thinking the guard needed to be watching his money. The other inmate would be there to break up fights and keep them from tearing up his building. Just then Billy got lucky. Boyd walked into Captain Frank's office. The warden had sent for him to help him kill hogs. Slick cautiously said, "What about that nigger? He's strong as a bull."

Slick and Boyd formed a bond that has lasted throughout their lives. Boyd believed that his life was pretty messed up. Though not quite nineteen Boyd had spent one third of his life behind bars. Boyd had no formal education and perceived of having little opportunity at getting one. He figured he had to learn something to make a living. He figured Slick could talk, get people to do what he wanted them to do. Boyd was impressed so he listened to Slick. Slick taught him every con he knew and his views on life. Boyd listened and learned quickly but he didn't buy into Slick's views. He had his own views on life and what he wanted out of it. The two of them looked forward to getting out and going to "work."

Chapter eight

Elaine sang loudly and played the piano. "Jesus keep me near the cross. There's a precious fountain. Free to all a healing stream flows from Calvary's mountain." Her singing was fair and playing at best below average. Her love of music non-existent but it got her out of the house away from Willie's raving and Laura agreeing. Laura had started to lose weight. "Mama, why don't you go to the doctor?" Elaine asked. Laura smiled weakly. Willie was frightened by the possibility of the loss of Laura. Unbelievably, he became more unrealistic and unreasonable. Demanding crazy things of Laura crazy even for Willie. He blamed Laura's lack of faith for her bad health. Willie got the preacher to pray for healing and demanded Laura that claim good health in the name of Jesus... she sincerely tried. Unfortunately, the infection was spreading and Laura got little results from her efforts, as she got worse Willie got more demanding. Elaine got more mystified.

The young girl watched her parents play out what seemed to Elaine to be a tragic foresee. Willie fasted, prayed, got prayer cloths, put his hand on the radio and anointed both of them with oils. Everything but seek badly needed medical attention for his dying wife. Laura quietly sat agreeing and getting sicker. This disease of agreement had progressed to a fatal point Elaine thought. Laura had been a sickly child. Her lungs had been damaged but for many years she had appeared healthy. Her system did not develop normally due to the pneumonia she had as a child. Still despite her childhood illness and poor medical attention, available to her at that time...home remedies and potions were all they had to treat her with. Her new problems still might have been corrected if Willie had allowed her to see a doctor. Willie's boss would have seen to it that Laura could get medical attention not available to most blacks.

Elaine sat singing at the piano. As Laura agreed and struggled to breathe as she slowly died. Willie was somewhere over in Zion far removed from real life misquoting the "the good book," not believing a word he misread. His hatred of God, was all he had he was afraid to let go of it. His selfishness warped his perceptions of his own importance... giving him the delusion that God was his private baby sitter. By making his wife sick and his daughter such a "brazen little whore" God was perfecting his soul.

Elaine escaped the madness around her by being number one in her class, learning to play three instruments. She played that thing that you held in front of you and hit with a stick in the school band and of course the organ and piano in church. She did chores after school, studied, ignored Willie, nursed Laura and tried to hang on to her sanity. Elaine thought about her "Uncle Redmond" a lot, he had been so different from her father. She could talk to him and he would listen...nobody had to be afraid when he came around. Sometimes at night she would lay there wishing that he were her father. The next six months were the unhappiest of her life.

Laura died right after New Year's...Elaine had conflicts in her feelings concerning her mother's death. She missed her mother...Laura was all she had that she could count on. But her mother had suffered so much...Elaine was happy that the suffering was over. Willie did a lot of complaining about having to cook and take care of that girl now that Laura was gone. Elaine wondered why Willie hadn't been the one that died. The teenager hoped that she could go to live with her Aunt Rosetta.

"Too much Willie had been fatal." Elaine said silently as she sat in the church at the funeral listening to her mother's eulogy. The preacher preached about what wonderful workers in the church she and her loving husband had been. They would be together again in Heaven. Elaine wept at that thought, as she tried not to throw up. However, she did hope her father lived a long time. James was allowed to sit with the family along with Rosetta. Laura's only living relative (her sister Ruth) attended the funeral...Willie never allowed her to visit while Laura was alive. She had taken James in after Willie put him out. Willie didn't acknowledge James or Ruth even being there. Wilma had driven Rosetta down from Augusta the two women were very glad to see Elaine. Rosetta asked if Willie needed help with Elaine. Willie said. "We'll manage." Willie had too much pride to ever admit he needed help with anything. Willie had plans of making a maid out of his daughter. That was his plans not Elaine's.

Elaine asked about James several weeks after the funeral. Willie slapped her and instructed her to never mention James' name again in his presence. Then he announced that he would be taking Elaine out of school to take care of him. That was it. Elaine had enough. The young girl wanted to see her brother very badly. Elaine also had seen Willie slap Laura when he felt like it or things didn't go his way. He had even hit Laura while she was ill. Elaine had no ambitions of becoming her father's punching bag, she deeply resented Willie for his treatment of James and her mother. That night Elaine packed her clothes. She then took the money her mother kept hidden from Willie. Laura had squired away twenty-five dollars in the kitchen cabinet behind the dishes. Elaine also had the five dollars Rosetta had given her after the funeral. Then she got on a bus to Augusta. The trip from

Jacksonville to Augusta was full of joy and expectations...she could hardly wait to she the people see loved so much. When Elaine got to Augusta, she called Wilma to pick her up. When they got to Rosetta's. Wilma suggested that Rosetta call Willie. "He's worried about his baby." She said. Instead he said, "I ain't got no daughter." Rosetta called him a "jack ass." Wilma laughed. Rosetta never used profanity, she had to laugh about it herself when she cooled down. Wilma was just as angry but both were glad Elaine would be staying.

Elaine wouldn't allow herself to think of Willie for several years, though a teenager she was mature beyond her years. She was going to be a great help with Redmond Jr. Things had worked out for Elaine, she knew that Willie meant it when he said that she would have been forced to quit school if she had stayed with him... she wasn't about to do that. Elaine really was too young to be totally responsible for the baby and Wilma was too old not to need a lot of help with him. Elaine, Wilma and Rosetta loved each other and each had something that the other desired to have as a part of their own makeup.

Willie now alone closed off from having to feel or interact with any loved ones. Willie could praise the Lord in his own perverted way. He was the supervisor of all colored workers; he tithed, sang loud and prayed louder... so everyone could hear him. Everyone except God that is but he was praying to the others in church anyway. Willie was miserable and thought that was pleasing in the sight of God. Willie tried very hard to convince himself that he loved the misery he was in. He felt he had to be in control of everything around him...he lived alone. What better way to have control than to be alone with no one to disagree with you? As the years passed, Willie withdrew further into himself...his only companionship came from his occasional visits to prostitutes. Those visits added to Willie's feelings of worthlessness. Willie wanted to be alone so he could feel sorry for himself. He rejected the company of anyone that tried to befriend him.

Rosetta would wake up on Sunday morning singing in joyous anticipation of going to church. Elaine knew she had to go to church on Sunday but it was different with Rosetta. She was happy having Rosetta in her life...just the thought of the baby brought her joy. Since Elaine came to live with her, Rosetta now knew for certain that God loved her... more importantly she loved God. Everyday she thanked him for sending her to Rosetta...Elaine thanked God for her new family as well. Rosetta's genuine joy was contagious...and Elaine caught it. Elaine's piano playing improved and so did her appreciation for music. She even sang solos in church and played the organ as well and was the church's musician as a teenager.

Wilma encouraged Elaine to take part in school activities. Redmond Sr. attended all the functions when a father was needed and all the school activities where no father was needed. He learned to love Elaine like a daughter. Redmond Senior, Wilma, Elaine and Redmond Jr. went places and did things most blacks had no opportunity to even imagine. Trips to New York, Atlanta, Washington DC just to see the sights. Yearly vacations every summer...they were the envy of most of the people they knew. Anything Elaine needed and most of what she wanted he provided it...without disrespecting Rosetta. Elaine continued to work hard on her studies and graduated first in her class. Number one in the class of '52 and again in'56. Elaine concentrated on the things she had and was grateful for what she had. When Elaine graduated from Paine College, Rosetta again invited Willie to the graduation but he declined to attend. Elaine had not invited him and was not disappointed when he didn't show up. Elaine pushed any thoughts of Willie to the back of her mind. She loved her father but was convinced that he didn't love her...she couldn't shake the notion that Willie was nuts too.

Chapter 9

Fresh out of jail, a pocket full of money they had gotten by taking part in every crooked scheme they could think up in prison; Boyd and Slick went on a con-playing spree, taking money faster than Boyd had imagined possible. The two bought a car and went on the road all the way to Pittsburgh, Boston and New York. Slick knew people everywhere so it seemed to Boyd anyway. He was impressed but not for long. "Life in the fast lane." Slick would say. "The fast track." Slick loved the fast lane, spent money, got high, and had pretty women. Boyd liked the money but the drugs and all those women didn't suit him. The two of them spent the next five years in the north getting money, going to jail and not being able to hold onto anything…thanks to Slick's self indulgence. Slick's expensive habits were keeping both of them broke. They would make a score. Boyd would try to save a little of the take but never enough to buy anything or change the way he was living.

Slick loved the lifestyle, the excitement danger and the uncertainty. The short trips to jail were just an occupational hazard. Slick loved playing cops and robbers. Boyd didn't play. To him it didn't make sense to risk his freedom and at times his life for the fun of it. Drugs had no appeal at all for a serious young crook that wanted to succeed. He didn't need any more problems than he already had. Boyd also didn't like all the moving around he wanted to settle somewhere and have some roots. Boyd wanted to buy some property…this cop and blow nonsense had to go (get some money and spend it just as fast). He wanted to have something substantial, with these frequent trips to the slammer he would be better off working. The last year of the time he spent on the road, Boyd looked for that big score that would enable him to go back down south and stay. While in jail for a con, game Boyd heard about a numbers operation in Florida, that could be robbed without much difficulty. The two of them had robbed drug dealers in New York and Boston. Boyd really didn't like robberies, but, he did anything he felt he had to do to survive if the chances of not getting away with it weren't too great. Boyd was big, strong, fearless and mean if he had to be. He had never hurt anyone in the crimes he committed but he knew that it might come to that this time if anything went wrong. Boyd planned things out before he did them with surprising conning for a young man with very little experience and exposure too much. Slick stayed so loaded on the street that Boyd did most of the thinking. Boyd told Billy. "Fuck this fast track shit. I'm going back down South and hold on to my money. When we take this place in Florida off I'm staying in Savannah." Slick agreed, he knew how Boyd felt for quite sometime. He had a couple of girls that he was pimping anyway. Slick didn't think he needed Boyd even though Boyd had been taking care of him.

Boyd went to Tampa about two weeks ahead of time and studied the movement of the numbers runners. He knew when they brought the money and how many of them came into the back of the restaurant. How many people would be there after the last runner made his drop. Rudy Lee Harris, a huge, midnight black man with a reputation for extreme violence and an ego as large as he was ran the numbers in a restaurant. He had as many as twenty whores working for him at a time. Rumor had it that he had beaten at least two rival pimps to death for stealing girls from him. Harris was a very feared man in Tampa. This big man never trusted anyone so Rudy was the last to leave each night alone though well armed. Boyd had seen numbers places in New York with armed guards and Mafia protection still get robbed. This would be easy. Harris was not careful. His reputation and the huge amounts of beer he drank each day had gone to his head. Boyd watched Rudy Lee go down a dark alley by himself every night without even looking.

Boyd had a friend who worked at a zoo. He had seen the keeper at the zoo control wild animals with the use of a tranquilizer gun. Boyd asked his friend at the zoo in New York. Though he wasn't a trained animal handler, Boyd's friend knew quite a bit about the chemicals. He could mix the stuff they used to control the beasts at the zoo. He even sold some of the animal tranquilizers to local drug dealers. He could mix the chemicals up just as well as the formally trained animal keepers. "How much of that would it take to knock out a 250 pound man?" Boyd asked. He then explained that he wanted to play a trick on a large friend of his. Boyd knew that it would be nearly impossible to trace the tranquilizer gun all the way back to New York from Tampa Florida. He then took a trip to Tampa to look things over and develop a plan. Upon his return to New York he told Slick about his plan. Boyd got everything he needed, tranquilizer gun and all, packed up his belongings and got ready to head south. The real key to the success of the caper would rest on his ability to get Slick to Florida quickly without him getting busted on the way down or creating too much attention after they got there. They had to get in and out of Tampa with as few people as possible seeing them. Slick's womanizing and drug using might make them a little too visible. Boyd knew he would have to bring a supply of drugs for Slick but he didn't want to bring too much and his partner get himself into a drug induced daze when it came time to do business. The two men talked about the upcoming caper and they decided that Slick would take two weeks to kick and have his nerves together for the job. They rented a room in a boarding house and Slick's main girlfriend nursed him back to health. She made the trip with them and drove the get away car.

Rudy Lee drank beer all day and most of the night, he was pretty high when he left the restaurant...for his walk down the alley to his house on the next street. Boyd and Slick hid in the alley behind some garbage cans...there was no light in the alley. They shot Harris with the tranquilizer when the big man passed. He turned toward them, took two steps and fell flat on his face...both Boyd and Slick breathed a collective sigh of relief. Rudy was a very intimidating site...he was huge and had already pulled an equally huge pistol from his shoulder holster. Slick and Boyd grabbed the money and left Tampa running. Harris stayed out for two days but when he recovered he had no idea what happened. On the drive out of town Boyd gave Slick the drugs he had secretly brought with him. Boyd knew that his old friend would need something to calm him down after the job was done.

Savannah in 1954 was as segregated a city as there was probably in the world. Whites with old money guarded their estates jealously. The few blacks with money or status shunned poor blacks... with at least as much disdain as any Klan member. Boyd knew he could operate with almost impunity as long as he didn't bother whites. No one cared what went on in the black side of town. Boyd also knew there was money on the docks. He remembered the policeman who had tried to help him when he was a kid. He also remembered that the cop had been down on the docks getting paid to look the other way when cargo got missing. Boyd set out to find Officer Bob Edmonds.

Chapter 10

Elaine stood quietly alone in Wilma's backyard thinking about leaving home for the first time. She had been accepted at a nursing school in New York. She was full of joy and fear. But more than anything she felt a sense of accomplishment. Elaine was sad that the happiest chapter in her life was ending but she was excited about the future. "Laine throw me the ball", little Redmond cried. "OK", she said. The playful child had brought her back to reality. She picked the ball up and threw it back to the anxiously waiting nine-year-old. She would be OK. "Yeah" said Elaine quietly to herself as she joined her son in a game of catch.

Elaine had been on lots of trips with the Perry's but always by car. A trip on the Jim Crow trains caused some anxiety on the part of Redmond Sr. But he knew a porter, Marcus Flynn and asked him to look out after "my daughter". Flynn agreed. He showed Elaine in what towns she could use the bathroom and after the train reached Maryland she could go on the train and get something to eat as well from the dining car. Elaine enjoyed the trip. She looked out of the window at the passing countryside. She had heard so much about life up north and looked forward to seeing "the Big Apple".

When she arrived at Grand Central Station, Wilma's cousin Macy Williams met Elaine at the station. Macy was also a student at the nursing school and a native of Harlem. Macy was a typical Williams, short, full of energy, talking a mile a minute. Elaine loved her from the time they met as kids...on one of the vacation trips to New York. Macy was so like Grandma Lillie...she never stopped talking.

Wilma's cousin Henry and his wife Betty lived on 128th Street. Elaine had visited them a few times but had never thought she would be living in New York. She was a little overwhelmed well a lot overwhelmed...like anyone from a relatively small town would be. Macy was a city kid full of confidence and a zest for living. She set out to wise her country cousin up in a hurry. Elaine listened and followed instructions. It was obvious that New York was not anything like Augusta...or any other place on earth she thought. Elaine stayed out of trouble by listening to her more experienced cousin. Elaine's hours of studying, her attention to finding out the nursing school curriculum had paid off. She again was first in her class. Macy improved her grades with Elaine's help.

The two young women went to work at Harlem Hospital. Elaine's outstanding grade point average got her inquiries from many places but when the young black woman showed up, the positions were suddenly filled. Harlem Hospital was an exciting place to work, especially in the emergency room, that is where they started out. Elaine quickly moved up. She had reached a supervisor's position in a little less than three years. Redmond Sr. died suddenly. Elaine was forced to return to Augusta. Wilma was now sixty and needed help with Redmond Jr. now fourteen.

Redmond Perry Sr. had been one of the most respected and well-liked men to live in Augusta. His funeral filled the largest Black church in Augusta to overflowing. The procession to the graveyard had over 80 cars. The Williams Family, all of its nearly 200 men, women and children attended. None of this outpouring of love meant anything to a 14-year-old boy who had lost his best friend, advisor, confidant and father. Little Redmond sat devastated at the funeral asking why, wanting to put the blame somewhere but what good would it do? "Crying won't bring him back, won't change things" Wilma said, fighting back the tears herself. The boy's world was crushed and for many years he had a nagging feeling in his gut. It seemed that a fear of life set in and nothing could erase that feeling.

Elaine landed a job at the VA Hospital in Augusta... the first colored nurse at that hospital. Her ability as a nurse was undeniable and she advanced slowly but steadily. It was difficult being a parent or an almost parent to Redmond Junior. The elder Redmond had been a male roll model and a very strick disciplinarian. Redmond senior never allowed the youngster to con him. Wilma and Elaine were suckers for anything that Red came up with...he had a game for everything and everybody.

Romance wasn't a part of Elaine's life especially after her return to Augusta. She had cautiously dated a few times in New York and had male friends but when it came to intimacy she couldn't put the memories of her early unhappiness out of her mind. While in New York she had a Lesbian experience but felt ashamed and dirty after...she found that she had issues with Willie not all men. The fact was in her own way she was every bit as controlling as her father. Sexual relationship made her feel vulnerable...Elaine hated to be vulnerable. She could control her work environment so she worked long hours and tried to be the best nurse she possibly could be. She had people close to her that she loved and had no real desire to take chances...it seemed that she wanted to be an old maid.

"But Aunt Wilma don't even know this man," Elaine protested. "What is it going to hurt having dinner with him?" Wilma questioned. "Okay but that's all." Wilma had fixed Elaine with a young man from their church.

Carl Watts, handsome dark skinned muscular man who worked for the railroad. Elaine couldn't stand him from the moment she saw him and the more intimate the relationship became the loathing she felt for him multiplied. Elaine reveled in her ability to hurt Carl. She got a delicious tingle when she saw pain in eyes after some vain attempt to please her was rebuked.

This arrangement lasted two years until Elaine started having a recurring dream where Carl would melt into an exact copy of Willie, Bible in one hand choking her with the other. One day while lecturing Redmond about his finding one girl he said, "Why so she can treat me like you treat Carl?" Elaine ended the farcical liaison.

Chapter 11

Boyd entered the outer office of now Deputy Chief Bob Edmonds. "Hello, my name is Boyd Tillman. I knew the chief a long time ago and I would like to talk to him if I could." "Well I'll see" his assistant said. She smiled as she knocked on the door. There is a boy out here to see you name Boyd Tillman. "Who?" He said, "Boyd Tillman said he knew you long time ago." His assistant replied. Bob then said, "OK I got a minute." As Boyd entered the office he said, "Sir, I don't know if you remember me. I was 12 years old and got in trouble and you helped me. "Have a seat." Edmond still didn't remember. When Boyd sat down the Chief looked at Boyd closely and said, "You're the kid with the wicked right hand." Laughing he said, "What can I do for you? You really grew up." Boyd then said, Well sir, I've been up north for a few years and I want to come back home. I need a job. I was hoping you could help me. Maybe something down on the docks, people respect you." "Thank you. I hope some do." Edmonds replied as he wrote a note and gave it to Boyd "to give to John Barrett at the Moore's Warehouse. I hope that will help you. Don't beat anybody up" Edmonds said with a grin. "Thank you. I won't." Boyd said.

Boyd went to Moor's Warehouse bright and early the next morning. Gave Barrett the note and he read it and asked. "Ever done this kind of work before?" "Yes, Sir", Boyd said. "I know how to do most of the jobs in a warehouse." Boyd said with just the right tone for the white man to listen to him. He got hired for $87.50 a week, good money for a colored boy in the mid-fifties. Boyd gladly accepted the opportunity. He knew that he was in with the right people and was on his way to a lot more money.

The work was hard and Boyd watched everything that went on in the warehouse. He watched and kept his mouth shut. But he saw who was stealing with permission and who was stealing on their own. He said nothing to either. He knew how to mind his own business and wait; over the years Boyd had learned patience. After six months, Barrett asked Boyd if he wanted to make a little extra money. Boyd said, "Yes Sir." Barrett got Boyd and Joe Chaney to help him unload a truck after hours and he paid them $50.00 each. Many of the dock's workers smoked marijuana. Boyd wasn't involved in using it so he asked Barrett if he could buy him some to sell on weekends at the small nightclub Boyd owned. Barrett agreed. Boyd also sold heroin; booked numbers ran crap games and bootleg liquor.

Boyd had been putting money aside waiting to hear from Bob Edmonds. One night the police raided Boyd's place. Officer John Carey drove Boyd to the police station. “Boy are you crazy trying to make all the money?” “No sir just don’t know who I need to see.” “See me.” He said. “Okay Officer Carey.” Boyd had $500.00 in an envelope in his pocket. Boyd dropped it over into the front seat. Neither man said anything. Boyd was released. Officer Carey came by every week.

About a year after that Bob called Boyd into his office and asked him, “Do you want to make some real money?” Boyd said. “Yes Sir.” “We’ve been watching you”, he said. “Your little club is doing all right. We really don’t like you selling dope but you won’t need to. The people I know can help you run your club, whorehouse and gambling houses; we will see to it that you have all the numbers that OK. We’ll look out for you. We want you to run a house with colored girls for us; you don’t talk about your business.” For five years Boyd prospered. Ironically the Civil Rights movement brought an end to Boyd’s whorehouses. Customers got afraid to come to the house. Boyd’s control of most of the numbers still left him OK. His backers had helped him hide money and Boyd made money off his investments. Hilton Head was a windfall for Boyd. His net worth was close to a half million dollars. He lived modestly and kept his job at the warehouse.

Saul Greenspan was very good at cleaning up dirty money. Greenspan was Boyd’s attorney for deals that his backers weren’t involved. Boyd trusted no one and that was to be his downfall. Boyd Tillman had over played his hand. His friends couldn’t help him. But he was able to hold on to most of his money and property.

Greenspan had his fingers in a lot of pies but his luck ran out. A deal he had with a state Senator’s nephew went bad and left the young man broke; Greenspan, a lot richer than he was before he met the young man. Investigations followed and Boyd was one of the firsts to be caught up in its wake. Add the fact that it was an election year and racketeering was something new to charge a black man with in Georgia. It was off to jail again for Boyd Tillman. Boyd asked his lawyer to see to it that his interest was looked out for if he got some time. It was agreed. Boyd said, “I know I fucked up. Nobody’s fault but mine.” He was ready for whatever happened. Twenty-one years the judge said. Boyd sighed that would be his only show of emotions about his fate.

The Civil Rights movement was changing the south. The chains had been taken off and the road gangs done away with. Boyd had never done time with whites in the South, he had in the North. The truth was, however, he had not known any white people on a personal level other than Edmonds. Integration made better living conditions and other reforms such as educational opportunities... prison life was now more bearable. The system had changed in some ways but prison was still prison. Life for a black man in Georgia was still different from than that of a white Georgian. Boyd's connections could not stop him from getting prison time. However they all thought a pre-trial arrangement had been made for an early parole in two or three years. The arrangements had indeed been made but events would change the ability of his friends to keep their word. Edmonds knew Captain Wells the supervisor of the guards at the prison. The plan was for Boyd to do two or three easy years and get out.

Marvin Wells was a twenty-five year veteran of the criminal Justus system. The tall slim, military looking man...everything about him was spit and polish. Wells ran the prison with an iron hand what he said was law. Though the warden was technically his boss, Wells was "The Man". Wells knew that gambling and drugs and every other vice went on in prison. Capt. Wells believed in order and he also had a fondness for money. The old guard wasn't about to let an inmate get rich and he not be a part of it. Wells knew the working of a prison probably better than anyone did in the prison system. He knew how to stop anything that he didn't want to get into institution. There was never any doubt about who was in charge and you didn't double-cross Marvin Wells.

His money was now secure on the outside, parole fixed he thought and a new friend on the inside. Boyd would make the best of it. For the first time in his life Boyd was financially secure. Though he didn't like doing time. Things were different this time... different from when he and Slick were going to jail broke and getting out broker. Boyd looked at his situation and was grateful for what he had. Then his circumstances improved. He hoped to go into legitimate enterprises when he got out. The last year or two he was lessening his involvement in the rackets...he had started to invest his money. Boyd accepted the fact that he had profited from a lot of illegal activities now he had to pay...he knew he could handle it.

Wells called for Thomaso Mialo and Boyd to come to his office. The men that Wells had running things had been released. Mialo was a New Yorker who had been caught up in a robbery gone badly. Thomaso had connections in one of the five Mafia families in New York. He had been an under boss but due to a change in hierarchy he had to relocate. He went to New Orleans then traveled throughout the south. He was still considered a man of respect he had been loyal to his old boss...a good solider. The new man in his position was a vengeful man. Thomaso had been promoted over him in the last take over. He was just letting things cool down. Mialo didn't want to disrespect his old rival. So, if he didn't make trouble or cause concern for the new bosses he would be left alone. His sources were still in tact. He could get what ever he needed. He would just wait to be summoned and permitted to go home. He even sent word that he would be loyal if the time came when he could return.

Boyd and Thomaso had watched each other like two animals in a jungle each probing to find a way to open communication. Both could see something in the other that was intriguing. The call to Well's office was unexpected but not unwelcome. "You know everybody needs friends. Wouldn't be where I am without my friends" Wells assured them both. Boyd sat looking around the room. "This is my prison. I run it, control everything. You boys can get along here real good." Wells announced like the two were not aware of that fact. The two convicts sat looking bewildered but each knew what the Captain was talking about. Prison has a language of its own. What is said and what is understood. " The Lord wants 10% but man wants 30%". He continued. "I guess he needs more help than the Lord." "Less people involved." Mialo joked "but I always liked 25% myself." The New York hood stated. "What church were you part of?" Boyd asked with a straight face. Then all three men laughed. "Well, I think we'll get along fine." Wells said walking the men to his door.

The two men had agreed to give Wells 25% of what they made. They had a free hand to do whatever they wanted. Wells would take care of the competitions, allow them to bring in whatever they needed and protect them. Wells had good reports on both. They could keep their mouths shut and be trusted. Both men knew how to operate and respect Captain Wells at the same time. Boyd and Mialo organized their distribution system. Each had a man between them and the actual sale of drugs, gambling, prostitution and protection of weaker inmates.

They found enforcers, two men whose viciousness was famous throughout the prison system. Wells' had unorthodox ways of doing it but he kept order. Virgin Peeler, a relatively small man about 5'10", 175 pounds but he was given respect afforded only the most dangerous menace in the penal system. He was a man of undetermined race. He was dark, had straight hair and keen features. A white family in South Georgia had raised him. He had been abandoned. They found him out front of a store wandering around naked. The Peeler family took him home. J W and Pearl Peeler had four girls and J W always wanted a son so they kept him. Things like that were not that unusual in the south in the 1930's. Virgin didn't take to school very much so he stayed on the farm and helped his father. The two were inseparable. J W was killed when Virgin was twelve. He stayed with the Peelers in a little shack in the woods on the farm's edge. Then one day in 1948, a Sunday he killed three people, his sisters' husbands right after Sunday dinner. He was given life without parole. He said he had a reason for what he did but couldn't remember what it was.

Virgin loved to talk about farm life, plowing mules and killing hogs. If Peeler liked you, he would do anything for you. If he didn't, he might kill you. He had the mind of a child, a very sick child. But he did have sense enough to cover up his crimes in prison. Peeler liked Boyd because Boyd would read the Bible to him and Boyd wasn't afraid of him, at least he didn't show it. Every inmate at the prison had some level of fear for this man he was unpredictable. For some reason Peeler idealized Boyd. Peeler didn't place value on material things the only thing that he owned was a amulet that he kept hidden and showed to no one not even Boyd. He was wearing it when the Peelers found him.

The other enforcer was one Rudy Lee Harris, the same one Boyd and Slick had robbed. Harris didn't even know he had been drugged. He thought he had passed out and passers by took his money. He didn't know Boyd from Adam. He was in for killing two men at a card game in Columbus, Ga. He beat them to death. Something seemed to be eating away at this giant man. If he lost his temper he would go into a rage that had cost four inmates their lives. Deaths were seldom investigated in most prisons. Things were not that way at this prison however.

Boyd also suggested that the two maniacs could make some money protecting the weaker inmates who could afford to pay them. Wells appreciated this type of help and Boyd knew it. Peeler gave Boyd his money he got for protection. Boyd got Wells to let Peeler have a garden. Harris and Peeler kept order on their tiers. Peeler was the only man that Harris feared in the prison; Harris thought Virgil was crazy and he had a fear of crazy people though he probably could have broken the smaller man in half with his bare hands.

The agreement that Wells and the two convicts made would prove to be a profitable one. Everything that came in the prison the three got a piece of it. Gambling was organized even prostitution girls from Boyd's houses in Savannah were brought in for the inmates who could afford them. Even the guards had to pay if they wanted to be with one of the girls. Wells didn't approve of prostitution, he didn't think any of the hand picked guards he had watching over the enterprise should take part in it. Therefore if one of them saw a girl they liked they had to pay if they didn't want Capt. Wells to find out. Thomaso and Boyd got whatever they wanted. Capt. Wells had granted them power over their fellow inmates and even some of the guards.

The next two and a half years Boyd, Thomaso and Wells prospered; the two convicts had to have their lawyers make weekly visits to the prison to take their money out. Boyd had one of the best lawyers in Savannah handle his affairs. Boyd's money was being invested in stocks in the form of mutual funds, bonds, real estate and various other, low risk but profitable investments. The Lawyer had holding companies set up so nobody knew that a prison convict was getting rich while he was incarcerated.

There really wasn't anything that Boyd didn't have in prison but he didn't want to spend the rest of his life there. Confinement no matter how much money or power you have is not what you want. Boyd had a mindset that he was only going to spend a couple of years behind bars. He had adjusted very well to that idea... he had given very little thought to the twenty plus year sentence, he had been given. But Boyd's parole hearing came up. He was sure he would make parole and go back to Savannah and take up where he left off. The make up of the parole board had changed. Bob Edmonds visited Boyd and expressed some concern about the changes but no one thought the changes enough to stop a parole that Captain Wells had approved of personally. One of the new members was a woman from the Atlanta area. Leigh Hollingsworth, a socialite, who had a rich husband and time on her hand.

Saul Greenspan had gotten beaten up at the prison where he was incarcerated. She found out several things in the course of her "investigation". She was given information that Boyd had paid to have it done. Her investigation consisted of testimony voluntarily provided by one Wesley Barker. When asked if he knew Boyd Tillman he said that he didn't but through the prison grapevine Boyd had gotten some money for him and a couple of inmates to do the job on Saul. Baker had killed a white man this time and was in prison. He said Boyd had a grudge against Greenspan and wanted him taken care of for putting him behind bars. In reality the attack on Saul was because Baker and his friends didn't like Jews. The fact of Boyd's conviction seemed to support this story even when Saul told her that he and Boyd had no antipathy toward each other. But the woman jumped to the conclusion that Saul was afraid to talk. Since Boyd had been sent up for assault on Tom Godwin and the details of the case were hushed up therefore she saw no connection.

Chapter 12

Boyd's parole was denied. Edmonds was as bewildered as Boyd. Wells summoned Boyd to his office. "Well sorry", he said blowing in the disgust. "Wesley Baker is being transferred here." Wells said handing Boyd a copy of the parole report "this is bull-shit" Wells said looking depressed shaking his head. "They suspect him of being in the Arian nation, a Yankee Klan or gang, something. Trouble anyway you look at it." "Do you know Baker" Wells asked? "Yea, from years ago when I was in reform school." Wells then admitted that he knew the whole story. "How is Mr. Wilcox, is he a friend of yours" Boyd asked? "Yes he's fine fella known him for years he asked about you sent his best said he had hoped you would have stayed out of trouble" the worried Wells answered. Wells liked to have people validate information he already had he figured that he could find out more that way and also get a sense of how the individual felt about the situation.

Peeler was sitting on the top bunk when Boyd returned to the cell. "What's wrong big man?" Boyd told him about the expected trouble. "Shit." Peeler said "I can take care of that and everybody will think he escaped don't worry about it" Peeler said.

Harris and Peeler didn't mix except for business. They talked very little to one another. Rudy Lee had made John Henry Jackson his sex slave and spent most of his time making Jackson perform all kinds of perverted sex acts. Rudy liked to make Jackson orally copulate him in front of other inmates while he was playing cards or dominos or charge $2.00 for Jackson to do the other card players at the game. Rudy would laugh and say, "Come here bitch." Jackson would reply. "OK Daddy" and come over to Rudy and kiss him. One day Boyd said to Rudy, "You make everybody uncomfortable with that shit." Rudy said, "That mother fucka's got some good head. You just too cheep to spend the two dollars."

That was Boyd 's last attempt at reforming Rudy. Peeler didn't approve of that sort of thing and the strange and frightening Peeler gave Rudy the creeps. Rudy and Baker had fought when they were imprisoned together. Both men cut each other up so badly they both ended up in the hospital. Baker had stabbed at Rudy's back but Rudy had turned at the last instant. The knife put a deep cut in Harris' side but he was able to turn and cut Wesley and by the time the guards broke them up Baker had been stabbed in the stomach, cut in the face, arm and neck. Rudy Lee had the side wound, cuts to the face, hand and arm. Both stayed in the hospital for four weeks.

Rudy had a score to settle he couldn't help but smile when Peeler related his plan to him.

Rudy Lee had become a vicious sadistic man who fed off the fear of others. He enjoyed hurting people... hearing them begging for mercy he would inflect more pain. He raped inmates when he felt that they were fearful or weak. Fear and intimidation were the way he coped with any situation. His jailhouse reputation meant everything to him no man had ever really beaten him in a fight but yet he seemed afraid and wanted everyone around him to be in fear. He respected Boyd's brain and the power he had in the prison. OLE Rudy was more intimidating to be that close to the powers that be.

Rudy's deep voice, his startlingly black complexion and huge size frightened even the most hardened inmates. Rudy's features were not fearsome in fact he had a pleasant smile and a really infectious grin. But he had to know you very well to let his guard down enough to let you see his sense of humor. He had known only brutality; his earliest memories were of being beaten and sexually abused by his stepfather and his family minister. Rudy told his mother what was going on she chose not to believe him. He spent many nights crying and pleading for them to stop. When he became a teenager he stopped it himself. He beat and sodomize both men in front of his mother." You should have seen the look on that bitch face" he once told Peeler. "You don't fuck with Rudy" seldom anybody did and he let everybody know it.

The plan to get rid of Wesley was simple; they would just make him disappear. Warden Mathews, was supposed to be the boss, but he left everything in the hands of Capt. Wells. The prison ran quietly the warden got awards and praise from all over the state and country he was happy. The joke among the guards was that the warden had his head so far up Captain Wells' ass that if Wells stopped suddenly the warden would break his neck. By keeping a low profile Wells was able to make his money on the side and run things like he wanted to. Wesley Baker wasn't about to ruin things at Captain Wells' penitentiary; he would disappear and things would go on as normal. Baker had caused problems as a member of the Klan, caused problems as an inmate at other places, had grudges against a man that was making Captain Wells' money and Baker couldn't be reasoned with. His death could almost be ruled a suicide by anyone that knew the good captain.

The prison had recently completed a building to be used as a reception barracks while prisoners were being processed. The building was completely finished the only thing left to do was to clean it up and bring the furniture in. Wesley, Rudy and Peeler were assigned to clean the building. Virgil was standing on a chair behind the door as Wesley entered the room. Wesley saw Harris standing in front of the shower room door. Upon seeing Harris started toward him saying "You Black" Before he could finish Peeler who could move as quietly as a cat plunged a butcher knife into the back of Baker's neck. The knife went all the way through the point of the knife sticking out of the front of Wesley's neck. Rudy ran over to him and stuck a knife in to Baker's chest. The two men grabbed Baker on each side and ran with him into the shower room. Throwing him to the floor of the shower. Virgil pulled the knife from his neck. Rudy chopped, chopped again and once more with a meat cleaver. The head was removed, blood splattering all over the floor of the shower and the walls. Virgil said, "Get the arm by the joints on the shoulders. Just like cutting up a hog." Rudy a country boy himself, remembered butchering hogs with his father and uncle. Both of them went to work filled with happy childhood memories. Both were kids again racing to beat their father's cutting up their hogs. The two maniacs split the body's torso down the middle, found the joints at the knee and they put the internal organs in a bag inside three other bags. They talked of those happy days, had found they had a lot in common. They finished cutting Baker up and bagging him in an hour and a half in time for the garbage truck at 3:00 p.m. They cleaned the building so well it was so spotless that the warden gave them special privileges and rewarded them with seven extra days of good time on there records.

Baker was missing at the evening count. Both Harris and Peeler swore they had not seen Baker they both lied with choirboy looks on their faces. Captain Wells put on the best performance saying he was very upset with the escape. But not to worry the escapee would be captured the Captain said with a straight face and in his most comforting tone. "I feel sure he will be captured before long. We will not tolerate this sort of thing"

This was Captain Wells' only commit to the press. Nothing was ever said about the escape again until American's most wanted aired it on a segment some thirty-five years later. They got tips from all over the nation but they still haven't caught up with Baker yet.

Chapter 13

Watch the ball into your hands, catch it, tuck it away, there's an opening. Redmond thought as he scored a touchdown. One of twelve he would score as a ninth grader. Another Jim Brown some said. Coach Phillips, however, wasn't one of them. All he said was work harder than anyone else and you might be pretty good one of these days. After the practice Red would run extra laps, lift extra weights and study the other team's films. Red liked being the best, didn't mind working to be the best because he didn't mind telling you about it either.

The crap games in the boy's room, smoking, drinking held no excitement for Redmond. He went to church every Sunday. "That's where all the pretty girls are," Red told his friend Bobby. Bobby went with Red and found something. Red wanted company basically because he couldn't handle all the girls he met at church… Red could talk Bobby into anything. But this time Bobby was the winner he really fell in love with church… the faith that he found there would be the foundation for his life.. Thereafter the two boys went every Sunday. They were in youth choirs, pageants, youth conferences and trips. Redmond got what he wanted as long as he kept his grades up and went to church; football was fun. Whatever he got he shared with Bobby. Redmond was class president and had everybody eating out of his hands. Everything that was left over went to Bobby his loyal vice-president.

Red's senior year he started drinking, not much at first just on weekends, not every weekend. Red's senior year he scored twenty-seven touchdowns and led his team to the State Championship game for the third straight year. They lost Red got hurt and blamed he himself for the loss this was the first failure he had ever experienced. His next disappointment was Red really wanted to attend the University of Georgia but it had not yet integrated he didn't want to go a long way from home. He chose to go to Florida A & M in Tallahassee, Florida. Red nearly decided to go to Michigan State but he wanted to be near family and friends. Bobby was not as good an athlete as Redmond and went to Hampton Institute in VA. Red had a good season as a freshman 494 yards rushing. Black college football in 1965 was as good as college football got. Grambling, Florida A&M, Alcorn and Tennessee State were the best of the best. Red was a little intimidated, he wasn't used to not being the best player and having to work hard just to get playing time. His confidence was shaken, he wasn't the big man on campus. His drinking increased. He started to experiment with drugs, marijuana, cocaine and heroin. Lots of pretty girls liked drugs and Red liked girls and they loved him. He started selling drugs and found that he liked money and the power having drugs gave him. Then add the excitement of breaking the law, Red was hooked. He was getting the perks of being a football star without the hard work. Red never considered the price he might have to pay. Georgia Red, as he started calling himself, imagined himself on the fast track, a player, super fly (he had seen the movie) high heel shoes, pimps clothes and all he was living a fantasy. Red was smoking and sniffing everyday. The fantasy was that he didn't have a problem and he could do anything he wanted to do.

Red had a pocket full of money when he got busted, possession with the intent to distribute. Furman White's son Tallmadge had to use all of his considerable legal skills to get Red five to seven years. Red knew he had made a mistake but still didn't think he was an addict. He had been caught, if he hadn't sold that dope to that guy he didn't know everything would have been all right. Everybody is a crook he thought I just wasn't slick enough didn't have the money to pay the right people off. He told himself over and over until he believed it himself. Then as his trial got closer he prayed the hypocrite's prayer "Lord if you get me out of this one I'll serve you forever."

Chapter 14

Bob died suddenly of a heart attack while mowing his lawn. With his death Boyd's chances of an early parole died just as suddenly. Boyd had no leverage on the rich white Savannah society. A few of his old friends wanted to help him. However, it would be hard to explain their interest in a black man associated with a house of ill repute and racketeering. With Edmonds around they could say they were helping a policeman who wanted to help a reformed crook. Boyd weighed the situation and choose to keep quiet. Captain Wells ran the prison and Boyd was in prison he thought as he lay on his bunk. "Boyd" a voice interrupted his thoughts. "Detrick Reynolds entered Boyd's cell talking quietly. "That I-tallian Molli is scheming to kill you." Yeah Boyd said dryly. Reynolds was getting paid but didn't have a clue of how Boyd and Thomaso ran things so smoothly. Boyd controlled his anger and said. "OK Man. Let's don't do nothing yet. Let's just cool it for a while." Boyd knew that only Wells could make a move like that and he knew that Wells wasn't interested in dealing with this young fool.

Tony Rizzo, one of the few other Italians, approached Thomaso with a similar story in the prison. Mialio felt close to the young man. They were Yankees and more important of Sicilian descent. The kid only had five years and Thomaso had plans for him when he got out. "What a shame, " Mialio sighed. The kid got ahead of himself. "Yea," Boyd agreed. The folly of youth the two men thought almost out loud.

Captain Wells was furious when Thomaso told him of the planned treachery. Wells normally reserved shouting to his secretary. "Get Boyd Tillman in here now!" Wells without his usual subtly said, "We got to take care of this ourselves. We've got to take charge of this thing. It could be a cancer; we can't let it spread. They must have someone on staff. When I find out who it is, I pity the poor bastard." Boyd said, "Maybe not, these guys are young. They may not be that smart. Thomaso didn't say anything for a while. He just sat there looking perplexed and somewhat far away. After a time he said, "Officer Adams," Wells pacing the floor in a rage turned to Thomaso and Boyd. "He's my problem and I'll take care of him."

David Adams had been with the penal system five years. He had risen through the ranks quickly and was a shift supervisor. Though not a part of Well's inner cycle he could get drugs in but was unaware of Captain Well's direct involvement. He might even be trying to get some evidence on Wells, in any case this young man had to go. Wells didn't like the new breed of correction officers, college educated without a clue of how to run a prison. Interest in becoming governor or "some such shit." These guys were just temporary jailers. Wells believed that prisoners had to be controlled and run by people who were committed to be prison guards for life. Young Adams had to be used to teach a lesson to anybody on staff who doubted who was in charge. Wells had a long reach in the system and out.

His thoughts racing Boyd returned to his cell...He had never killed anyone, avoided violence whenever possible. Yeah, he had been in fights, had hurt people seriously but had never set out to kill anyone. Thomaso sensed this but could not say anything in front of Wells. Thomaso had gotten his "bones" several years prior and had handled three contracts but he didn't relish the prospect of what had to be done. Thomaso respected Boyd and would do his best to make up for Boyd's inexperience. He recalled throwing up after his first.

Boyd hadn't understood how Thomaso knew about Adams. Adams had approached Thomaso with a deal, which he turned down thinking it was a test. He hadn't mentioned it to Wells. Thomaso felt he had caused the situation to get out of control by not telling Wells. Adams would have been taken care of and he would have been able to teach Rizzo some things he surely needed to know. Boyd had no such affection for Reynolds. Captain Well, Mialio and Rizzo came to Boyd's cell at 2:00 a.m. Rizzo asked, "What's going on?" Where are we going? "No one answered. They entered the barely lighted tier no guards were at the tier door. "What's going on?" Rizzo again inquired no response. None of three stern faces even looked at him. Wells broke the silence handing Rizzo a knife from his gloved hand; "Here boy you got some work to do." Reaching Detrict's cell the door opened. The men rushed in. Reynolds sat up as Boyd hit him in the face with his fist. "Stab him" Wells whispered to Rizzo. He did, "Do it again. He wanted to kill your boss." Rizzo stabbed Reynolds five more times. "Cut his throat," Wells instructed. He did, Mialo then cut Reynolds wrist the long way so he would be sure to bleed to death. Rizzo stunned and in shock backed up in a daze. Thomaso slipped a slim rope around Rizzo's neck twisting it with a precise move, that he had been taught by an old assassin that had accompanied him on his first hit. Boyd then pulled a six-foot length of rope from his pocket. They then tied the rope to a pipe near the ceiling placing Rizzo's feet in a chair and kicked it out from under Rizzo's feet breaking the neck of the already dead man. The two men pulled down to make sure and cleaned up all traces of them having been there.

Murder suicide would be the verdict. Rizzo's belongings had been moved to that cell earlier. Thomaso and Boyd showered. Captain Wells disposed of their blood stained clothes. Boyd and Thomaso returned to their beds and slept better than they had in a week. Boyd was exhausted and in shock but somehow relieved that the plot against him had been thwarted. Thomaso prayed for forgiveness and hoped he wouldn't have to kill again. Captain Wells relaxed. He had maintained order in the insanity of prison. His control and power was again established; that is the only way that a prison could be run, that was what the people of Georgia were paying him to do. Wells drove home prepared for the Sunday school class.

Officer Adams got the message. He tried to transfer but could not. He resigned but not before two pounds of marijuana were found in his car. Then one night six months after he lost his job he was shot to death while being robbed. Wells told Mialio and Boyd, "I told you boys I'm your friend." His kind of friendship sent chills down the spine of the two inmates.

Chapter 15

Billy Robinson, Redmond Perry, Jr., Curtis Dwight were shackled together as they disembarked the bus upon entering the prison. Redmond was frightened although he didn't show it. He could smell the odor of prisons. He could feel the vibrations of hatred, fear, dishonesty and insanity lingering in the air around him. Human beings reduced to their most basic animal instincts; human refuse reduced to their basics, evil. Everyone in prison isn't bad but everything about prison is. Men in curlers, tights and make-up, blow kisses to the three new men when their lovers aren't looking. Others inspect the new men for weaknesses or preferences anything that could be taken advantage of. Slick was accustomed to the madness. He wanted to get to his room and get settled in, find Boyd and get plugged in to what's happening. He had some news for his old friend just didn't know how to tell him. Slick had found out about Red. He had beaten James Posey out of some money at cards. The men had talked and somehow Boyd's name came up. James told him the story even about Red's arrest.

"Your name Slick Robinson man?" A heavy thick voice called out from behind Slick and Red. The voiced startled Red, as he was lost in the spectacle of the insanity around him. "Yeah that's me." Slick answered. Slick had seen this huge gold toothed unusually black man before somewhere he was sure of that. "Follow Me." The black giant instructed. Slick only request is. "O can my homeboy come with me?" "I guess so." The giant concedes. Come on young blood Slick directs Red. "OK." Red gladly agrees he didn't want to be far from the more experienced man. "Where are you from?" Slick asked. The huge man glowers down at Slick and says "Tampa, why?" A cold chill runs through Slick as he recalls that night in that alley. He continues to follow the big man but he asks where he's going. "Somebody wants to see you. He sent me to get you. You ever been to Tampa?" The midnight giant asks. Slick quickly lies "no can't say that I have." That was the only caper that Slick had never bragged about...the only way that this guy could know about it was if Boyd told him...Boyd never told anybody anything.

Boyd is seated in a room with a few card tables. Nothing on the walls the room was spotlessly clean. "Hey Slick" back home um?" Boyd laughed. Slick then makes a request of his old friend after exchanging pleasantries. "Just passing through won't be here long. This is Red look out for him." Boyd agrees to Slick's request "Fine have a seat both of you." Well it's like this. Captain Wells runs this place. We can put you on this tier but we don't tolerate any bullshit. If you are into boys OK but don't rape anybody on this tier understand what I'm talking about." Red of course didn't have a clue but he continued to listen. "We don't steal from each other. Settle arguments in the yard. The rest of us won't let you get ganged in the yard. We're kind of like family here. You are a little younger than a lot of us so listen and you'll learn. If you are for real people, it ain't that bad for jail. Slick, man, don't cheat these mother fuckas at cards on this tier. Slick looked surprise that someone might think he would cheat at cards. "Really man", Boyd said, "Young blood if you ain't never been in prison before. Well I know it sounds crazy but if you follow what we tell you it'll be all right."

Boyd assured Red. "One more thing, don't fuck with Captain Wells cause if you get on his bad side you're fucked and I can't help you. Anything else I might be able to help you with if you are good people, school him Slick." After what seemed an orientation everyone then sat down and began talking. Slick told stories about he and Boyd in the good old days mostly lies or exaggerations. Boyd laughed the two men were genuinely glad to see one another. Red was fascinated by the stories; they all had to laugh when Rudy told about the time his wife had sewed him up in a sheet and tried to set him on fire. He said he woke up just in time to somehow roll out of the bed. She missed with the gas she tried to throw on him he kicked the bed over and somehow managed to get his feet out of the sheet. The mental picture of this ebony giant chasing a car clad only in one white sock at three in the morning. He was throwing rocks and cursing at the top of his voice. Rudy laughed and said I'm just glad I didn't catch that bitch that night. Then he seemed a little sad he had to confess that he missed her and his son. Then he talked about that time when he got drunk and lost all that money when he passed out...Slick now knew where he had seen Rudy.

The conversation quickly turned to the light side when Willie James announced that he was pregnant. Thomaso congratulated them both then told a story about forgetting to put bullets in his gun on a hit. They wound up pushing the guy in front of a subway train. The victim was afraid to get back into the car to go to Brooklyn. He said he would only take a train where plenty of people were around. He didn't completely buy Thomaso's story of kidding around; but he wasn't sure even after he was shown the empty gun. "Why would I come on a hit with an empty gun?" What do you think I am an ass hole?" Thomaso questioned. The men all laughed and agreed that Thomaso was an asshole.

As Red listened, strangely enough he started feeling a little safer than he had before. These men, though twisted in their thinking, seemed to accept him.

For some reason he sensed closeness to Boyd in particular. It was like Red could trust Boyd even if Red didn't know him and Red could see that if you won Boyd's favor the rest of them would go alone with whatever Boyd wanted. Lied about he and Boyd being like brothers.

Boyd usually didn't warm up to strangers but it was something about this kid...something that made him think about his first time being locked up. Just before they were all to go to bed Boyd pulled Slick aside and said. "Take care of that kid he looks like he don't belong here. " The walk back to the cell seemed to be a journey of a thousand miles into the very heart of hell. The laughter of the day was over and the realization of being in the penitentiary was setting in on Red. Slick could sense what was going on but he knew that each inmate had to find his way himself. Red looked around and tried not to show the deep regret, fear and uncertainty he was experiencing. He was just beginning his seven-year sentence. He wanted to go home more than he ever wanted anything in his life.

Just then he heard someone crying out for help. Slick told him to keep walking and mind his own business. "In here you got to know how to take care of yourself you can't get caught up in nobody else's shit. If you going to make it, if you don't remember anything else I tell you remember that. This place ain't like most prisons there is more order here... the way that Boyd explained it to me. We'll watch your back from the niggers trying to take advantage of the fact that you haven't been here before they will try to get you in a cross. Don't be no fool I've done a lot of time and I know every bull shit game there is. Watch these motherfuckers you will get used to it here; don't take anything for granted. Show no fear or weakness, watch everybody, be alert, learn how to take care of yourself. These guards are not here to protect us they are here to protect society from us. They don't even like snitches in this joint, stay away from them motherfuckers too. You are lucky to be here really if you did time before you would know what I'm talking about. Boyd and I go back a long time he's the man here him and Mialio we can get anything that we want if we just be cool and wait for it. "Doing time ain't nothing you want but you are here so make the best of it." Red wondered if Slick always talked this much. But some of the things he was saying were making him feel better.

Red was big and strong and more than able to take care of himself. He didn't fear being raped not by any one man not even one as frightening as Rudy. Red was not the type to be taken advantage of physically. It was not fear that was on his mind, he questioned whether he could kill if he had to or was put in a kill or be killed situation. Slick started again "Stay away from them fags, they will get you killed quicker than anything in here. Tomorrow I will show you how to make shank, you never know what's on these crazy motherfuckers minds. Don't sleep on anybody in here. Any of them is capable of anything at any time. A lot of these freaks need to be in a crazy house. Boyd got whores he can set you up with, just wait a few months to get your dick sucked. Punks are going to try you, some you won't even know are punks. Then some of these sick ass niggers are punks and they don't know it, they just been fucking men so long they have flipped and don't realize it. All they know is that you look good to them. These are the most dangerous motherfuckers in the joint whoever they are fucking might try to kill you; it might be a guard. Think about it, how would you like making a living looking up niggers ass holes, stirring through niggers' shit looking for dope that mother fuckers swallowed before they got here, them mother fuckers are the real freaks."

Red was trying to listen but Slick was telling him so many things at once and some of it was scary and funny at the same time. The whole idea of this life style was foreign to him this was all more than a little crazy to him. Red was a pretty good kid growing up he sold a little dope but he wasn't a criminal he thought not bad enough to come here anyway. He did not understand all this treachery and deceit. He was basically honest he thought and had been around mostly honest people. Now he was in an environment where virtues were thought of as weaknesses, any act of kindness was viewed as stupidity, femininity or an attempt to bribe some one to gain favor. Nothing was as it seemed, trust was not an option. When you were dealing with the people in this place… ninety-nine per-cent of the time." Why was Slick being so helpful? What did he want? Red was starting to think in the paranoid fashion of the rest of them. Red wanted to ask Slick why he was so helpful, if you were supposed to mind your business.

Slick started up again "you ever been to Savannah." "Yeah" Red answered, "I have an uncle that lives down there his name is James Posey. Do you know him?" "Does he work for that sugar plant down there?" Slick asked. "Yeah that's him. He's been there for twenty-five years." Red replied. "I know him I met him in a gambling house a couple of years ago… he's not much of a card player. I knew you reminded me of somebody. Maybe that's why I took such a liking to you. He said he had a nephew on Florida A and M's football team." "That was me; I played cornerback and running back, boy that seems like a long time ago." Red said. "Yawl had a good team he said you were faster than Bob Hayes" Slick reported. "Not quite I was pretty fast though," Red said with a chuckle. "Uncle James exalts his family's capabilities a little much that's what Elaine likes to say but we had a hell of a team. We were the first black college to play on national television.

The two reached their cell, Red took a deep breath before he entered. This was home for the next few years, however, the idea of this place, as being home both depressed and frightened Red. The idea of confinement is more frightening than its reality. The reality of human storehouses where the worst of us are held for periods of time and then inflected back into the larger society. A larger society can be more dishonest, immoral and self-serving than prison with all of its perversions. Just by telling itself this madness helps the prisoner or society.

Yea, Slick is right this is home until I'm free Red thought I've got to learn to deal with this. Red was worried about losing his mind and his self-respect. Red was a great deal more dishonest than he realized but he was a babe in the woods in here. The first time he saw a fight between two inmates it made him shutter. He was in the reception station waiting in line for something when a fight broke out. The idea of a fight didn't bother him two guys fighting it out with their fists wasn't too bad. But what happened next made his stomach turn. Red was pretty good with his hands so to speak but each of these guys set out to kill the other; the winner lived the loser died. A relatively small inmate, who appeared to be a trustee or something, he had more freedom than the rest got spotted by a prisoner that must had been acquainted with him on the street. The two must have had some kind of grudge. The larger man rushed the trustee as soon as he saw him knocking the smaller man down. He pinned the smaller man's right arm down with his knee. Then he began to beat him viciously with his fists then suddenly blood was everywhere; the trustee had plunged a shank into the larger man's upper abdomen just below the ribs with an upward thrust penetrating the man's heart. Blood spurted all over the place and the man was dead before he hit the floor. Red stood starring at the scene as Slick grabbed his arm and told him to mind his own business. Pulling him away before the guards got to the body. No one was even questioned about what happened.

He asked Boyd if he could arrange for him to learn how to use a shank and make one as well. Boyd got Peeler and Rudy to show the kid how to make and use the homemade weapon. Red liked to have the best; Slick didn't hold a candle to these guys when it came to violence. Red wondered how long would it be before he could sleep at night. Boyd and the others had told Slick that the cell doors were really locked in this joint and Wells didn't play that shit of bribing guards to leave cell doors unattended. If anything happened during the night, the cellmate was responsible. Wells didn't want a man in his charge to think he could get away with anything. The guards were to be looked upon as gods, everything that the inmates were allowed to have were gifts from the gods. And Capt Wells was in charge of the gods "don't fuck with me" was the warning that each inmate received upon entering the gates of the prison from Marvin Wells. Most heeded that warning, the ones that didn't soon learned that it was no idle talk. Punishment was swift and painful and without exception. If an inmate killed another inmate he was caught and punished. If an inmate killed a guard the other prisoners might kill the guilty party for the guard, just so they could have some privileges. Wells would not play when a guard tried to be slick, either; he was the only slick one in his penitentiary. He told you only once to call him Capt. Wells after that it was a trip to the hole if you addressed him in any other way. He decided everything.

Slick and Red's room was small: a bunk bed with dresser draws under the bottom bunk, toilet, a writing area and sink. The prison building was new about ten years old. The walls were clean the floors were shiny. Then the unmistakable reminders of prison life intrude in their dehumanizing way; the toilet was in a closet like structure. The sink was on the outside wall of the enclosed john; there was a door that closed to reduce the smell and give an illusion of privacy when someone was using the bathroom. All the cells on this tier were kept spotlessly clean Captain Wells saw to that. The showers were on the far end of the tier and could be used only at scheduled times. Red watched Slick make himself at home and he seemed fairly pleased with the accommodations. "You take the top bunk," Slick asked Red, as they put their few belongs away the drawers. Slick laughed at the look on Red's face. That look of a deer caught in the headlights of an oncoming vehicle. Dazed and confused Red climbed up to his bed sat down wearily on the bunk. He knew that he wouldn't be sleeping tonight.

"That fast life, don't seem so great now does it?" Slick inquired with a laugh. Red didn't answer. He vowed never to go to prison again silently. How do people survive in here without going crazy he thought? The confinement alone could bug you out he speculated. Red didn't know quite yet what he could talk to Slick about. But Slick knew what Red was thinking and looked in Red's direction and said. "Pray really pray man you'll be alright". Red said. "OK" And he really tried it. To his surprise it worked; he managed to function a little better each day. It got a little easier or less difficult might be a better way to put it as time creaked by. Jail is not easy; there is an underlying desperation in the back of anyone's mind the whole time that you are locked up. That need for freedom burns inside of us all. Nothing in Red's past experiences prepared him for incarceration, the unnatural thought patterns that seem to be formed in self-defense. It's that way for most people from a normal background. Prison is anything but normal or natural it is degrading, demeaning and is designed to be that way.

The first three months no one was allowed to visit new prisoners. Red adjusted as best he could to the restrictive lifestyle of confinement. Red was drawn to Boyd and talked with him everyday and listened for the first time since Redmond senior died. It appeared they were building a father son relationship without knowing it. For sure Red would not have made it emotionally without Boyd; and Boyd found himself looking forward to the talks. Red didn't come to Boyd crying about being in jail. The two of them just talked; the older man didn't allow self-pity. Boyd had been alone for a long time and he liked the kid for some reason. A man in his twenties has his life in front of him if he learns to make the right decisions. Boyd told Red. Boyd discovered that he regretted not having somebody to steer him in the right directions some one to care about. Boyd figured it might have helped him if he had someone to guide him. But he didn't and he sensed that he and Red were different, this young man has a family. Bob Edmonds had been the closest thing to family Boyd had in Savannah. Edmonds not only was Boyd's silent partner in crime, the two them were friends. Bob was Boyd's father figure, really it was Edmonds that taught Boyd who to deal with and who to stay away from. Bob knew how to treat people and get what he needed from them. As long as Boyd stuck to what Edmonds told him, he did fine. It wasn't until Boyd went against advice, that got him into a situation that Bob couldn't control. Boyd passed this information along to Red. Boyd's down home savvy and Red's natural charming personality was gaining him points with the powers that be (Captain Wells). The older man cautioned Red not to try to move too fast. Red followed instructions to the letter and got put in the mailroom, one of the cleanest and best jobs in the joint. In the mail room you can stay on top of everything you can get anything you want into the prison and keep most of what you didn't want out. Boyd said in one of his talks with Red. "No matter what let Wells think he in charge never question that he is the authority because if you question that he will show you who is in charge and believe me he is crazy enough to do anything. His ego is so big that nobody can do anything without him and everything is his idea." Wells has a thing about being boss, he is the head cracker in charge. No way is he going to let anybody black think he's not. Play along with his shit cause it ain't nothing you can do about him, not in here. Use the system to your advantage fuck what them Niggers on lockup think or say! Fuck what Wells and the rest of them think too, look out for number one, this is the penitentiary." Never take anything for granted was the recurring theme of Boyd's advice to Red. Think before you act Boyd told Red, but when you make up your mind get on it. "Have all the angle's covered have a way out. Don't burn any bridges. Try to make friends and be one if you can. Take it slow, check things out but when you make up your mind move." Each day Boyd would repeat his advise to Red one way or the other. Boyd would say kid you can't hear good shit too much or too often. "Trust yourself but listen to somebody that you see is doing better than you are and have a mind of your own, your mind can be a gold mine. Don't let it be an empty hole in the fuckin ground." Red respected Boyd because he was doing better in jail than most people do on the street. Boyd however told Red "Square up, all that slick stuff winds you up in here. Jail is no place to be for a smart young man like you Red." Slick and Red would talk at night and Billy Slick would share his wisdom with Red as well. Slick did have some wisdom to share most of it gained from making some really bad decisions. Slick had his same old theory about people he would say that, its only twelve different types of motherfuckers. When Slick would explain the twelve different types of motherfuckers there was a certain type of amount of truth to what he said.

Then he would say that he learned this theory from the Bible with the twelve Disciples. Slick had an unusual way of looking at things but along with Slick's gift for gab it made sense or was entertaining anyway. First type of motherfucker is the commonsense motherfucker does the right thing for the right reason. This type didn't wind up in jail but when they did he would be OK. 2. The religious motherfucker self-righteous and most of the time a hypocrite. Can quote the Bible talk about it all day down deep this type is really a whorish motherfucker but is too scared to live the way he wants to live. 3. The whorish motherfucker that's the type of mother I once thought I was a whorish motherfucker, maybe I still am...whorish motherfucker usually don't know he is one 4. Neurotic motherfucker crazy but nobody don't know it just think he's different this type of mother, can be controlled 5. Insecure motherfucker don't trust nobody this type of motherfucker is normally so crooked that he will cross his own self. 6 Larceny hearted motherfucker nobody can trust him will steal from his grand mama will cross you in a minute this is a good and easy fool to beat. 7. Lying motherfucker can't tell or face the truth this motherfucker only believes a lie. 8. Gullible motherfucker believes anything; this is a born fool 9. Honest motherfucker don't want nothing for free this is a rare motherfucker
10. Dishonest motherfucker wants everything for free. This motherfucker is weak and lazy, you can beat this fool out of anything. 11. Controlling motherfucker want everything to go his way this motherfucker has a need for power 12. Psychotic motherfucker crazy don't fuck with him under no circumstances freaks, killers them motherfuckers that are locked down in the

hole for years and can't live in the population. A fool is anybody that believes anything a con artist tries to run on him. I have studied this for a long time Slick said...those are the only types of motherfucker that exist.

Slick in a moment of candor admitted he was still a whorish motherfucker. He said Boyd was a common sense motherfucker most of the time. Slick explained that whorish meant anybody who let their wants for something over rule their senses drug addicts, alcoholics, gamblers and anything like that and that he let looking for something outside themselves to make them feel better be his downfall. You could be one type of motherfucker most of the time but slip into another type if the conditions were right. "Looks to me like you are a whorish motherfucker too." Slick told Red one day. Red reluctantly agreed that he is most of the time but promised to change. Slick said "Man that's a hard thing for one of us to do. You are doing the right thing talking to Boyd that a start in the right direction." The two men laughed and had to agree

Slick went on to explain the importance of communication and being able to be understood.
I speak seven or eight languages Slick told Red said he could be understood in those languages. "Italian, Spanish, a little French, a tiny bit in Greek and four different types of English'' the English poor crackers speak, they are the ones that bust your ass and watch you while you are in here. Two educated Crackers, the ones that try you ass. Three, that street talk bullshit we talk in here. Proper nigger English what we talk like when we're trying to show crackers that we are not like the niggers in here." The ninety days crept by but Red was adjusting slowing; he missed his freedom and his family.

Visitor's day arrived finally after three months. Red had always taken his family for granted in the past but not anymore. He missed Elaine and Wilma but especially his daughters and Paula too. Red sat there thinking I would marry Paula just to have a conjugal visit. Yeah, and divorce her ass as soon as I get out. But then he thought of people like Slick who had no one to come to visit them. Plus Boyd could probably hook something like that up for him after a while. Redmond Perry, Jr. a voice called out. "You got visitors." Red and 12 other inmates including Boyd went to the visitor's room. Boyd had a visitor, his lawyer with more bad news about his parole. Just about Red's whole family came to see him many couldn't get in but they came. They bought him food and clothes and at least a dozen books.

As Boyd entered the room he went straight to where his visiting attorney was sitting. Boyd was talking with his lawyer, the parole was getting complicated. Bob and a few of the other partners had some problems before his death. The profits from their variety of enterprises weren't very good. Bob had said it was because they needed you to run things, some of the others questioned Bob's honesty and said that they didn't need one man any nigger could be told what to do. The lawyer advised Boyd to be careful. Boyd assured his lawyer that he wasn't about to try and cause trouble he would do his time and that would be that...besides he didn't know any names anyway. Then quite by accident Boyd spotted Elaine staring at him. Boyd knew immediately who she was but he couldn't believe his eyes. Elaine nearly choked as she tried to talk embarrassed she said, "Excuse me is your name Boyd Tilman?" "Elaine is that really you? Boyd gulped, "Yes" Elaine exclaimed. Boyd nearly fainted as he stood there with emotions flying at him like rockets on the fourth of July. Wanting to run, wanting to hug her, wanting make love to her tell her that all the years meant nothing. He realized he still loved her after all these years thinking that he had suppressed his feelings. After summoning up all his courage he managed to say. "Hi, how are you?" Overwhelmed with emotion Elaine tried to answer but she broke down in tears. Crying as she ran from the room. Elaine was confused because she knew much to her surprise that she still loved him. No other man had been close to her. She was afraid of her feelings but she was now aware of why she couldn't feel anything for other men. She still loved a man that she had not seen in over twenty years and knew him only as a boy. What had this boy she loved so long ago become? What had she done? What would Red think? Father and son meeting this way after all these years of not talking about what happened. Not telling Red the whole story. She kept running when she got outside in the prison parking lot she got into her car and drove home alone. She needed to think the others could make room for Wilma. More than anything she was running from herself but somehow she recognized that she would have to face things; things about her self that didn't fit the life she had lead for since she was a girl really. "Boy what a mess I made of things." She said as she started her car.

Paula asked Red what was happening? Red though confused said "I have no idea really but I think Boyd must know my real father. That's the only thing that would make Laine act like that she never talked to me about any of that stuff. When that topic is brought up she gets real quiet. She seems so upset that I never asked her anything. For her to show that kind of emotions at seeing someone. It must be something like that."

Boyd stood there stoned faced for what seemed like an eternity to him, then Rosetta said,“So you is Boyd?” Smiling warmly at the confused hollowed eyed man standing in front of her. “Yes ma’am,” Boyd said. Wilma walked over to Boyd hugged him and said, “Take care of our boy. God knows what he’s doing let him work with both of you.” After a moment of searching for just the right words Boyd said. “OK, yes ma’am.” Tears’ now filling his eyes Boyd was almost unable to say that.

Paula and Red by now completely confused sat looking but trying not to look at Boyd or Wilma. “I don’t know” Red said to Paula when she turned to ask what was wrong. He continued “Evidently they know one another I’ve never seen Elaine this upset. I’ve never seen her with a man really. Maybe” Red stopped in mid sentence. “He can’t be; but he is from Savannah”. Then Red looked at Paula and said. “Yea I think he’s my father and he didn’t know it. Slick did; that’s why he’ been so nice to me. Ain’t that a bitch” Red thought maybe that’s why I felt so drawn to Boyd; it was almost like I know him from somewhere.

Then Red remembered Slick saying that he knew Uncle James he must have known about it. He wouldn’t have taken me under his wing the way he did if he didn’t. Mind your own business was Slick’s motto but he watched over me like I was his son. Paula knew Red had been told Elaine was his mother after he got out of high school. And that he never asked about his birth father. Everyone thought he’d ask when he was ready or that it didn’t matter to him. To Paula this was a terrible way for Red to find out. At the time I guess everyone would have agreed. But in time everyone would come to think of this day as one of the best days of his or her lives.

Red had wondered about his birth father but felt that they might think he was ungrateful if he wanted to know too much about him. Wilma never forced the issue, who would have thought the two would meet like this. Red hadn’t allowed a thought of father to enter his mind for many years. Unresolved feelings hit him harder and more unexpectedly than he had ever allowed himself to believe it might. Red had never finished grieving the loss of Redmond senior. The boy had tried to please everyone around by being strong but he was just hiding his feelings he had so many conflicting feeling, about his whole situation. He had put them away so to speak and now they were out. It was a full time job dealing with prison now this but at least the truth had come out.

Slick was the first to see Boyd entering the tier in a teary eyed daze; “Man you found out I didn’t know how to tell.” “Yeah” Boyd murmured. “We’ll talk later, OK." Boyd had thought of prison like occupational hazard. He had never felt ashamed, he felt that he had to do the things he did to survive. But shame is what he felt, because he now knew that he didn't have to live the life he had led. Elaine seeing him, his son locked up with him. Boyd had never felt the need to apologize for his life to anybody until now. He thought he had no choices so thinking about what might have been wasn't a consideration until now… but what could a girl of thirteen and a seventeen year-old boy offer a child? Willie put him in jail but maybe somehow he could have stayed in touch. So many ifs but that was the past anyhow he knew she had the baby but that was all. What in the world could he have done? Now maybe he could help the kid he seemed like somebody that got fooled by fast money. The kid wasn't a bad sort just young and impatient. Boyd vowed to go straight and set a better example for his son when he got out.

Peeler entered their cell. The sadist maniac said to Boyd, "Pray." Boyd looked at Peeler and smiled. Then Virgil said " It came to me in a dream last night. God told me to tell you that is a fine boy you got. Be there for him he's he going to have some more trouble but in the end everything is going to be all right. Ain't nobody told me nothing. Saw it in a dream." Boyd wondered about his own sanity. He believed Peeler.

Red sat in the visitor's room as Wilma returned and sat down. She said, "Boyd is your father." "In a way but " Red said. "Redmond Perry, Sr. is my real father." "Yes, he is but Boyd is also. Don't be angry with us. He couldn't". Red interrupted, "I not mad. I just don't see him that way you understand at least not yet. Being adopted was fine but now meeting my father in jail I feel a little disoriented."

For the next seven days the two men avoided each other, neither knew what to say. Despite Virgil Peeler's constant prodding. Even though the fact was that both Red and Boyd wanted very badly to talk to one another, neither one of them knew where to start…or how they felt. Early Sunday morning Peeler packed his belongings and went to Slick and Red's cell. "Pack up and move in with Boyd." Virgil demanded. Red looked at Peeler. He had heard the stories about how crazy Peeler was and how loyal he was to Boyd. Slick knew the stories to be true, even Rudy was a little afraid of Peeler. "Don't argue Red you need to talk SB anyway." BS advised. [That's what Slick and Boyd were called BS and SB], Billy Slick and Savannah Boyd. Red packed and moved. "OK I'm here" Red announced "Virgil sent me he put me out of my house." Red said. "I'm glad you didn't piss that man off." Boyd assured Red. Then after a moment Boy said "I couldn't take care of you and Elaine I was just 17 and your grand father put me in jail." Red said, "I didn't know that but Redmond Perry was a good father I didn't want to ask too many questions about you. I don't blame anybody I had everything I needed as a child and just about everything I wanted. Maybe that's why I in here. He was good to me we would talk and he was like my best friend. I really can't think of anybody else that way." Boyd listened then said, "Yeah, you're right Red. I won't try to take his place. In a way you were lucky things turned out the way they did. I really don't know what I'm trying to say or what to try to be to you. Maybe in time we'll find out. If you want to go back to school, I got the money to send you and I'd like to if its what you want." Red said, " Thanks I sure don't want to come back here.". Red and Boyd's relationship slowly grew into one of mutual respect. They both loved to read and along with Slick discussed books and exchanged their views on just about everything. Though in the prison environment it was best not to let ones feeling be known, Boyd was very proud of Red.

Peeler was now convinced he had Holy visions. He was predicting things with a great deal of accuracy. He was told Slick that he was a prophet; Slick didn't argue the point. Especially after Virgil told Slick that he had a vision of the events of the next day and everything happened the way he said it would. Most of the other inmates figured Peeler was planning an insanity plea. No one could think of whom it might be because of the way that Peeler's mind worked. Everybody was on edge, "Who's he gonna kill," Thomaso asked Boyd. Boyd laughed. "He got religion." Thomaso said with certainty, "That crazy fuck gonna kill somebody,"

With everyone so on edge about Peeler, Captain Wells agreed to let qualified inmates take college courses from the University of Georgia. Boyd and Thomaso recommended Joey Batilio, Red, Billy Ray Thomkins and George Ware all qualified for the college classes now available. Captain Wells didn't like these classes but Boyd and Thomaso convinced him that these guys understood friendship and would make him look good. Also, John Eckman, a college professor in for killing his wife and her Lesbian lover could help or do whatever was needed to insure the young men passed. Wells warmed to the idea.

Red worked very hard, stayed out of trouble, helped the other inmates and even completed two elective computer courses. Computers fascinated him. It seemed Red was on his way at last. Elaine and Wilma were never happier. Paula had dreams of living happily ever after with her perfect husband. If Red, had a soft spot it was Elaine and Wilma he would do anything to please them or try make them he was trying to please them; a view shared by Peeler and Red's oldest. Wilma and Elaine loved Paula and thought that the girls desperately wanted for Red and Paula to be together. Well Red's youngest daughter did anyway so they weren't completely off base.

Red adjusted to prison life because he was so busy for the next two years he again suppressed his feeling he could lose himself into a sort of numbness. He studied harder and longer than anyone else in the program did. The pre-engineering course was difficult even the somewhat watered down prison version. Red got his teachers to give him extra work some for extra credit and some for the benefit of extra knowledge. He wanted to go on and become an architectural engineer. It seemed that all of his dreams were coming true. Red's life was back on course jut like high school follow the rules get the rewards. Now his dream of going to UGA had come true he was getting all the things that had caused him disappointment. As long as he was busy Red was fine so he stayed busy. The luxury of free time was not a part of Red's life for the next five years. He knew what he wanted and he went after it with a determination that few people possess. He didn't want to think about anything other than his goals. But life is not just meeting goals, he still had a gnawing emptiness in his gut.

Red stayed out of trouble away from drugs and taught a Bible class. He memorized the Bible but he did not have a clue of what it meant. Red watched Peeler with great interest, he was the only man in the whole penitentiary who was at peace all the time. To Red it seemed that the prophet of Milliageville was the only one not convinced of Red's perfection. Peeler always said you can have the world and all that's in it but it's no good if you lose your soul. Red said he didn't know what the madman (that's what Red called Peeler behind his back) was talking about but inside he could feel the missing piece that he needed to make him whole. One day Peeler said to Red "Why do you call me a madman? Is it because I have killed people or is it because I love people?" Red was so surprised and caught off guard that he couldn't think of any thing to say. He only used that term with Boyd or Slick he knew that they wouldn't antagonize Virgil.

Red completed his courses with a four-point average; the governor gave him a pardon. Red had earned admittance to the Georgia Tech School of architecture where he would again have a four-point average. This time there was no watered down version. He was at Georgia Tech and the same was expected of him as anyone else.

The unlikely prophet Virgil was now gaining converts other inmates listened to him and followed his teaching. Although Peeler was unable to read he knew all the books of the major religions and he helped others to contact spirits and forces outside themselves. His prayer vigils stopped a potential riot at the prison. Slick and Virgil started praying together everyday. Slick was convinced of Peeler's conversion. "No weapon formed against me shall prosper," Peeler preached in the yard during exercise time. Some days he attracted a crowd. But as time passed Captain Wells transferred Peeler to the maximum-security building. Wells only let Peeler in the yard when no one was there to hear him. Slick looked with curiosity and for the next two years. He and Peeler had roomed together without incident. Slick missed his talks with Peeler and their morning prayers. They got to see little of one another but after Slick got the job of bringing the canteen they talked each day. The day Slick was released Peeler said; "You will be back in 6 months. Gods working with you." Peeler was right about that the back in six months part anyway the old con man thought. Slick was putting up the fight of his life not to have God run his life.

During the years that Red was incarcerated Bobby had visited Red at least once a month. That was no small feat for the busy young assistant pastor of one of the larger black churches in Atlanta. Bobby had finished Hampton and gone into the ministry, moved to Atlanta. He always brought Paula or one of Red's many female friends to see him. Boyd had arranged for conjugal visits. "Rev. Bobby" Red would say. "Put in a good word for me." Rev. Bobby said, "Red, I don't like to bring these women to see you. Paula is a good friend." "OK." " She loves you, this doesn't seem to matter to you" Red replied. "I know she does but so do the rest of them, I'll be out in three months… when I get out I'm going to straighten all that out". Red got out but things went on pretty much as before. Red couldn't understand what everybody told him about this monogamy stuff. Red often said "what she don't know won't her." Red also didn't realize Bobby was in love with Paula and had been ever since high school. One day Peeler told Bobby "Remember the story of David and how he was in love with another man's wife your friend would forgive you a lot easier if you told him now. But you would never have her if you do. Now you are just hanging around until you get the chance to have her." Bobby acted like he didn't know what Peeler was talking about. Virgil prayed for Red the day he was released. "The road to salvation for you will be bumpy." Virgil told Red. "You are of the flesh. Wicked women, weak men, weak women wicked men glory be to God. I know you don't hear a word I'm saying." Red lied "I gonna miss you." Peeler laughed and said "If you could turn your life over to God now you would save yourself a lot of pain and heartache, but your path to Him hasn't been revealed to you yet". Red started to say something but Virgil stopped him. "Don't lie to me just remember my words the time will come when you will seek my counsel." Yeah-right Red thought the counsel of a mad man. "That's right the counsel of a madman" Peeler said before Red could finish the thought. The Mad prophet of prison prayed, dreamed, preached and prophesied to all that would listen. He helped everyone who he could. He once told a guard not to take a plane. The guard heeded Peeler's warning, when the plane crashed the guard was very grateful that his life had been saved. From then on this young man consulted Peeler about all of his major decisions. Still the talk, he's planning an insanity plea. The more Peeler helped people the more the talk persisted.

Abulah Raham the Iman of tier three asked Virgil a question about the Koran. Peeler not only answered but in flawless Arabic. The young would be Holy man declared Virgil a prophet because he knew that Virgil couldn't speak a word of Arabic or read any langue. For the next four years until his release he studied the Koran under Virgil's guidance. Now Raham is one of the foremost American experts on Islamic Holy writings. When he studied with long time students of the Koran in Mecca they were amazed at his knowledge. A leading Imam proclaimed that he had never seen an American with as much understanding of the Islamic holy Book.

Chapter 16

Captain Wells watched Peeler with at first curiosity then concern finally paranoia. The Captain figured that since Virgil was sticking to this "act" for so long it had to be him or the warden. None of the prisoners saw much of the warden so it must be him. Wells convinced himself that Peeler was going to kill him. The truth was that Wells was a hypocrite. For years Captain Wells had committed every crime in the book and gotten away with them. Now a truly reformed inmate, who had knowledge of many of these crimes, presented a dangerous situation to the veteran correction officer. Peeler had marked him for death Wells told everyone on the staff. He ordered protection and never went anywhere without three or four guards with him. Virgil would tell Captain Wells whenever he saw him; "No weapon formed against me shall prosper." And laugh his chilling laugh. Wells became more unnerved. The fact was that Virgil really respected the old guard. Wells' guilt and his paranoid personality proved to be his undoing. Asked Thomaso and Boyd to kill Peeler. They refused. They told Wells that Peeler's lawyers had evidence on them. He had saved one of Baker's fingers in alcohol. It would be used if he were killed. This drove Wells further up the wall. Then when Wells tried to get a guard to kill Virgil and none of the guards wanted anything to do with trying to hurt Peeler. With every apparent miracle Wells' fear grew and his control over his now neurotic fear of Peeler increased with each passing day.

Once a young hoodlum spat in Virgil's face. Later that day he fell down some steps and broke his leg in three places. Virgil visited him in the hospital and he was up walking in three weeks without crutches. Peeler selected this young murderer to be his Bible student. The Rev. J.T. Bloodworth released after 10 years and the pastor of a 2000 member congregation somewhere in the Southwest.

That was the final straw. Captain Wells now was totally out of control. He hired death row inmate Ruben Garfield to kill Peeler. Garfield was a remorseless six-time killer of girls ranging from 6 to 17 years of age. Garfield was considered the meanest man in the Georgia penal system. He wasn't like the stereotypical child killer, he had killed men in prison. Wells convinced Garfield that he could get an indefinite stay with another murder. The trial appeals and so forth. Also $5,000.00 for his family would help his aging mother. Garfield took the deal but wanted 2 ounces of cocaine. Garfield added "my poor dear mother could go to hell." Ruben was to stab Peeler when he came to pray with him barely 3 weeks before his execution. Peeler entered Garfield's cell, turned, and looked directly into the eyes of the at least 6-time killer. Garfield's knife in hand kneeled down with Peeler and prayed. Three weeks later he walked to the electric chair singing, "Nearer My God To Thee." Peeler walked beside him singing loudly. Captain Wells missed the execution and went on sick leave. Captain Wells then tried to resign but his many friends didn't let him throw away his retirement. They arranged for him to be on sick leave until retirement date came up in six months.

Marvin Wells though unorthodox kept order. His record spoke loudly and for itself. Wells knew that the men he was guarding were for the most part incorrigible so he kept the staff under strict control; he felt that the prisons could influence them for bad long before the staff could influence them for good. He therefore controlled which prisoners were allowed to interact with the staff and that was strictly controlled. Wells knew that if he had a staff he could trust he would have little need for prison informers. Wells wanted no doubt in any inmate's mind about who was in charge... everything was a privilege. You could get most of the things you could pay for as long as you didn't forget who was in charge. Like it or not Captain Wells' system worked. Thomaso told Boyd, "I miss the old bastard. Maybe you should have whacked Virgil," Boyd said. "Hell no, no weapon formed against him shall prosper." They laughed. Deep down they wondered what was really going on with Peeler. He had changed. He was no longer frightening but there was something that seemed to discourage other inmates from harming him. Virgil had always been odd but now he was a good odd. Something seemed to always be with him... like a presence that was around him. You knew that you felt something different. One could not recognize whatever it is through, you had only a feeling that you would get when you were around him. That intangible quality that some people have, you know that they believe in God and you can see God through them.

"Marvin Wells the devil himself," Peeler declared but only the devil kept the order in Hell. Only the devil could know how to deal with this much evil in one place. Truer words were never spoken. With no one running the staff with an iron hand corruption became rampant. The vices of the prisoners and guards took over the every aspect of life in the brig. After Wells left the prison became pure chaos. Inmates killing inmates, guards killing inmates, cell doors opened for a few dollars. No one was safe from the carnage. Boyd and Thomaso had gotten their money out before Wells went over the edge. These two were too street wise to get caught up in any of the madness around them. They watched out for each other they were always in a state of heighten alertness.

Chapter 18

Peeler was the only inmate who had no fear. The prophet said that Slick was going to change and do great things for the Lord. He prayed daily for Slick to stop resisting the will of the Master. "I gonna call you Odfus from now on," Peeler revealed one morning after learning Slicks real name in a "dream." Slick still thinks Boyd revealed the name to Virgil. That name represented everything that Slick hated about his true self; the country boy from rural Florida with no education. The polar opposite of the image he wanted to project. "Call me Billy if you don't like Slick," Slick insisted but his pleas went unheard. Peeler declared, "Nope, not a fitting name, you got to be for real when you come to the Lord. Rev. Odfus Muse, is your name, if you can't even tell Him your real name how can you say you love him. God don't like Ugly." Slick laughed but slowly he began to realize that he had to change so he started with his name. It was a long hard battle but it had started when the con player stopped saying. "Not me it's too late for me and I'm too set in my ways." Slick had told Peeler that for nearly five years but in truth he did want to change.

And the change had begun without his knowing it. One night Odfus had a vision and he knew the time had come to change. He started with his name. Slick even took the chance of telling the prison officials his true name. He had risked another charge but when no other States wanted him under his real name, they accepted his reason for the confession. He hadn't been called Odfus since he was seven years old. Needless to say it took a lot of getting use to for everyone.

Thomaso had a wife and four grown children. They visited often. His daughter, a nurse moved south near Augusta and Elaine was helpful in finding her a job at the VA Hospital. Vincent followed in his father's footsteps. Domonick and Carmine ran a successful legal business in Florida. Vera (Thomaso's wife) had moved to Florida as well. Mialio decided to retire to Florida and live in peace.

The prison environment turned out to be the perfect place for Boyd and Elaine to rekindle the spark from long ago. The couple talked, went on long walks on visitor's day, some of the older guards still gave Boyd special privileges. It was almost like an Old World courtship with family members always watching. It worked for them. Elaine was in therapy for her sexual repression and resentments toward Willie. She didn't need to be pushed. She knew she loved Boyd. The space built into their relationship allowed her to heal and grow. Seeing Boyd in the visiting room had started the nightmares of Willie again. She worked through it and with effort, she no longer saw all men as Willie and therefore a threat to her. She wanted to resolve things with Willie but the Doctor told her to work on one thing at a time. He said "There is an extreme probability that your father might reject you as he had done in the past. Given the fact that your relationship with Boyd will be difficult at best, do things one at a time.

Boyd had his own demons that haunted him. He found a refuge in just knowing Elaine loved him, a fact that he found amazing. He struggled to keep the thoughts of his ill-lived life at bay. How could he ever be good enough for her? Maybe she is just feeling sorry for him. This beautiful decent woman loved him; it was hard to believe. Boyd went and talked with Peeler he told him how he was feeling. Peeler said "God will bless you in ways that you could never imagine, she loves you and she has since you two were teenagers, have faith, God is with you both, act on your faith everything is going to work out."

Chapter 19

Red and Paula moved to Atlanta. He had gotten a job with Whittler and Howell, a large architectural firm. The American dream for Red, the handsome, "almost single" man about town. Red had not wanted to move to Atlanta by himself. Paula was there, Elaine loved her, so why not marry, Paula, at least Elaine will be happy. Paula, Red and Grace, older daughter, Mary refused to come. She remained with Elaine and Wilma where she had always been. Red wished Grace would have stayed too but she didn't. He'd have to make the best of it, he didn't or couldn't in all fairness to Red at the time. Grace worshipped her father, no matter what he did she still loved him and wanted to be part of what ever he was a part of. He often thought of her while in prison he had a dream about her. The dream was strange and he did not understand it. He somehow had become a spirit and invaded her mind. Then he led her to happiness though a maze that only he knew how to get out of. Daddy will fix it was what Red told her whenever she cried. Most of the time he did when he was around but he wasn't around enough.

Red worked just as hard when he got his dream job but after he got settled things started to change. Slowly Red started to drink a little more then he started to experiment with free base cocaine. Red had always been like a magnet for gorgeous women. Now the cocaine life style freaks (women that are uninhibited sexually) were all over the place. Not just freaks but the most beautiful freaks in Atlanta. Red became a victim of his strengths and his weaknesses. The construction of Atlanta in the 70's and early eighties was an architect's dream. Red had been on the fast track to success… the legal fast track this time, respectable but just as fast. He partied, worked and partied. Women threw themselves at him. He caught them as fast as he could. Paula and Grace seldom saw Red. At first he was working but after a while he was having "fun".

The day Boyd was released; Elaine met him at the prison receiving room. Boyd was a terrible dresser. Slick told Elaine, "Get him something up to date." "I'll get rid of all this polyester shit he brought in here, it was out of style nine years ago." She had Red pick out a jogging suit and running shoes. They didn't tell Boyd what the clothes cost. Boyd was as tight with a dollar as he was tacky. Slick said, "He still got the first dime he ever stole."

Boyd shaved, brushed his teeth, combed his hair, went and said, "Good-bye"

to Rudy, Slick and Peeler. Peeler said to Boyd, "I dreamed again that you and that lady gonna be happy. Stop worrying about the past. God's forgiven me! It's gonna be all right."
Boyd confided to Peeler "I'm scared man for the first time in my life really scared". Then he walked down the tier to Rudy and John Henry's house and said "Thanks, believe it or not I gonna miss you. Especially you John Henry" blowing a kiss to the teary eyed Jackson. "
"Hold it mother fucka I know its time for you to go. I thought you was fucking my woman anyway." Rudy joked in his most menacing voice.

Boyd met Elaine in the receiving area. Free after nine years. Really scared for the first time in his life. For a brief second he wanted to stay at the penitentiary and watch life and not really be a part of it. Then Elaine kissed him and her body touched his her firm but soft breasts rubbed against his chest. He knew he had to try to make it on the outside.

Peeler and Slick continued to be cell-mates. Billy Slick had grown tired of his lifestyle in and out of jail. No home, only the road and the game. But even more than that nothing inside, nothing to hold on to when the ill winds of life blew. Slick started to have frightening dreams and visions about his life. He would see all the people he hurt, the aftermath of his "harmless con playing". The young girls he had pimped, one had been killed pulling a trick while Odfus had her. He had made her go out, she had stolen two ounces of heroin form a dealer the night before. They had money and dope but he sent her anyway just to prove a point. Slick and the dealer had a dislike for each other. The pusher thought that Slick's girl could be persuaded to leave him but instead she fooled the distributor and stole his dope.

The dealer saw her he forced her, into his car. Unknown to him at the time he was being followed by a police special drugs task force and was tailed. The pusher when to where he had another stash; he wanted to find Slick. The police waited to get back up before they went in the apartment after him. Had it been the age of the cell phone, the events that transpired would never have happened. A cop that was being paid off by the drug dealer came as backup he wasn't able to stop what was going down but he did delay it; he said they needed a warrant. The drug-crazed gangster beat the girl up and tried to get her to tell where Odfus was. But when she wouldn't tell, and he shot her in the head. The police heard the shot and had to break down the door, the dealer panicked and shot one of the officers. Ironically, the crocked cop had to return fire and killed the pusher. Odfus left Boston with his other two whores and never returned. They traveled south playing con down I95 in Baltimore one of the whores left with another pimp. The other stayed all the way to Savannah, like she always had for many years Iris Brim and Boyd were the only constants in Slick's life. Slick and Iris committed every crime in the book together except murder including her being the driver when Boyd and Slick robbed Rudy. Iris was kind of a protector for Slick; she was a lot more violent than he was. She drove the car during the Tampa robbery but the truth is Boyd would have felt safer with her with him. They had robbed several dealers. She could be counted on if things got rough; it was only Slick's ego that sent him with Boyd that night because he was scared to death.

Chapter 20

Slick's dreams frightened him because he would see himself as a broken old man, homeless and alone. That was the fate that was awaiting Odfus if he did not alter his ways. The old crook dream of horrible creatures chasing him but not quite catching him; most of the time he woke up or something saved him. Every time in the dream he would wind up losing all his material possessions or getting nearly killed or crippled. When he got money, it would catch on fire or blow away. The dust from the ashes would then make everyone sick that came in contact with it.

Then dreams of God of peaceful valleys, with clear water and happy people haunted Slick. "Jesus is calling you," Peeler told him. Slick never used drugs in prison. He started to crave the euphoria and almost got some. But he didn't he had reached a point in his life that he knew he had to change. He discovered that he desired to feel at peace and that was all he really ever wanted. "Jesus is calling" Peeler would greet Slick each morning. The two convicts studied the Scriptures. Slick convinced was of Peeler's right to call himself a prophet. Now Odfus began to seek his own spiritual path. The dreams were changing though Odfus could not understand most of them. Peeler would simply tell him, "Jesus is calling. You'll understand in time." The peace that a once maniac like Peeler had found intrigued this Odfus.

Odfus had a dream of a man riding a horse to the north and ending up in the west and wind blowing and trees not moving. People running around saying and doing things that made no sense all talking at the same time. Peeler told Odfus that was the story of his life. Odfus again questioned Peeler's sanity. "No I'm not the one that's crazy." Peeler said. "Jesus is calling."

Peeler's change of heart didn't go unnoticed by the powers that be. Oddfus and Peeler were scheduled to see the parole board the same day. The night before the hearing both men had dreams and awoke at the same time. Each man sat up on his bunk at the same time. Odfus was in a cold sweat his heart beating loudly against his chest. Giant gargles were chasing him the faster he ran the larger the demons became. Finally they caught him that's when he woke up.

Peeler had dreamed that the parole board set Odfus free and a voice told him to tell Odfus go to Savannah to a house on Albocor Street. He saw the house in his dream. If he blew this chance that would be the last time God would intervene. Peeler told Odfus what he dreamed and described the house and then told Odfus that he would be locked up five more years. At the end of that time Odfus was to come back and get Peeler and take him with him. Odfus would go to Savannah for two years to learn how to live on his own. The strange thing was that Odfus had dreamed the same thing the night before. Odfus hadn't told Peeler about it because he thought Peeler wanted to get out and it might upset him. Peeler laughed and the two men prayed and believed that they had been given a sign.

Peeler told Odfus that he had committed the murders he had been convicted of doing. He had killed people that the law knew nothing about. Before he went to jail he shot hunters that people thought of as accidents or others never found. Peeler buried them in the woods. Four others since he came to prison, including Baker. Peeler confided to Odfus that he could not use that name Slick anymore ever. "Billy Slick Robinson is dead and the only way that he could bring his true spirit to life by saying that name and that man was dead. Odfus Muse has always been your name, you were sin free when got it but that wasn't the way the folks that gave you that name intended for you to live. Your sins are forgiven so be Odfus in your new life, the spirits of those people will be with you. Don't call Boyd or Iris for help no matter how hard things got. "Learn to depend on God and do what He tells you to do." "Jesus is calling, "Peeler told Odfus as he was preparing to leave prison for the last time.

Chapteer21

Nobody was there when Odfus boarded the bus to Savannah. The trip was full of thoughts of the future, doubt, fear and dread. Faith wasn't really what drove Odfus to go to the house that he had visualized. It was desperation. The neat large house in the middle of the black section of Savannah with the sign, "Rooms To rent" seemed like an oasis of hope for the desperate ex-convict.

"Hello, my name is Odfuse Muse. I saw your sign." Odfus said shyly. "Come in " an elderly black woman invited. I'm Mrs. Blake. "Well ma'am, um um, I" "What is it?" she said with a laugh in her voice. "I'll tell you the truth. I just got out of prison. I don't have any family. I need a place to stay. I had a dream about this house. I hope you don't think I'm." again laughing she said, "God works in mysterious ways. I knew you was coming. Maybe we both are crazy." "Thank you, " Odfus sighed. "Let me show you your room'' she said.

"A man in my church needs someone to help out at his café. You go by there in the morning. Now get settled in. We eat at 6:30. Mr. Greer and Mr. Maxwell get off from work at 5:00. I don't hold dinner. We eat at 6:30. Get you some rest. It's 3:00 now. Remember 6:30".

"Yes, Ma'am." Odfus replied.

Calvin Greer, a short heavyset man of sixty and Fred Maxwell, a slight built balding man of forty-eight were both seated when Odfus entered the dining room at 6:25. "Hello" they both said in unison. "Hello" Odfus replied. "My name is Odfus Muse. Glad to meet you both." "Same here." Both replied flashing smiles like twins from Hell. "Sit over there."" Mrs. Blake said pointing to her left. "Thank you" "Can I help you with anything?" "No." she said. "I don't let men in my kitchen. " Yawl don't clean up after yourself." Greer and Maxwell both laughed. Maxwell said, "Don't ask that again. She'll tell about her dead husband. It will take a hour for her." Stopping in mid-sentence, Mrs. Blake re-entered the room carrying a serving bowl. "You need not have stopped talking. I heard you." They say I talk too much." "No ma'am" Greer said. "Lair." Mrs. Blake said laughing. "I do talks a heap. I cook too. Did they tell you that?" "No Ma'am." Odfus said. "Well, you is gonna find out she said proudly. Two more serving bowl and a platter for the pork chops. Odfus found out she was about the best cook he had ever seen.

Chapter 22

Boyd and Elaine drove the 75 miles from the prison to Augusta blushing like two kids on their first date. Nervously talking about the clothes Elaine picked up for Boyd. The repairs needed on Rosette's old house where Boyd would be staying. "I got some furniture, cleaned the place up. I hope you like it." "I'm sure I will," Boyd replied. I didn't put up lace curtains or anything like that. I didn't know your favorite colors so I stuck to the basics." "I am glad you did." Boyd chuckled.

"Nine years is a long time Laine. A lot has changed since 197O." Boyd observed. "I hope I don't embarrass you. It's gonna take a while to get prison out of me." "Just don't wear those clothes Slick told me about. That's the only thing embarrassing I can think of." "Seriously," Boyd continued. "I don't even have a driver's license. I was sitting here with you thinking about Slick, Peeler and them." Elaine laughed. "It'll be all right." She said.

"Well here we are as you see the house needs painting, the lawn needs cutting. It's a lot of work around here and things will talk care of themselves. "OK?" ''Yeah, OK" Boyd smiled then he said. "The house looks like it is in fair shape the roof looks new" inspecting his new home. "Come in. Let me show you what I did on the inside." Elaine said grabbing Boyd by the arm. Elaine had found some used leather chairs and a couch, a heavy wood coffee table for the living room, basic simple table and chairs in the kitchen, pots and dishes, cutlery. Everything needed to set up housekeeping. "I got the receipts for everything I spent." You can open a bank account tomorrow.

Then she led him to the bedroom. There was a large bed with a comforter, matching curtains. Everything had a decidedly feminine flavor to it. Elaine looked into Boyd's eyes and said "I plan to spend a lot of time in here" as she kissed him gently. Sometimes God creates a man and woman to be together, it is impossible for either of them to be happy with someone else. They made love that seemed to melt them into one mind, body and a shared soul… a spiritual experience each knowing what the other needed. At 43 she had not really made love since she and Boyd had secretly met 30 years before as children experimenting with forbidden fruit. Now she was a mature woman that felt loved and wanted to please Boyd in every way conceivable. Boyd was frightened and really didn't understand how she could love a man like him but he knew she did. Lying there in each other's arms each knew the depth of the other's passions. They had an unspoken language between them one deeper than words could express. Every dream of happiness and fulfillment that one could get from another human being they found in each other.

Boyd felt secure in knowing Elaine loved him. But he felt that he didn't really know himself. At least he had never let anyone know him and by always wearing a mask he hid himself from himself. Boyd decided to tell Elaine all about the things he had done. Hell he had close to ½ million dollars she knew nothing about. She had never asked why he was in prison. He knew she wouldn't stop loving him but numbers, drugs, prostitution, even murder was enough to frighten any decent person. Boyd knew he could never truly be happy until Elaine knew him and he understood himself. Being completely honest with someone being emotionally naked and against everything he had been conditioned to believe. Prison, crime and living without a spiritual guiding light had hardened Boyd's protective shell around his heart. He also had a pocket inside his mind where he put unpleasant feelings or secrets or tenderness he felt for others.

For months he tried to summon the courage to talk to Elaine. The words wouldn't come no matter how hard he tried. Elaine felt a wall between them and asked Boyd what was the matter. "Nothing" he replied. Then one day Elaine reminded Boyd that Red had been in prison with him. "I know all about you." "Redmond and I talk," Boyd told her, "no you don't know all about me." "Did you know how I was involved in killing three men in prison?" "Yes, weren't they plotting to kill you?" I know about the whorehouses, the numbers con games with Slick and even the selling drugs; I'm not a child "I love you maybe you should pray for forgiveness and learn to forgive yourself." She said. Boyd looked into Elaine's eyes and said "Yea, but it's not easy you know. I did what I did. I knew what I was doing. I didn't really care who I hurt not really now that's the truth." Boyd confessed. "Do you care now, "Elaine questioned?" "Yes, I do. Ever since I saw you something changed inside me. I want to be decent. I never cared about anything just money." "Well Boyd you don't have that much money." Elaine said. "I've got more than you think. I own property in Savannah, land in South Carolina, houses, an apartment house, and stocks and bonds. I got some more land on Hilton Head all together about a half million dollars. The money I sent out with you was like a gift. You could have kept it for raising Red. I didn't want you to know how much money I had. If you knew, I thought, you might get scared.

I've got a couple of bank accounts and I have to go to Savannah to get things straightened out. Will you go with me? Boyd promised "no more secrets." He hadn't told Elaine about the other two apartments houses or annuities his lawyers were managing for him. Old habits die hard he would surprise her later. A surprise, isn't really a secret not if it's a good surprise.

Actually the surprise was to be on Boyd. His real estate had increased in value. Through careful management his investments had more than tripled in value. There was an offer on the table for the old apartments for six million dollars as part of a commercial development all that was needed was his signature. Boyd and Elaine both nearly fell off their seats when they heard about the deal.

Chapter 23

Red was now in Atlanta doing a very poor imitation of a family man. He and Paula had gotten married and along with Grace their youngest moved down there. Red made it a point to meet everybody in Atlanta who liked to party from Bulkhead to the various housing projects throughout the city. For the next two years he spent more money had more affairs and indulged in anything he felt like doing, most of the time Elaine sent Paula the money needed to pay living expenses. The 85,000 dollars Red made went on cocaine, hotel rooms, and trips to exotic places for weekend trysts.

Red 's idea of a good deed was to find a pretty girl, well let's say young woman from the projects. Take her to a couple of the more expensive stores buy her a couple of outfits. Then take her to some far away place, for the weekend. If he really enjoyed her "company" he would give her number to one of his friends on the Hawks or Falcons or in the entertainment business...maybe a business associate. Everybody loves a good time; Red would say I'm not hurting anybody.

Once when Bobby asked did he feel a married man should be going on trip to Las Vegas with someone other than his wife Red said quite seriously "Paula don't like Vegas how is it going to hurt her if she doesn't know where I am?" Red even talked Bobby into going on a trip with him. Once they went to New York for a weekend under the pretense of a business conference. Red had a very young, very beautiful woman waiting for Bobby when he got there in truth they had a great time and even saw each other when she came to Atlanta. Red had gotten worried about his buddy he wasn't seeing anybody Red thought he might be gay.

Red had known a lot of preachers that were. Red also suspected that deep down all were con artists anyway. He was happy when she told him his old friend was straight. Red still hoped Bobby would wake up to the game and start making some real money. A lot of people were caught up in that church game and his old friend could make a killing "promising a bunch of niggers something for nothing." Red figured that had to be the best hustle of all time.

Red's reputation as a ladies man was growing to near legendary status women almost looked forward to being seduced by him. The stories you would hear were right out of a playboy magazine fantasy the Swedish Twins the three stewardesses and so on. Most of it was true though embellished. Red only had one rule never tell them your real name most people thought his was Red Robins or Red Rollins the best protection against unwanted pregnancies, Red always said.

The Swedish twins is a true story, almost, the girls were of Swedish descent but had never been to Sweden. Each was over six feet tall and beautiful they did modeling in the Atlanta area; Red did have sex with both of them at the same time. However, Red confided to Bobby that they nearly fucked him to death Red never tried that two at a time thing again. He did remain friends with the ladies but convinced one that he had more feelings for her and wanted it to be special for she and he. The girls never knew of his near death experience. Red still managed to have sex with them both just at different times. The three stewardesses again true almost; he did spend the night with all three women. He had sex with only one the other two had sex with each other. The late 70's morays were a little different than today, you might say he saved their reputations. Well the truth is he did have sex with all three but at different times. All three women really adored him. Red had a gift. His gift wasn't what he thought it was at the time.

Red confided everything in Bobby; at times he tried to tell Red he didn't want to hear about his sexual encounters. It was tearing Bobby up inside hearing all this while the woman he loved was being treated so cold and callously. What could he do about it? Bobby didn't know that Red wasn't taking care of his responsibilities at home...Bobby thought that at least Red was supporting Paula. She confided many things in Bobby but not her money problems. When it reached a point that the house was three month behind in mortgage payments she had talk to someone... she was too ashamed to tell Elaine. Somehow Bobby mustered up enough courage to tell Paula how he felt. He also came to realize that he had ceased to be Red's friend a long time ago, maybe that man at the prison had seen through him but what mattered most was that he loved Paula. Though surprised to hear it she had to admit that she had grown to expect more caring from Bobby than Red. Without knowing it she had fallen in love with Bobby and really needed him. They struggled with doing the right thing. The couple wanted to be together but what about the children and what about Elaine's feelings? So many people would be hurt. Their decision was sealed after Red and Bobby returned from Coach Phillips funeral.

Chapter 24

Coach Phillips, an immense bear of a man whose character and strength of will helped to shape the lives of most of the boys he coached, died suddenly of a massive stroke. Bobby and Red played for him and Bobby thought each loved and respected the coach after all he had taught them a lot. He had been almost a surrogate father to Red after Redmond Sr. died.
Two hundred forty five pound of pure muscle distributed over a six-foot frame. His daily training regiment of 200 sit ups, 100 push-ups and a five-mile run to work rain or shine showed his players he practiced what he preached "Get in shape and you'll win in the forth quarter". Leroy Phillips meant business and he got results wherever he went… his first love was his alma mater… he still is considered by many as the greatest athlete in the history Laney High School of Augusta Georgia.

Phillips' military career began in 1939 as a member of a Negro Transportation unit. He served both in the Pacific and European theaters during WWII. He had climbed to the rank of first sergeant long before the army integrated. When the army integrated he was transferred to an infantry unit. The Sergeant quickly developed a reputation as an outstanding Non-Commissioned officer. He was among the first black soldiers selected for Special Forces training.

He led reconnaissance patrols into North Korea served as an advisor in Viet Nam in the fifties. He again served in nineteen sixty and won a Bronze Star, Purple Heart and a presidential citation. Coach leads by example, he never asks you to do anything he was not willing to do for you. Sgt. Phillips had a way of inspiring loyalty; it was simple, he was loyal to you. When he told you something you believed it. You believed it because it was true. If you told him something he never passed it on. Men who had served with Coach would travel hundreds of miles just to tell his players stories of the war and how Coach had saved their life or changed it.

In those days you didn't have to be a student to play on a team at a black school. Red played in eight-grade he was good enough; also he had just lost his father it was like a lifeline for Red. Coach took an interest in Red at a critical time; Red would visit coach's home. Bobby thought Coach Philips was respected by all, especially Redmond Perry Jr who seemingly idealized Coach. Things are never as they seem with Red. He wanted to be a part of five straight championships. He mistakenly thought that if he was the best football player in the state it would help him get into the University of

Georgia…it didn't. In Red's mind he figured that all Coach wanted with him was his football playing ability.

Coach's wife was the first Japanese person Red had ever met and was fascinated by her as she and coach speak in Japanese. Red even learned a little of the language himself. Meko was several years younger than coach [mid twenties] and was quite pretty. She was a challenge to Red and something different a nice trophy so he pursued her very carefully.

Coach is what everybody in Augusta called Sgt. Phillips. The whole back community loved and respected Coach ever since he returned to coach and teach ROTC in nineteen sixty-one. The Bronze Star and the Purple Heart he won cost him the use of his left arm. Coach had an ability to see people as they really were and inspire them to make the most of what they had to offer. His insight into human nature was part of what made him such a good leader. You could seldom fool Leroy Phillips; he loved Red like a member of his family. But he always felt something disturbing in the way that Red used people. As a teenage Red seemed to lack empathy or any real concern for the feelings of others; Bobby remembered coach commenting to him about it, but said he'll grow up, he's a good kid. Bobby thought at the time that Coach had something troubling him but he didn't say anything else about it. Now he knew what Coach meant.

Red's total self-absorption was part of his charm and he seemed oblivious to what he was doing, Red almost made you feel sorry for him until you were on the receiving end. Coach loved Red and apparently never found out about the brief affair Red had with his wife. On the way home from the funeral Red told Bobby about it, you would have thought she raped him. He blamed her for seducing him but even at eighteen he was a lot more experienced than she was. That was her only affair and the sad truth was that Red was the biological father of her only child. I guess the silver lining was that Coach really loved his daughter…she was a big part of the joy he got out of life itself.

When Bobby heard this he knew that he had reached the point that he had to distance himself from Red. When they returned to Atlanta he and Paula made plans to leave. Red though, charming laid back and seldom angry could be extremely violent. Bobby had to stop him from killing a man that had in a fight, on one occasion right after he got out of prison. If Red felt threatened or wronged, he was down right dangerous. They decided to leave the next time Red went on one of his extended weekends. Bobby rented a truck, called some church people in Philadelphia and made arrangements for them to stay until they got on their feet.

Red had gotten some money from a couple of old friends to buy cocaine while at the funeral. Red had nearly two thousand dollars to party with and a good story to tell his old buddies Tuesday when he called them. The fellows Red went to school with thought he could get anything so he promised to get six ounces of coke for the two grand. He had a friend who had a lot of coke, loved pretty women and believed anything Red told him. Red really meant to get some amount of cocaine for his friends but he blew their money, used ounce and a half the dealer gave him so he called his friends; told them he had been robbed. Got more money from them and did the same thing. This time he took one of the guys with him; they had so much fun that Red's old friend didn't even notice he paid for everything.

Bobby made arrangements to Pastor a church in Philadelphia; he and Paula packed up as much as they could get in a rented truck and left. They took Grace to Augusta for the "weekend", they knew she wouldn't go with them she was a "'daddy's girl" and Red would really be out of control if they took her. It was best if nobody knew where they had gone for a while. This was a bad situation for everybody.

Elaine loved both Bobby and Paula since they were kids. But she hadn't wanted to see how bad things had gotten for Red. She also had tried to keep as much of it from Boyd as she could. He never questioned what she did with money. When they got married she said she wanted to continue working, he asked her to quit. He wanted to makeup for all the years he had missed when Red was growing up. She enjoyed her work and so she made a promise to spend her money on herself and the grand kids. Most of it went to take care of Paula and Grace. Boyd would have been upset if he knew Red had gotten involved with drugs again.

Chapter 25

Red oldest daughter Mary was an extremely gifted child; she had been number-one in her class nearly every year. Her best friend was a girl named Judith Smith. The two engaged in a friendly rivalry all through school. Judith's grandfather had been governor of the state and her family was very well connected. The two girls were so gifted that with Red pleading, Elaine invested the money she had gotten from Boyd when he was in prison. The two girls had an eighth grade project called "Where is technology leading". The two twelve-year-old girls had researched the best investment in new technology. Mary and Judith asked Red to read it over. He was so amazed by their in depth and precise research that he showed it to Furman White, Jr. president of the People's United Bank who commented that he was going to invest some of his own money based on their research.

Even though Boyd had more money than he ever really dreamed of having, he knew that there is no such thing as too much money. He was still a relatively young man. Making money had always occupied most of his thinking. Even if the things he had done in the past did hurt some people and were illegal but helped some others just as much. Now he wanted to be legal and a positive for his family, community and himself.

Mary and Judith with the help of Judith's Uncle Jim were enrolled at Hillmont Preparatory School, one of the most prestigious private schools in Georgia. Only the richest and or brightest were considered for enrollment. Attending Hillmont meant political connections that if used properly would ensure a lifetime of success. Judith's uncle, his wife, her brother and a number of Judith's family members had attended Hillmont. Because of jealousy and the fact that Mary was the first black to attend Hillmont; Judith and Mary were each other's only friends for the four years they were there. However, they were all they both needed. These two knew what they wanted and how to go about getting it. This experience bonded them in a life long friendship. Judith and Mary were a lot closer than they were to their sisters.

Although Boyd had little formal education, he had vision, foresight and courage. His vision was to have a company that handled every aspect of the construction of a project. The grounds structure, climate control, technical systems and the maintenance of all. With the age of computers come new ideas. Records of everything can be kept and utilized with the pressing of a button. With the proper systems in place it is possible to keep up with everything involved with the continuing use of a property. When the grass needs cutting, temperature changes systems updating and the proper use of utilities. In the age of computerization, every office, every school will be run with computers or controlled by them. Boyd saw that very early on. Though many of his conclusions were based on the girl's project. Boyd was also practical; the girl's research had tripled his money in three years.

He started small with the construction of homes, small offices; the landscaping side was now number-one in the south. The computer side of his business depended mostly on government contracts and minority set-asides…until markets opened up in Europe and Asia. The construction business began to grow because Boyd insisted on quality both in materials and craftsmanship. The vision still remained, Boyd had turned the six million into forty million in three years. He knew that in computers he had just begun and the world was his market. The racism factor of America was not a consideration in other parts of the world. Boyd decided that to be a factor in American business, he would have to buy his way in.

Chapter 26

Jack Smith, Judith's father was a personable, carefree, extremely incompetent lawyer. He had just been let go by the third law firm in five years. No one in Augusta was more entertaining at a cocktail party or just plain likable. Boyd was an easy touch for Jack whenever he needed money for Judith to stay in school. The two men had become friends. Jack took Boyd on a skiing trip and as it turned out Boyd really liked to ski. When Boyd asked Jack to come to work for him, He said," Jack, I'm not a salesman, you have a way with people, and you know everybody. And if this company is to get where I think we can go, we need you."

Jack always felt he lived in the large shadow of his father. He desperately wanted to accomplish something on his own. Jack never felt needed or for the most part even wanted. Jack sensed Boyd's sincerity and he respected the things Boyd had accomplished. Boyd told Jack, "Let me be frank with you, OK. You like to have a good time, you have connection that we don't; we do very good work and will handle all the details. All you have to do is be yourself...I need you." Jack said, "I can't argue with that; Jack Smith knows how to throw a party but." Boyd interrupted "No buts you're hired." The two shook hands.

Boyd's no nonsense approach impressed Jim, Jack's older brother and Georgia's Attorney General. Jim suggested that Jack's younger brother Bob contact Boyd as well. Bob's real estate's company had been one of the largest and most successful in the south. But Bob's partner had developed a mid-life crisis and had misspent company funds. The company had nearly defaulted on a couple of loans...Bob spent a great deal of his personal money on bailing the company. Bob went to Boyd in a hope to get the money to operate his real estate business but wound up coming to work for Boyd. Comp-Tech. bought the company, got rid of the partner and double its annual profits.

The combination of Jack's personality, Bob's real estate expertise and Boyd's leadership and vision plus a brief fling with affirmative action equaled money. However, Boyd knew that anything not based totally on performance was a house of cards. Jim was now a deputy ambassador to England. Boyd decided that it was time to open up international markets.

With all the success that Boyd had enjoyed, some things troubled him Elaine felt uneasy about her father as well. One morning both woke up at the same time and sat up. Elaine spoke first "I had this dream about daddy and you know it's been almost a year since Aunt Rosetta's heard from him. I've got this feeling I need to go and see about him."

"Yeah Boyd said "I have been thinking about Slick, I'm worried he hadn't been in touch with me even to borrow money let's take a couple of days and go to Jacksonville first and check on Willie. Then go to Savannah I've got some business I need to take of down there anyway." Boyd called the office told them where he was going and unless it was life or death Bob Smith could handle it.

Chapter 27

Boyd and Elaine arrived in Jacksonville on a sunny Monday morning not a cloud in the sky. The weather made them feel optimistic. However, when they got to Willie's house what they found was disturbing his yard was uncut and his beloved roses dead. Elaine recalled that the only happy memories of Willie she had were helping him tend his roses. Something was different about him when he was in his rose garden. Now she was really worried her steps quicken as they approached the porch. Elaine summoned all of her courage as she knocked on the door. No answer, knock louder she thought fighting back panic. She had dreaded the possibility of rejection but now she feared he might be dead. Willie... "Willie Posey"... now with desperation in her voice she cries out "Daddy." Elaine snatched open the front door, she went straight to Willie's room. A weak but determined voice called out "who is that in my house." " Its me, Laine; daddy its me" Elaine said.

When they saw each other they began to cry. The joy of an old man who thought he'd die without seeing the family that had meant so much to him. He nearly had lost them forever because of his selfish pride. Elaine knew she had always loved her father; the fear that she had lost him was overwhelming. Both tried to speak but couldn't for several minutes. The words I love you no longer stuck in Willie's throat. Willie said the words over and over again as they cried in each other's arms. Boyd waited on the porch as the reunion unfolded. He couldn't help sneaking a occasional peek...but he didn't over hear what was going on inside.

Willie had not allowed the members of his church to help him after Rev. Spencer died. Willie was old and set in his way and didn't trust the new minister, Rev Battle. The preacher had done his best to help, but Willie was not the type to compromise. Neither was Rev. Battle he enlisted the aid of another member Lucille Dorman. Mrs. Dorman got a friend of hers Velolla Johnson involved. Mrs. Johnson ran a nursing home and was in truth a kind and loving person. But Willie didn't see her that way to him she was a bloodsucker. Willie wasn't about to get neither his blood sucked nor his retirement or social security checks used by anyone but him.

A blue Volvo pulled up to the curb three people emerged from it. Rev Battle, Mrs. Dorman and Mrs. Johnson as they approached the porch Boyd greeted them "Hi I'm Boyd Tillman Mr. Posey's son in law." Boyd extended his hand to the reverend; they shook hands as Rev. Battle introduced the woman to Boyd. "I didn't know he had a daughter" Mrs.

Johnson hissed. "Seem like he did yes, he did I remember people say she run away a long time ago. Mrs. Dorman reported. "Glad she came back maybe she can talk some sense to him". " Lord I hope so" Mrs. Johnson exclaimed. After a few minutes they entered the house; the tears in the eyes of he old man said it all.

Willie was sick, but he was more in the need of loving attention than anything else… seeing Elaine again telling her he was wrong was the best medicine he could have. Willie said to Elaine " I had to get to be eighty years old to get some sense. Do you think James will forgive me"? Elaine laughed as she wiped her eyes. "Yes I guarantee it."

When Willie saw Mrs. Johnson he nearly jumped out of bed "what is she doing in my house?" Calm down daddy" Elaine said as she gently coasted him back into bed. "We just want you to get the proper care Mr. Posey" Mrs. Johnson said.
"Well get out of here then," Willie shouted. Rev. Battle shook his head and everyone had to laugh at Willie stubbornness. Even Willie was amused "Lord forgive me for being so rude. It has been so long since I've seen my baby" Willie sobbed as Elaine stood fighting back the tears… the nurse in her had taken over. Daddy we have got to get you to a hospital." She said with authority. Rev. Battle and the three women went to make arrangements for Willie to get into the hospital. Boyd got Elaine a hotel room and rented her a car. Willie's old neighborhood had gotten run down and a bit rough. Boyd didn't want his wife to stay in the house by herself. He had an important meeting scheduled for Friday and he was going on to Savannah to check on Slick. Elaine called James and told him the good news about her and Willie's reconciliation. When she told James that Willie had asked her to have his son come so Willie could apologize to him. James was overwhelmed with emotion. Willie hadn't called James his son since he thrown him out forty years ago. James said he would be there in the morning and they could put Willie's affairs in order.

Willie though nearly eighty and suffering from a slight case of pneumonia was otherwise healthy. Up until the pneumonia had sapped his energy he had been active. Willie loved to work in his flower garden. He walked three miles a day even in the rain if it wasn't a thunderstorm. He was strong as an ox. They say he was twice as stubborn but he was no match for Elaine when she made up her mind; he was coming back to Augusta with her. She told him "Daddy we want you to come home with us. Aunt Rosetta is there and we can find you a nice little place you can tend to your flowers. Your family will be around, the doctor says you are in good shape. And I say if you want to stay that way you will come home with us. It's your home too."

Willie looked at his daughter and said "I'll go but I want to take care of myself I don't want to be a burden to anyone." When James arrived the next day he and Willie had a tearful reunion both men blaming themselves for letting it go on this long. Elaine said "Well that's all right we'll all put it behind us." The three of them vowed to be a family from that day on. This is what mama always wanted a choked up Elaine blurted out as tears flowed down her face. The time had come for them to be a family God had blessed them with the true knowledge of what it meant to have one another Elaine thought.

The joy of their reunion was temporary; Rosetta called with bad news about Red. Paula and Bobby had been through and left Grace with her. Rosetta said "I knew something wasn't right so I asked Paula what's going on, she hemmed and hawed but she finally told me the truth. Red had been messing up, they were about to lose the house and then she started crying. Paula and Bobby are going away together, I always knew he was hanging around for something, I told you that a long time ago."

Chapter 28

Boyd drove up I95 toward Savannah but when he got to Brunswick, he stopped and drove by the house where he had lived as a boy. The happy reunion in Jacksonville had gotten him to thinking about his family, maybe his sister was still alive. The house was run down no one had live there for a long time. Boyd paused for a moment then drove on; making himself think of something else. He had learned to do that in prison, those years when he got very few visitors. No sense in getting upset about something like that you know something you can do nothing about. He thought as he drove on to Savannah. . "Man I used to love this town Boyd chuckled as he passed the city limits sign. The money I made the people that I have known Boyd thought. He would always remember all the good times he had in Savannah. Boyd hadn't seen many of his old friends for a long time. "I guess a lot of them are dead" he thought. He'd look some of them up while in town, some of my old numbers runners should still be around. He smiled as he recalled several old friends.

He wondered how Thelma, the woman that ran the whorehouse for him was doing. She would be in her seventies now, times flies he lamented. She could fight like a man nobody got out of order with her she wasn't scared of anything either. She ran that house and we made money especially when all those white tricks used to come to the house. She knew everybody and they say she had some of the best pussy in Savannah in her day. Young Niggers would spend a lot of money on her and boy, did those white guys, pay. Boyd thought of Thelma's daughter; May was the only woman other than Elaine that gotten to Boyd. Then he felt a slight melancholy come over him as he remembered how she had gone to New York and gotten killed. "Those were the days and that was the game they played," he whispered softly to himself as he drove toward his old haunts. Thinking about all those old acquaintances made him long to see Slick.

He became more determined than ever to find his old friend. Boyd decided his first stop should be Al's Poolroom, if it was still there, more than likely Slick had been by there, he would have at least have stopped by. Al was a loud mouth man in his sixty's who smoked cheap fowl smelling cheap cigars. He nearly always wore a knit shirt barely able to cover his ample belly. He knew everybody. Every hustler to come through Savannah came by the crap games in his back room; everything was sold out of his front or back door. The only reason the police let him stay open was they knew that sooner or later every crook would come by Al's. The police knew where to find them.

There was Al's it looked the same, ragged but not the look of a place that had all the things going on that Al's did. Boyd walked into the dimly lit room, there at the back was Al running his mouth. Boyd laughed and thought some things never change. Al turned and looked in Boyd's direction squinted and said; " Boyd, Savannah Boyd I'll be damned is that you?"
"Yeah it's me" Boyd replied. Al was the owner of the loudest and filthiest mouth in Savannah. "Mother fucker I heard you got out and went straight made a million dollars". Boyd laughed at Al's obvious attempt to set him up for a loan.

"Well I went straight;" Boyd answered, "I'm looking for Slick have you seen him?" Al quickly answered "No not in quite a while, they say he preaching, you know I don't go for that type of shit, I don't play with God. He's got a little storefront church over on Martin Luther King. Remember Iris, that bitch he used to fuck around with? She seen him about two weeks ago she had just got off the chain gang. She said she thought that he done went crazy didn't want no pussy just wanted to preach to her she said she told him she didn't have time for that shit. Wait a minute." Al said almost as an after thought "Come here Jaffa I want to ask you something. That little storefront church over on MLK what time do it be open?" You mean the soup kitchen" Al interrupted "Yeah nigger the place you told me about". Jaffa said "Al you know if you wasn't so old I'd kick your ass." Al interrupted again "Nigger, just answer my question. A dumb young ass nigger like you need to be kissing my ass trying to learn something I told you I'm probably your daddy anyway". Jaffa just shook his head and laughed. "Yeah it still there and growing they got that store next door; and they serve lunch now too. Not just breakfast and dinner... most of the hustlers give him donations and some churches are getting involved, I think they have a church building now too." "What kind of game do you think Old Slick Billy is running?" Al inquired. Jaffa said "Ain't no game they are helping a lot of brothers." "See how dumb that Nigger is," Al said to Boyd. "You probably give him money yourself with your stupid ass".

Chapter 29

Boyd and Al's conversation turned to other old friends, but when Boyd asked about Thelma, he got some bad news. She had been stricken with a stroke and was in a wheel chair she was staying with some people over on Connors Street. She was in pretty bad shape
"I did hear that Rev. Slick was trying to help her." Al reported " Preacher at Conner Street Baptist Church is trying to get her into a nursing home. Her son shot up all that money she had from working with you". Boyd really was hurt by what he heard. He knew he needed to help her, she had taught him the game, so to speak. They got a lot of money out of that house and if the rest of the backers had taken he and Bob Edmonds advise and let her run things, they wouldn't have fallen apart the way they did. Boyd owed her a great deal. He'd get her into a nursing home the best money could get. He could do that he, owed her that.

Boyd asked "What abut Charlie Harris how is he doing?" Al shook his head as he said, "You don't know man he got twenty five years fed time. Something about interstate trafficking of dope they say he had a hundred pounds of heroin. If that mother fucker had gotten here with that dope we would been on". Then Iris walked in carrying a black garbage bag. Al shouted to her "Look at who is here." She came over to them and spoke she wasn't in the mood for small talk she was too near the end of her mission. Her eyes were tearing her nose running and her disposition was surly and abrupt. "Yeah good to see you both, I've got to find LD, have you seen him I got these suits and a couple of dresses you can get all of it for two hundred dollars." Al and Boyd knew that she would take fifty. Boyd gave her the two hundred for old time sake. "I still need to see LD." She protested. " Jaffi's got the same thing he working for LD". Iris told Al "don't bullshit me". Al had the reputation of having the worst dope in Savannah no matter how weak the dope was he cut it. "I ain't got nothing to do with it Jaffi's got it you can get off in the bath room." She grunted "OK". Iris knew that Al didn't want any trouble with Boyd there. Boyd put the bag down next to the seat where Iris could steal it back he had no use for the suits or dresses. This was a little game they played in the old days. With all her faults she still didn't like asking anybody for anything. She was proud.

Iris was a very bright woman, she was extremely well read though most of her reading was done while incarcerated. If she had put her talents to productive use, she might have been a woman of great renown instead of a woman of ill repute. She had unbelievable energy and more pure nerve than most of the men she encountered. Though she was still attractive when she dressed up, in her youth she was a knockout. Slick and Iris stayed together longer than any couple “in the life”. They were closer than most straight peoples’ marriages. They were loyal to one another in the strange way of the streets. She never fooled around on Slick unless she was getting paid for it and that meant she gave the money to him that was the rule. The two of them played by the rules with each other. Boyd knew that his old buddy would always have feelings for her. She was family to him as well.

After about ten minutes she returned in much better spirits. She slurred her words rubbing her face, scratching her neck and faking a smile “Hi, Boyd baby. When you get to town baby? Seen the Rev yet?” Boyd said “No not yet. You know Slick was the best man I ever had, he helped mama with his two chaps. You know Felicia and Eric are both in college? Eric goes to Savannah State he helps the Revered out at the soup kitchen. Them two are real close.” Boyd conceded. “No I did not know that’’ Iris went on, “That man was the best thing to happen to my kids you know he would send them all money for Christmas even the two that wasn’t his.” Boyd never knew that Slick had taken much interest in his children. Iris went on to tell him how Slick would send money every time they made a good sting. Boyd remembered that Slick only made a real effort to pay him back was around Christmas. Iris went on to say that her oldest was on death row in New Jersey and the other son was “working for the city of Asbury Park in the mayor’s office or some such shit. Barry always had a lot of shit with him.” Iris’ mother lived in Asbury Park for many years. “Mom came home when she heard that Slick was preaching.”

Chapter 30

Jaffi who had been standing by the window waved his hand. Iris said, "Oh shit"

And ran from the table and hid under the bar near the back door. She discretely took the bag with her.

Jaffi walked to the back room and got the shotgun that Al kept there for emergencies. Two young imitation gangsters barely out of their teens entered the poolroom. The two young men came in trying to act like characters in a gangster movie. "What up" the taller of the two called out "ain't nothing" Al responded. " We are looking for Iris have you seen her?" Al turned to them and said, "You know I can't stay in business seeing nobody." The shorter one scowled and said "Don't try to be funny old man." The taller one with the gold turned to Boyd and asked "What about you." Boyd had already started looking for a defensive position he wanted to get where he could get close enough to one of them so he could knock him out before he could get his gun out. Not really hearing the question he answered, "What" "Have you seen a bitch name Iris"? The short one asked with an annoyed tone.

"I wouldn't know her if I saw her." Boyd answered. "He's been out of town he's telling you straight, but you don't know who you talking to." The short one said, "I don't give a fuck."

It had been a long time since Boyd had been in this type of situation. He was uncomfortable but not really afraid, his survival instants were taking over. He should have known better than to come to a place like this he thought. But those survival instincts pushed all other thoughts from his mind. Boyd smiled as he got in just the right position. The young man was between him and the other hoodlum if they made the wrong move he had them both he figured he could get to the youngster's gun. He could break that one's neck and shoot the other even if the other kid got off a shot he'd hit his partner.

The tension in the room reached a level that if you spooned it out you could stress out a small city. The front door opened a tall thin man entered the room. He was dressed in the hustler custom of the period; the wide hat, bellbottom pants, the fur collar on his leather coat, all of it burgundy. He strutted right over to Boyd and said "My man Savannah Boyd what's going on SB."

Then he turned to the young men and scolded them "This is the man that taught me the game you were just about to get fucked up both of you. I told you to come in here and look and not to fuck with nobody." One of them tried to say something but the thin man stopped him and told him to wait over at the other table but first he must apologize to Boyd. The tall hustler extended his hand to Boyd, the two men shook hands. Boyd said hiding his relief "How you doing Squirrel". Squirrel said "Fine just fine, I heard that you was straight now" Boyd answered. "You heard right and I don't want to get mixed up in nobody's business." Squirrel turned and gazed at his two henchmen, with discuss, then said to Boyd, "I don't blame you, those guys don't know how to talk to people and I don't want no trouble…the kind of people you know. Its good to see you, its been too long."

Boyd figured that Squirrel was under the impression that he was still involved with Thomaso or his son and they were connected to the Mafia. Boyd knew that it was time for him to leave his old friends alone for good. He said his good byes and left this would be his last visit to Al's. He and Squirrel walked to their cars at the same time. Squirrel's was a El Dorado lime green in color. The car had every option available inside and out even a phone, which was unusual for that time and fluffy white covers on the dash and in the area in front of the back window. Of course he had leopard seat covers with something hanging from the rear view mirror. Two very nearly naked women were in the back seat, one more in the front passenger seat and another scantly clad woman driving. The two thugs were following in a less ornamental El Dog.

Chapter 31

Boyd had enough of memory lane but he was going to help Thelma and he found out some things he didn't know about his old friend. Slick never talked about his kids now Boyd understood why. Slick was not cold toward his children, he loved them. Slick took responsibility financially, at least for his children.

Boyd drove over to the storefront but as he drove, memories of his old life raced across his soul. Slick and Iris were always getting into some jam, having to leave town…but not before calling him for money. Boyd was lost in thought when he entered the storefront soup kitchen. Then the realization of what had just almost happened hit him. He got scared, he could have lost everything associating with his old cronies. He thought about the time in Miami when four Cubans tried to rob him. He was there trying to buy cocaine he had all the money but they only had half the coke. He sensed something; positioned himself like he did today. When they tipped their hand Boyd grabbed the closest one to him taking the gun from the surprised combatant shooting two of the three would be robber's one did get to shoot. But he shot his own partner in crime. Boyd left the hotel with the money and the coke. The three were hurt seriously but only the one the Cuban shot died. That was the closest he had come to killing anyone before he went to prison. "Hi" a voice behind Boyd called. Boyd trip down memory was suddenly interrupted. A man in his late twenties dressed in a cook's outfit emerged from behind a counter. He looked at Boyd with curiosity "is your name Boyd Tillman" He asked. "Why yes that's me" Boyd answered "I'm Bobby Dykes my father used to work for you (running numbers) years ago. Surprised, Boyd said to the young man, "You have quite a memory that was a long time ago, you couldn't have been more than six or seven back then". "I was nine," he said. Boyd now relaxed, spoke up "I'm looking for an old friend, Odfus is his name," The young man laughed as he replied "You mean Rev. Clean? That's what we call him now. When he first came home he got a pot-washing job in my father's café; he washed the pot so good that we started calling him Mister Clean and the name stuck. He started this ministry we changed it to Rev. Clean. I have been involved in this part of the ministry a couple of years now."

" He lives over on Albacore, 221 I think, he'll be there in a little while". You remember Charlie Blake don't you? Well, he died but his wife runs a boarding house, that same place where they used to live. She is a sweet old lady. Charlie kept her in the house away from everybody he even changed churches when he thought the preacher was looking at her. He was a possessive and jealous man I used to cut their lawn, he stopped that when I was fifteen."

Bobby showed Boyd around the dining room and the chapel. Then he asked Boyd if he wanted to see the church. They drove to the church building; the small structure freshly painted no church bulletin in front. The old church had a new roof, repaired steeple and fresh blacktop in the parking lot. We did a lot of the work ourselves Bobby said proudly.

"My father died last year; he was so happy and proud of what we are doing he left us the storefronts. I think he believed that we could be successful more than we did. We bought this building last year and it is almost paid for we have one hundred fifty members. You ought to hear Rev. preach he can set the building on fire. He's really something else." Boyd didn't know weather to laugh or cry. On the other, he was sure that his old friend could talk and be convincing.

Then Bobby Dykes told Boyd about when Odfus preached his first sermon; "the reverend was out walking one evening and passed a storefront church when a service was going on. For some reason; he went inside they were singing and praising the Lord. They didn't even have a preacher. He joined in and someone asked him to testify. He did; he told them about leaving home at seven years old. Being a con man, a dope addict spending years in prisons all over the country. Then he told them about being in the cell with a murderer, a man that nobody thought could be saved; more than just a lifelong sinner, a man seemingly possessed by the devil himself led him to Jesus. The people asked him to be their minister right there on the spot. We have a radio show on Saturday mornings. You should have heard that first sermon "Slick is dead" Lord, he preached that morning that was the day I joined him. We've been rolling ever since. I think he preacher about you one time too; a sermon about a true friend."

Chapter 32

The two men then drove out to a vacant lot. Bobby Dykes said, "My father left us this; it's about four acres. This is where we want to put our shelter. Bobby happened to turn in Boyd's direction and was startled by the look on his face. "What's the matter?" Bobby asked. Boyd said, "Have you had any offers on this property?" Bobby replied, "Not in about five years." "What" Boyd exclaimed he then explained to Bobby that he had sold the run-down apartments across the street to a developer for a substantial price. Bobby said. "I heard rumors of a development in this area but I heard they went belly-up."

People were still living in the apartments and he could see that no maintenance had been done on the property in a long time. Boyd told Bobby that he had to talk to Slick about what he had just found out. Boyd had seen the plans for the purposed development and he knew that it could be a benefit to the community and somebody could make some money why not he and Slick?

They drove back to the storefront where Bobby Dykes gave Boyd directions to Mrs. Blake's boarding house again. Boyd drove the six blocks to the boarding house. He parked, admired the yard, then entered the gate and walked to the porch. Climbed the four stone steps, walked across the porch to the door. Boyd rang the bell, waited a few minutes and then knocked. An elderly woman opened the door, Boyd said, "Hello, I'm looking for Rev. Muse." And who might you be?" asked the old woman looking a Boyd carefully. "My name is Boyd Tillman; I'm an old friend of his." Mrs. Blake looked at Boyd with a look of joy and surprise and wonder the she ordered him to come in." "Oh, my Lord! Come in here," Boyd did as he was instructed, but as he looked at her there was something vaguely familiar about her. "Lord, have mercy, she said, I'm Vinie Tillman." Boyd stood speechless for a moment, then they hugged, "Lord, she said, "You was ten years old the last time I saw you. You was the wildest boy. I was wild in those days myself I guess, but, that was before I met Blake he was a good man but jealous. I went along with him cause his first wife hurt him so bad." Boyd stood there struggling to keep his tears of joy inside him. But, somehow he still managed to say, "I'd never thought I'd see you again." Mrs. Blake said, "I looked for you after mama and daddy died. There is a lots of things I gotta tell you, the lawyer gave me some things to give you. Oh, where are my manners? Want something to eat? You thirsty? Sit down." "No, thank you", Boyd said as he sat down on the couch. "Don't be shy around here, she said. My little brother all grown up." They both laughed.

"Odfus will be home soon, he has been here for four years, pays every week on time; see how pretty the yard is, he did most of that work by himself, he's a good man." Boyd sat there in disbelief of the change in his old friend. "The Lord is good," Mrs. Blake said. Boyd told his sister that he knew her late husband but he guessed that old Blake didn't make the connection. Vinnie said "He knew but he didn't want to share me with nobody and he thought I was too good to met his friends except in church." "When you was a baby your people left you with mama and daddy. Your mama passed when you was two weeks old. Your daddy couldn't go back to Florida where they were from; so he asked them if they could take care of you. My mama loved chulins. Your real name was Williams. Your daddy left a letter; he asked that we keep it till you was grown. See he got in some more trouble and some white folks lynched him. They had him in jail and he wrote you a letter. Mrs. Blake went up stairs and got a metal box and gave it to Boyd. He opened the box; there was a letter, some faded photographs and some kind of Indian amulet. Boyd read the letter. It read

Son,
I am a dead man in jail. It won't be long before they come and get me. The man I killed was trying to kill me. I didn't do what do what they say I did; but it doesn't matter. I'll die a man maybe you can live as one. My father got lynched; I don't want it to happen to you. Bessie and Henry will take care of you. I got two much hate inside me but what not hate is love for you.

Poppa

Boyd looked at the pictures first of some tall Indian woman standing next to a short black man, then he nearly fell out of his seat. The short man he saw in the picture was Grand mama Lillie's brother Charles his grandfather. He had never seen the resemblance but Elaine always said there was so there must be. Boyd cried silently as he looked at the rest of the pictures. This trip had altered his life in a way he had never dared to hope or imagine. Boyd sat thinking of the twists and turns his life had taken, for him to find out, who his parents were. He felt overwhelmed.

Wilma and the rest of the Williams family had always accepted Boyd some even wrote him while he was still in prison. He had a deep appreciation for all of them. The Williams family was known for their kindness they were always there for stray people who needed love and companionship. Boyd had been happy to be one of those strays. The kindness they had shown him over the years filled his heart with joy, but family, real relatives was more of a blessing than he ever dreamed. For the first time in his life he was part of something on the inside and he belonged and no one could put him out. Boyd felt with a great deal justification that he was the luckiest man in the world. Who could argue a million dollars forty times over give or take a few thousand. The love of his life was just as much in love with him. The sense that he had been forgiven for past wrongs… what else is it could he ask. Slick walked in, and he knew, old friends.

“Boyd” Odfus called out “Man how are you” Boyd turned as his old friend walked toward him Odfus extended his hand. Boyd grabbed him and hugged him with all of his considerable strength. “I never told you this before Slick” Boyd said without the slightest hesitation “I love you Slick you are like a brother to me.” If it’s possible to imagine a black preacher, at a complete loss for words, then you can see the emotion these two had at that moment. The word love had never past between in all the years they had known each other. But love was what each felt for a long time because for many years all that they had was each other.

The two sat around and reminisced asked about this or that person. Most of their old buddies were dead or doing life. Boyd got his old friend to promise to handle whatever arrangements to take care of Thelma. He would get her in the best nursing home by somebody there would have to see to it that she got the little things she needed. Rev. Muse talked about New Life Ministries his plans and where he thought God was leading him. That’s when Boyd, ever the cautious businessman. Talked about the deal he had made with the developers when he first got out of jail. Boyd told Ofdus not to sell or develop the property until he found out what’s going on. Boyd explained that when he sold the land that development was certain. Odfus said that no one had contacted them about it. He said, “a little before Mr. Dykes died.” He had heard that some people had some interest but they hadn’t contacted him. Then Odfus asked Boyd if he had heard about the trouble Bob Edmonds son was having? Boyd said. “No.” Odfus got him a paper there was a story about his problems.

Chapter 32

Tom Edmonds had been the lead attorney on a task force investigating corruption in South Georgia. He had stepped on some important toes in the process. Tom had many of his father's strong points but he had a different way of looking at the role of public officials. Bob honestly believed that if the police profited from certain illegal activities, they would control them better; everybody gambled. States had lotteries, off track betting, even churches played bingo. The poor cop was expected to survive on less while the public had fun. Tom had a different prospective, honesty was simple to him; you were either breaking or obeying the law. He made no exceptions, the law was the law. He was going through a bad divorce at the time his wife didn't have his scruples. Some evidence had been manufactured against him while not enough to prosecute him. It would do a great deal of damage to his reputation. They accused him of having avoided taxes on a substantial amount of money. His ex-wife's collaboration was all that was needed. An investigation would prove him innocent but the damage would be done. Who believes a lawyer anyway?

When Boyd finished reading about Tom he went to bed. Boyd woke up about 7:30 the next morning. He dressed and went downstairs. Odfus had already gone to work at the storefront. "Good morning Boyd," Vinnie said. "Or is it afternoon? You stay in the bed this late every day?" Boyd said, "no but I don't think I get up as early as you do." Motioning with her hand Vinnie said, "come on breakfast is ready." Boyd sat down and while he ate his breakfast of three eggs, ham, grits, homemade biscuits, jelly and coffee, he read the paper. There was another article in there about Tom.

Boyd had always been very grateful to Bob Edmond for helping him back all those years ago. Bob had asked Boyd to keep a large envelope in a safety deposit box. And if they ever had any more trouble, what was in the envelope would straighten things out if Bob weren't around to help. The wily old cop knew that he was dealing with people who might turn on him at any time. Boyd didn't use the information at the time of his trial basically because he felt that he needed an insurance policy to keep him alive if anything happened to Bob. Boyd had never even opened the envelope but he knew that what was in it would blow the lid off of Savannah.

Bob had always insulated his son from the more unsavory dealings he had been involved in. Tom was not even aware of his father's indiscretions. Boyd knew that it would be a very delicate situation approaching Tom with this information that probably cast Bob in a completely new light. But Boyd knew that he would have to the right thing because he knew how much Bob loved his son. The things that Bob and Boyd were involved in were not legal but their friendship was genuine. Boyd called his old lawyer then went to the bank and retrieved the envelope. He then went to Lloyd Granger's office a lawyer and long-time associate of Boyd. The attorney had handled all of Boyd's legal transaction, but not the criminal proceedings. The two men trusted one another. They each knew secrets that could harm the other…but more than that they respected each other. Lloyd was gay and Boyd had found the attorney discrete partners for as far back as the fifties. The last of which became his life long companion. No one questioned the loyal chauffeur who had to be everywhere the attorney went.

They discussed how to get Tom this envelope. Lloyd also suggested that Boyd open the envelope read and copied it contents. They perused the information and then made copies and took the proper precautions to safeguard themselves from a potentially dangerous situation. Lloyd took the papers to his safety deposit box and they also returned the originals to Boyd's box. Boyd then drove to Bob Edmonds' house. He was hoping to find out where Tom was from Bob's widow. Bob had made Boyd a regular visitor in his home and Bob's wife was always very hospitable. Bob never discussed their activities while he was at the Edmonds' home.

Boyd was in luck when he got to the house. He saw Tom in the driveway Boyd recognized him from his photo in the paper. Tom was in college when Boyd visited Bob at home; the old cop would share his vast experience and insights into human nature with Boyd. This advice would go a long way in making Boyd a success. Boyd pulled to the curb got out of the car and called to Tom.

"Yes, can I help you" Tom inquired? Boyd said, "I hope I can help you. My name is Boyd Tillman; your father was a very good friend of mine your mother will probably remember me." Boyd said as he handed Tom the envelope, he said; "I hope this can help you. If you have any questions call Lloyd Granger, give your mother my regards." Boyd then turned and walked back to his car opened the door pausing to look at Tom once more. He drove off glancing in the rearview mirror as Tom entered the house..

Tom called Lloyd although he knew his father's handwriting. Mrs. Edmonds confirmed what was on the papers…she knew a great deal more than her husband thought she knew. She told Tom that his father wasn't a bad man but he had been involved in a lot of thing that he never talked about. But she knew or sensed that something was wrong, they lived quite well on a policeman salary. Tom then told her Boyd had sent his regards she confirmed she knew him as well. She said, "Bob thought the world of that boy." Bob had always told his wife that Boyd was there helping him do some kind of work in the yard or on his car Bob had always told his wife that Boyd was there helping him do some kind of work in the yard or on his car…she knew better.

The envelope contained damaging material on all of the people causing him problems. Tom used the damning information to get the vultures off his back, trough his reputation had been damaged Tom had insurance that he would have no further problems with this group of thieves. There was a cloud over Tom his ex-wife had seen to that. A lot of people knew Tom, enough he thought to start over again.

Private practice without Savannah's elite for clients was the only future that he could look forward to at least for a while. However a messy situation was avoided. Political and governmental service was over for now also, his reputation was damaged. The divorce left him broke financially and in debt but not broken emotionally. Tom let her have the house, half the savings, a car and their lake house. The children were spared the spectacle of an ugly divorce. Tom's ex-wife loved the high society and longed to be a part of the "old money" Junior League types that are so visible in Savannah. She married six months after the divorce unfortunately the old money she thought her new husband had withered away.

Boyd then went by the courthouse to check on the deeds to his former holdings. What he found was a shock, the land was in the process of being sold for back taxes; which he quickly paid. This prevented any one from selling the land without his knowledge. Now he had time to find out what was happening and come up with a development plan of his own. Boyd called Granger and asked him to investigate and get back to him as quickly as possible.

Boyd went to the storefront mission just in time for lunch. Odfus and Bobby greeted him at the door. They ate lunch that was pretty tasty given the small budget of the mission. Bobby and Odfus invited him to stay all day and see the work they do, Boyd agreed. He told them what he had found out at the courthouse. He said. "If you are patient this might be the answer to your financial prayers." People were in and out all day with all kinds of problems. Mothers that had too many children and not enough money, sick people who didn't have any money, drug addicts needing treatment with no money. The homeless, those in need of hope the lonely and the lost came all with no money. Boyd's heart went out to them all. He knew that he could do something to help he had capital. After a few hours Boyd asked Odfus if he had anything against Boyd setting up a foundation to fund New Life. Boyd said, "We give away money each year for tax reasons we will be giving it away so why not let us fund your programs here. A lot of times when you give to large organizations you don't know where the money is going; I've seen what you do here and want to be a part of it." Odfus agreed " I can't deny the need for help and we know your heart is right."

That evening when they returned to the boarding house Boyd got a call from Elaine. She wanted him to go to Atlanta to check on Red. She explained what was going on and why she hadn't told him about it sooner she didn't want to upset him, Boyd was very sensitive when it came to Red. She didn't want to think about it herself because of her father's condition. Boyd was very upset he felt responsible for many of Red's shortcomings but at the same time he couldn't understand how Red could get involved with drugs again. Boyd got angry to mask is true feeling, he told Odfus. "I feel like breaking Red's neck." But in his heart he wanted to put his arms around his son and protest him from his self.

Odfus knew how Boyd was hurting inside so he asked to go with him to Atlanta. Odfus also suggested that they stop by and see Peeler. Odfus knew God worked through the old convict to save him he wanted his old friend to be thinking about helping Red not killing him. Boyd, while not a religious man, agreed saying "I need to calm down seeing Virgil again will do me good". They decided to leave the next morning.

Chapter 33

Odfus got up at four thirty and went to help with breakfast at New Life. Boyd got up at seven dressed and ate another of Vinnie's huge breakfasts. Boyd thought when he got to the mission he would ask Odfus to drive. Boyd could hardly move he had eaten way too much. But when Boyd got there the reverend had some disturbing news. It seems that the Mutt and Jeff team of would be outlaws had been by the soup kitchen and had roughed up Odfus' son. The young man had no idea where his mother was; he seldom did. Boyd and Odfus were both very angry about the intrusion. Odfus nearly decided to take personal revenge but his reformation was real and he could not go through with it. Boyd talked his old comrade into letting him handle the situation.

Boyd decided to call on an old friend at the police department, a visit. Boyd went to see Bob's former aid and now deputy chief, Frank Williams. Boyd asked if the former colleague could help to keep those two thugs from harassing the New Life staff. His old friend agreed. Slick "OOP's I mean Odfus," had helped the police keep the peace during a near riot. Some High School kids had gotten into a fight, adults got involved and the situation nearly got out of hand. Odfus walked down into the middle of the trouble at no small risk to his life and quieted the uprising. Another time a mentally retarded man wanted by the police turned himself in but only after Rev. agreed to go with him. The man who once considered himself a hopeless drug addict was now a highly respected member of society. People all over Savannah regardless of their race respected Rev. Muse and what he was trying accomplish in his ministry. Odfus loved to say Christianity is a way of life, a way of service to your fellow man. Odfus' old nemesis said he would make sure that pair would bother neither Odfus nor his son again. Boyd thanked his old associate. The irony of the situation struck both Boyd and Williams. They had to laugh at the turn of events. The long time cop had arrested Odfus when he was known as "Slick" over twenty times.

Boyd was still protective of his old chum Odfus. Boyd decided not to tell Odfus about his conversation with Williams. The preacher had prayed that God would work the trouble out and might be offended at Boyd's attempt to use a crocked cop to straighten out the problem, a situation that might lead to violence. Boyd figured that anything he could do to help avoid trouble with those two young toughs was worth a little hurt feelings. He knew the type; they wouldn't be satisfied until they killed somebody. They would be easy for the cops to find something to keep them off the street, they probably would resist arrest. In a way the police wished they would, a permanent solution in a case like this was always good.

Never one to leave loose ends, Boyd called Al. Boyd was aware of an old hiding place where Al had more than likely put Iris. There was an old tunnel under the bar that ran under the ground to Al's house on the street behind the poolroom. Boyd told Al that he was going to call Jim Qualls in Atlanta a private detective; who had been one of the first black cops in Savannah. He'd know how to get Iris away from harm. Al told Boyd that Iris seemed too scared it must really be something wrong. Squirrel was involved in a lot of things with a lot of people, the fact that he had been there looking for Iris was a bad sign. Iris had told Al that she didn't know why they were after her but somebody had tried to kill her. She was not the type to be afraid without reason. She really was scared and said that she had plenty of cause to be but she didn't elaborate any further. Knowing Iris it was more than a pimp to make her run in fear. Boyd called Jim and made arrangements for him to get some money to get Iris out of harms way. Odfus was concerned about his old flame but he knew that he might be followed if he tried to see her so he let Boyd handle it.

Chapter 34

Then Odfus and Boyd drove to Milliageville to see Peeler. They each owed the old convict a lot, he had helped each of them. They missed him and hoped one day he could get out, at least before he died. Peeler wasn't concerned about getting out; he would tell them that he had done too much wrong to ever be free. Being able to help his fellow convicts gave his life meaning. Peeler accepted his fate and tried to be humble; he always dressed in prison clothes, he refused to wear anything else. "Don't send me clothes or money, I don't smoke or eat that canteen stuff; give it to someone who needs it." Peeler greeted them in his usual fashion, he looked serious as he said to Boyd your son is in trouble a lot more trouble than Odfus'. Red's family has left him Boyd didn't know that. I want you to have something God told me to give you a sign because this is important. Peeler reached into his pocket and took out an amulet just like the one that was in the box Vinnie gave to Boyd two days earlier. "Keep this along with the other one, there will come a time when you will give one to Red." Boyd agreed he knew better than to question how Peeler got his information. Boyd decided to have the two amulets mounted in gold in a setting that could be worn as a charm.

Rudy Lee Harris still hadn't been able make parole. Boyd had joked that Rudy was too black to get out of prison, but Rudy was up for parole again; Boyd agreed to give him a job. This time Rudy wanted to get out, he had been reunited with his wife and son. The child had been born after Rudy had gone to the penitentiary. The ever, paranoid Rudy, couldn't deny him, the boy looked so much like him. The youngster was huge and black with a capital B like his daddy. But he wasn't mean he was very good in school, he was smart; even Rudy with all his bluster couldn't hide his pride he felt at the accomplishments of his offspring. Rudy's wife had raised the boy by herself and when he became curious about his father she brought him to see Rudy. She and Rudy had never divorced and both still had affection for the other so slowly they rekindled their relationship. Annie Ruth was one of the few women who were a match for the giant inmate in fact he was a little afraid of her.

Boyd promised to find a place for Rudy and his family to live in Augusta when he got out. The four men had a deep respect and a great deal of affection for one another. Boyd always needed help on construction crews and Rudy had learned to lay bricks in the joint. The years of incarceration had mellowed Rudy, he now wanted a home and the love of a family. Boyd knew that a few dollars in the right place would insure his friend's release.

Just before they left [Boyd and Odfus] Rudy said, "my son plays High School football and he's just in the 8th grade. He's good too plays first string, he gets straight A's too."

Odfus and Boyd then drove to Atlanta straight to Red's house. Red had not returned from his weekend spree. Boyd had a key so he let Odfus and himself in. It would have been a shock to find an empty house Paula had taken all the furniture except for a couch and a bed. The kitchen sink was there but the kitchen table wasn't. Thank God for Peeler they both thought. He had told them how the house would be when they got there. Paula had left a note on the bed addressed to Red. Neither Boyd nor Odfus read it. Boyd sat there waiting for Red he started to get really upset. The more angry Boyd got the more he knew that he couldn't be there when Red got there, he got Odfus to take him to a near-by hotel.

Red could get any woman but he really didn't care if he kept her or not. Women to him were sex objects, a convenience, someone to do his bidding. Whatever it may be at whatever time or place. He could almost read their mines could manipulate them, wine them up like toy robots. He could touch places in their soul, make them believe they were his only reason for living then he would be gone. This time Paula was the one not there but she wanted to be. Reverend Bobby knew that he was really a second choice…he didn't mind though.

Just as Odfus was returning from the hotel Red was pulling up. When he saw Odfus he shouted, "Slick my man Slick glad to see you, where is Boyd or did you play him out of the car?" Odfus said, "Before you go in the house I need to tell you something" Red look at his former cell-mate and inquired with an annoyed tone in his voice, "What has that crazy bitch told yawl?" Odfus told him, "your wife has gone she left a note in there on the bed." Red went inside got the note off the bed and read it. He sat down and almost began to weep. But then he got up and said "Read this man ain't that just like a bitch leave you after you do all you know to do to make them happy and they piss on you." Red continued to rant and rave as Odfus tried to talk to him. Odfus said "Calm down, lets deal with your problem first." "What problem" Red asked. Odfus looked Red straight in the eye and said "drinking and drugs, we know all about it how you lost your job everything." Red said in disbelief, "what I lost job because I fucked my boss's daughter" Odfus retorted, "Come on Red let's be for real you were fucking his wife too nobody in their right mind would be doing that and expect to keep a job, unless the were on something." Red looked bewildered how did he know that he thought. Then Red blamed his boss saying, "he was getting on me before that started that why I fucked those whores." Odfus said, "You know that is a lot of nonsense look at yourself. You made eighty five grand last year how much do you have now?" Red stood there looking amazed and misunderstood as he said, "that bitch Paula spent money faster that I could make it.'' Odfus fought back his urge to laugh and said, "Red she had to get money from Elaine to pay the house note." Red now lying to himself in an attempt to run from the truth said, "that lying bitch wait until I get my hands on her. Bobby was supposed to be my friend and a preacher on top of that; was smiling in my face and fucking that stink ass whore behind my back." Odfus interrupted Red's tirade saying, "forget that, what are you going to do about your problem?" Red then decide to blame Boyd saying "where is Boyd what kind of father is he; he's the one who should be here not you." Odfus repeated, "what do you want to do about your problem?" Red still trying to justify his selfishness said, "man if you had this shit happening to you that I've going through; you would want to get fucked up too." Odfus said, "who do you think you're talking to Red this is your old cellmate. Don't run that weak stuff on me. What do you want to do about your problem?" Red went and got the last beer out of the refrigerator opened it and said what problem.

As Odfus shook his head in disbelief and said. "This house is three months behind, all your bills are passed due. You don't have a job, if you want help you had better start helping yourself." Red looked at the reformed crook and said as tears started to form in his eyes "man I never thought she would leave where is my baby Grace?" Odfus told him "She is in Augusta with Laine. What do you want to do about your problem?" Red then conceded, "maybe I have been parting a little too much lately but I can handle it." Odfus said, "Red go look in the mirror you are not handling it." Red now in a melancholy funk said, "what is it you that think I ought to do about this problem you think I have?" Odfus said, "man you know you need help. Boyd called this place they can take you and he will pay for it." Red now assuming the rule of a victim said, "yeah that's all he ever does, pay for things, why isn't he here?" Odfus said, "he's not here because he loves you and he can't stand to see you like this". Odfus gave Red the phone and told him to call Boyd and talk to him. Red called they talked and Red cried when Boyd told him about how worried the girls were and how hurt Elaine was he agreed to go to Green Haven... a treatment center for the rich and famous drunks and or dope fiends.

Chapter 35

They drove the nearly one hour trip to the country club like facility, swimming pool golf course and all. Without question the finest treatment available in the south for drug addiction. When they arrived at the center and were directed to the detox unit. Red questioned "Detox, I don't need that cocaine isn't habit forming". Odfus pleaded, "just cooperate they know what they are doing." A tall thin black man greeted them "Hi my name is Lee, if you need anything just call." Red said "what about a beer?" Lee laughed, Red really wasn't kidding but Lee knew it so the joke was on Red. Red didn't know that; his life had been a joke he played on himself...Red didn't know that either.

Red showered dressed in a designer sweat suit and the flip-flops the center gave him, he felt better already. He lay down on his bed and fell to sleep. He slept four or five hours, when he woke up he went to the nurse's station, he was hungry. They seemed to be expecting his request and he was directed to the cafeteria. He ate three ham sandwiches, a bag of potato chips and drank three glasses of juice. Really, he was still hungry but it was late and he was tired.

Early the next morning Red had his first counseling session. His counselor was a man in his early fifties; he asked Red about his family, hobbies, friends, how old was he when he had his first drink. Red did his best to be as dishonest as he could; he didn't know how all that information was going to be used. When asked about his hobbies Red said sports and reading, but he knew he should have answered chasing pussy and getting fucked up. Those were the thoughts that crossed his mine when the question was asked. Friends, his answer was he guessed he really didn't have any but he was thinking anybody that has something I want.

When they finished the nurse came in; she was a very attractive young woman. Her name was Amy she had long blonde hair, delicate extremely feminine features from her pert little nose to her firm looking breasts. She exuded a caring, sympathetic, and compassionate attitude that made her very popular with clients, that and a nice ass Red thought. Most of the clients fantasized about making love to her. When she asked Red about what he had using he told her about the free-basing in an attempt to impress her with all the famous people he knew.

Red immediately sensed that was the wrong approach so he began to cry. "I've been such a fool my wife left me, I lost my job it's just not fair." Amy thought she had said something that got through to him. She sat up in her seat and listened intently to the rest of his story. Red was on a roll, the boss's wife and daughter seduced him. He was a mortar, a victim of circumstance. " Those freaky bitches loved black dicks OOPS excuse me." Red was just checking her reaction to the word dick; she squirmed a little. "That OK continue," she said in her most professional voice. Red apologized again with the hurt puppy-dog face that had gotten to at least a hundred unsuspecting but helpful women. "I hope I didn't offend you I need someone I can talk to so badly," He could see it was working, he continued, "nobody understands me maybe if I had just spent a little more time with my wife instead of working all the time." Amy said, "don't blame yourself, some things are not meant to be". Red said shyly "No I better not say that". Amy asked "What?" Red was thinking about where he could have sex with her. When he said "It is so nice talking to you like this, I never talk to a woman like you before, I guess I was getting carried away.". Amy was blushing as Red poured it on about what a good listener she was. Red looked into her eyes and said "Thank you so much for being here for me"... as he thought to himself, I wonder if the head any good. Red went back to his room and got a good night sleep thanks to Amy. At least I'll get some while I'm here, Red thought as he drifted off to sleep.

The next morning the medical staff checked his vitals, although he was shaky they felt he could be moved to the community. The community was down the hall from the detox. It was an in-patient care unit made up of sixteen two-man rooms. The unit had a door to the outside where the tennis courts, swimming pool, a couple of basketball hoops, a walking path and a golf course [nine holes] were neatly arranged on the two hundred acre beautifully kept estate.

The treatment consisted of group therapy, talks with the staff psychologist, physical activities and most importantly interaction between the clients. They were told to stick with the winners. Lee the orderly Red met when he came became an important part of Red treatment plan. He seemed to be immune to Red bull. And of course there was Amy, his first victim. Red used to loved to say, "another one bites the dust." Lee and Red developed a strange admiration for one another Red could not believe some one could see through him. Lee couldn't believe the ease Red fooled people and his incredible power over women. Lee was the only staff member to figure out what was going on with Red... at least three female staff including a staff psychiatrist bit the dust. Lee would just shake his head and ask, "whose next." Red always acted like he didn't know what Lee was talking about.

Red shared a room with Marty Raferty a stockbroker originally from New York City. Marty was a handsome, fun loving, good-natured Irishman. His red hair, infectious smile and sharp wit concealed his total moral corruption. At twenty-eight Marty had risen to the top of his profession but drugs, alcohol, gambling, and general lust for everything that felt good to him had gotten him in deep trouble. First in New York, he got involved in money laundering and barely escaped prosecution. Moving south didn't help, in fact Marty got a little worse.

Marty's gambling problem was totally out of control he would bet on anything. He played liars poker with his fellow clients until he ran out of victims, he had a dollar with seven nines in its serial number. He bet on sports on television, other clients playing tennis, who would walk into a room next. Red won every bet they made which of course made Marty that much more eager to find new ways to bet. Red told him "Marty you would even bet that you could stop betting."

The two Reds as they started calling themselves, hit it off from the start. Both thought of themselves, as great lovers but Marty couldn't hold a candle to Red. Poor Amy got in the middle of a bet. Now Red would have hit on her anyway but he loved to show off. After the bet was made the sweet little nurse was a game for Red to play. Red loved games and Marty had given him two weeks. Two weeks to go to bed with Amy it seemed unfair to win a bet like this, two days would be a challenge but two weeks that wasn't fair to Marty, Red thought as he entered the nurses' office.

The bet was that Red would go to bed with Amy and bring back her panties as proof. The getting her to have sex with him was easy the only problem was Amy didn't wear panties. Red enjoyed the sex and would have dropped it if Marty had been willing to let it go. Marty wasn't, he teased Red and I guess he insulted Red's honor code (never lie on a woman the truth is bad enough). So Red decided that he would have to get Amy to come to their room. Red had to play hard to get a couple of days. Poor thing she feared Red might be suicidal the guilt from having sex with her now that he is so upset about his wife. He was probably feeling used and abandoned. When he wouldn't talk to her, she went to his room. Red always said there is beauty in simplicity.

Red convinced her that Marty was asleep, they had sex in the room while Marty looked. A strange thing happened, as Marty watched, he wanted Amy more just looking at her sensuous movements. Watching her passion rise as she wrapped her slender legs around Red's body. The sounds she made as she hungrily asked for more. Marty wanted her more than any woman he had ever known.

While at the center the two Reds, Sam Jefferson and Jose Ruiz were each other's constant companions. The four young men were all very at their chosen professions. Sam was a declining star on the Hawks, Ruiz the shortstop for the Braves. All four felt set apart from the other clients… who though successful were older and mostly drinkers. The fab four as they dubbed themselves sat and talked about everything. Lee was the only staff member who could enter their inner circle, all four of them were determined to fool him about something. They prided themselves on the games they could play with the staff members. Lee told them time after time "You are just playing with your own lives." The four of them knew it but they were having too much fun to stop.

Sam had been the golden boy coming out of college, the savior of the Hawks. His first two years he played great, they made the playoffs. Then a contract dispute, idle time and poor choices in friends. The small town boy had been introduced to drugs and divorced from reality at the same ceremony…Sam was way out of his element. At first it seemed to Sam that the coke made him play better but he wasn't, he had more energy but no concern for his teammates. The truth was he didn't get into shape, had a series of nagging injuries and an awful season. The career that should have made him secure for life nearly killed him. He had a five-year no cut, no trade deal, fame and fortune. Everything he always wanted but had no clue how to handle any of it. The team had no idea that Sam had just been introduced to free base cocaine. Most of the time Sam had no idea where he was and missed planes, practices and games.

Jose was basically a family man with a very large extended family. He was a hero in his native Dominican Republic. He wanted to please everybody, take care of everyone and still play baseball. The pressure of trying to be all things to all people. Trying to adjust, trying to speak English, and adjust to his newly acquired wealth coupled with a batting slump. Jose needed to unwind so he did for two years. He nearly lost everything. But he was that rarest of creatures a shortstop who could hit. The Braves went to great lengths to keep him.

One day at their noon day bull session they were laughing at Marty who was still doing Red's chores. Red remarked that two weeks wasn't fair he said to Marty "I can get her to fuck your brains out in two in two weeks". They all laughed except Marty; he wanted Amy. Marty told Red OK I'd bet you couldn't...the first bet Marty ever wanted to lose. Red shook his head in disbelief what do you want to part with this time? They had no money and everything they owned was in hock so they decided. That the loser of the bet had to go to the chaplain and listen to him once per-day.

Red told Amy how much Marty needed to talk to a woman, he was on the brink on Gods knows what. "He needs you I'm really scared for him" he said. Red told Marty not to open his mouth no matter what Amy said. "If you fuck this up don't blame me." Red cautioned Marty. For the first time in his life Marty followed instructions. Red told Amy
"Marty was sexually abused as a child and he hides his fear behind a mask of being over confident; he's hurting inside and wants a mother to love him. Not hurt him the way his mother allowed him to be hurt." Amy was so touched she decided to help Marty, she understood why he acted like a jerk. Marty and Amy started spending a lot of time with each other and both started to get a genuine affection for one another.

At least Amy started to care for Marty, because she was emotionally capable of caring about another human being. Marty on the other hand felt only some sort of sexually induced obsession for her. Marty had not gotten in touch with his inability to feel any thing unselfish. But once while in one of his daily session with the fabulous four his conflicted feelings came to the surface. Marty had allowed his feelings for Amy or more accurately his hurt ego to get in the way of his friendship with Red. Both Jose and Sam told him that he made the bet, he got what he wanted. Also if he had asked Red to set him up with Amy from the beginning straight up he would have. Marty's meetings with the chaplain started him to think but he wasn't ready to change or even really listen. Thoughts of the development of spiritual conscience frightened him.

All four men seemed to be impervious to attempts at getting them to realize they had a problem. The fad four was convinced that they and the staff were engaged in a battle of wits. Each would listen to the things they were told not to benefit but to find a way to manipulate a staff member. Amy got caught in the middle but so did several other well-meaning staff folks. Lee watched the circus with dread and amusement.

Lee had been in recovery for twenty-five years, he said simply "I don't know a lot but I do know bull when I hear it." Lee told them that as a group they were the biggest lairs that the center had ever housed. Red couldn't believe that Lee didn't buy any of his well-conceived stories. Lee told Red one-day "Man you're so dishonest that your brain is biologically incapable of absorbing truth." Red cracked-up and said, "Man where did you learn to talk like that." Lee confessed he had heard that at an AA meeting but it applied. If you stay clean and sober Lee told Red "That will take a miracle and prove there is a God all by its self."

The strangest experience of all happened to Jose. The fab four were watching Saturday Night Live. Garret Morris did that routine about "baseball has been berry berry good to me." For the first time it dawned on Jose what he had to lose. Baseball had been very good to him, through it the lives of his whole family had been changed. He realized that it must be something wrong with someone who would risk all that to get high. He decided to take a look at himself and found he needed help. His way of dealing with the staff changed he started letting them help.

Jose got out; went back to his career and did very well. He helped others... did volunteer work at the center. Became very active in helping other ball players. Helped to form groups that assisted other Latin-American players make the adjustments to the big leagues. He played twelve more years finished with a .289 batting average. He is now a coach in the Detroit organization.

Sam left the Green Heaven thinking he didn't have a problem. He would fake a religious conversion and garner as much sympathy as he possibly could. Sam lasted three more years in the NBA and was then banned for life. He did play two more years in Europe. When he returned to the United States he was in and out of trouble. Eventually he was estranged from his family even lived on the street for a while. He was able to get in touch with Jose who got him into a halfway house. He has been clean for several years now. Sam and his wife are back together in their hometown in North Carolina. Luckily she had gotten everything in their divorce.

Marty got back on the financial fast track, he and Amy got married. But the lure of fast money got him into trouble again. His reputation as a crook ruined his career, his drinking and drugging got worst. He lost Amy and their two kids first, then all his money, which he had gone to a great deal of trouble to hide from Amy during the divorce. He went back to New York, got involved with some childhood buddies and was killed in a drug deal gone bad.

Red moved to Augusta; he wanted to become actively involved in Boyd's business; now growing at a rate nobody ever thought possible. Jack and Bob Smith had worked out better than Boyd had even hoped. The international opportunities opened up when Jim went to England and made the world the customer base for the company. Boyd bought a few European companies and set up offices in London. He needed someone to work the European shop that he knew and trusted. Red had experience in the construction business. He also had his uncanny ability to influence people so Boyd sent him to Europe to work with a management group Jim had put together. Red was to identify and procure companies, individuals or technologies that could benefit Comp-Tech.

Chapter 34

This job and Red were a marriage made in heaven. Red had a great deal of technical ability, his courses in computers coupled with his construction and architecture background served him well. They acquire companies not only in Europe, they went truly worldwide. The emerging countries of Africa, the Caribbean and Southeast Asia had a hunger for technology. Construction of the infrastructure of emerging countries meant they built everything from sewage systems to computer systems. Red found the people, materials, and ways to cut red tape and equipment to get the job done.

Red had put the drugs behind him, he went to support group meetings and made a personal commitment to stay clean. He was doing great except that he didn't understand addiction. He had traded drugs for the addiction of work and money. He was good at what he did but still somehow he could never get enough. Women by the score chased him all over the world and most caught him. Still, something wasn't quite right, something was missing. Any happiness that Red could feel was as superficial as his relationships.

Boyd always liked to cover all the bases. His operation had gotten so large that he knew he had to have a way to keep an eye on things. Again he got lucky. Tom Edmonds had problems; his divorce had left him broke and his law practice wasn't bringing in enough pay to take care of his wife and various boyfriends. She was enjoying living in a style of which she was completely unaccustomed. Tom was also paying for his kid's education. Boyd needed somebody he could trust to be security director.

Boyd knew the value of information and that if properly used was, maybe the most powerful weapon on earth. He didn't like surprises; they could be very expensive. Boyd also was aware that not everyone could be trusted. Tom called him one day about a year after their meeting in Savannah. Tom's call was to thank Boyd for his help and business Boyd had sent his way through Granger. Boyd had been thinking about Tom and wanted to seek him out and see if Tom had any interest in coming to work for him. God knows with Red and Saul out there, a very great potential for trouble was present.

Boyd, always the direct straight to the point person, asked Tom to come to Augusta. Boyd told him what he had on his mind. He explained to Tom that his operation was growing so rapidly that it was becoming difficult to keep up with what everybody was doing. "I need people that I can trust" Boyd said, then asked Tom to think it over and at least come and look at the home office.

Tom thought it over and agreed. The two men setup an appointment for the following Monday. Boyd said "Come early, stay all day if you can and look us over top to bottom. That is the only way you are going know what we do." Tom made the trip to Augusta by car; he could not have imaged the events that were to transpire that day. Before that day was over his life would be changed. Tom had built his law practice into enough to make a living but not the kind of money that Boyd was thinking of paying him. Tom also had no idea how large an operation Boyd had built. He didn't know what he thought looking back but he didn't think Comp-Tech was as vast as it was.

Chapter 35

Tom is taken aback as he drives up to the front of Boyd's luxurious suburban office building located twelve miles outside of Augusta. The Comp-Tech building was constructed on what had been the old Williams farm. The four-story structure stands directly behind a small lake. Road leading to the front entrance runs through the old pecan orchard and is lined with trees on either side. The front has columns like an old plantation house. As you approach the building, you are given the impression that the structure is a house though impressive but only as a dwelling not an office complex. The back of the building is on the down side of a hill...when approaching from the front you can't see it all. When you enter the foyer of the front room, one cannot help being overwhelmed by the feeling that you are entering another time. The front room has a high ceiling that gives the impression of being in an antebellum ballroom. The conference rooms are on both sides of the huge room. The rooms are furnished with antiques or replicas of furniture of the civil war period of the south. The front of the building is quiet and everyone seems to be relaxed. The reception area is equally serene and beautiful at the back of the ballroom. A marble bar like structure stands at the end of the room like a warning that an era is about to end. Three polite and charming women are busily answering phones as they usher you into the new south. The back of the building is a series of long hallways with offices on either side. This is where the action is where the modern south strikes you in the face; it is like entering a different world from the front. Boyd's office is at the end of the third floor hallway. The office itself is a stark contrast to the luxurious front of the building. Though well furnished the office itself is understated, the furniture is practical but comfortable; everything is functional.

To Tom's surprise Boyd has a white secretary... makes a mental note "I'll talk to her later." The others that work there are of different races women seem to have key positions, as do black and white men there are also quite a few oriental executive types. Tom is relived that Boyd isn't asking him to be his token white. Mrs. Higgins, Boyd's secretary greets Tom warmly as she notifies her boss that his appointment has arrived. Boyd comes out right away, the two men exchanged pleasantries as they walk back into the office. Boyd asks Tom to sit on the couch to the left of his desk near the window with the view of the lake Boyd sat on the comfortable looking chair near the couch. As the two men talked Tom felt somewhat at a disadvantage because Boyd seems to know a great deal about him personally. He also wonders how he has such a good view of the lake; driving up the drive he could not see the back of the building at all, Boyd explains that the property has two lakes. He chuckles as he tells Tom that most people wonder about that. I live on the other side some family members and a few key employees live nearby, too.

In many ways Tom's father was like family to Boyd. Bob had talked about Tom a great deal and was very proud of his son. Tom was surprised that his father had bragged about him hitting four hundred in his senior year in high school; he only came to four games. Bob had been equally proud of his son when he won a debating medal in college. He never came to a single debate. Bob wanted his son to go to med school; Bob always said lawyers are a bunch of crooks.

Chapter 36

The discussion of the job begins after a few minutes just as Tom is impressed with what he had seen so far, and then they are interrupted by a phone call. At first Boyd seems annoyed at the interruption. After being satisfied that the call is important he begs Tom's pardon. He invites whomever he was talking to come in and join them. Boyd told the caller "I want this man to see everything in our operation. I know you are busy but this is more important so drop everything and come in here please, all right? " Boyd then turn to Tom and said, "I don't know why I didn't think of this sooner." Boyd offered Tom a tour before he made a decision to take or turn down the job. Boyd was sensitive to the process that most whites go through before they see Comp-Tech offices many have prejudices toward black owned businesses but they often don't realize it. Tom thought that he should take the tour as a courtesy to Boyd for helping him out. Only something out of the ordinary could make him take Boyd up on his job offer.

Tom felt more that a little wanted and needed sitting there as Boyd sat talking on the phone to whoever had interrupted them about how crucial Tom was to the growth of the business. Boyd again asked Tom not to give him an answer until he looked the operation over. Then that something out of the ordinary happened. Breathing became difficult for Tom. Boyd's cousin Macy had entered the room and Tom felt his senses leave. "Hi" was all that Macy said but it sounded like a concerto her voice sent chills through him. They looked at one another struggling to say something; anything the silence was unbearable. Tom managed a hello; Macy blushed and struggled not to giggle as her face became flushed and her pulse rate raced. Tom and Macy stood there staring at each other in with their hearts in their mouths. Boyd watched the two with amusement then he took full advantage of the moment, Boyd thought, we've got him now.

"Macy show Tom around" Boyd said. "You really run things around here anyway. Take him to your office; show him a few construction sites and so on OK. ""OK " she said not hearing a word that Boyd said to her. "I'll be right back" she went and washed her face to regain her senses. She freshed her makeup put on a little more perfume as she scolded herself for loosing her composure. "God he's cute," she said to herself. Tom is an attractive dark-haired man with a fairly athletic body but to Macy he was a mixture of Bert Reynolds, Adonis and God. Macy questioned herself " what is wrong with me? I don't even know that man".

Tom was still a little confused as he asked Boyd who was that. Boyd told him.

"That's my cousin she is also my administrative assistant. After her divorce she moved south all she does is work. We could not manage without her. I guess she is lonely her children are grown you know how it is." Boyd could see the sparkle in Tom's eyes as he heaped it on about how available, trustworthy and wonderful his beautiful cousin is. "She is a great help she really does run everything and can show you everything you need to know about us. Are you at all familiar with our operation?" Boyd knew about Tom's divorce and Elaine's constant attempts at match making for Macy a roll reversal from their college days.

"No not really just what I saw today." Tom replied still bewildered. His mind was still on the petite Goddess that he had just seen. "This would be a great time to start getting to know us," Boyd answered.

When Macy returned to the office Tom went back into the trance he had been in before she left. Boyd told Macy "Take him to the international wing and show him whatever he wants to see." As Boyd talked, he realized neither Tom nor Macy heard a word he was saying; the company had no international wing. Although Red's efforts in Europe were beginning to have promise at that time and would prove to be one of Boyd's better decisions. The international wing was an exercise in positive thinking at that point; they had one secretary that handled all international calls. When the couple left the office neither knew where Boyd told them to go anyway. Both were too embarrassed to go back and ask. Tom said, "Let's go to lunch" Macy agreed though it was just ten thirty. This was the beginning of a love affair that would last a lifetime. When the two finally came to their senses, she did show him around Comp-Tech. Tom was impressed with what he saw of the company not just Macy. He had underestimated the operation and actually wanted to join the firm. Tom could see the growth potential and the need for someone like him. Tom has one of the finest legal minds in the country but more importantly he has a simple code of honesty. Tom also has the ability to organize and implement new ideas and organize systems that adapt to the needs of a growing company. Though he had no international law experience, over the years he has amassed a great deal of knowledge on that subject it had been sort of a hobby with him. It seemed that he was somehow destined to have this type of position with someone, in truth this position was a dream come true. Tom had the ability the vision and determination it took to be an indispensable part of Comp-Tech but still his most important quality was his integrity.

Tom came to work at Comp-Tech two weeks later. He brought his old staff from his days at the Attorney General's Office. His whole staff had run into problems because of their veracity. The first thing Tom thought was to find people who were trust-worthy. He personally went to every one of Comp-Tech offices and instated security measures. Boyd gave him full authority to get rid of anyone that was incompetent or dishonest. Every transaction anywhere in the world could be monitored for its effects on the ecology and the people in whatever location that Comp-Tech was doing business, moral values of the company and of course the legality of each transaction itself were understood by each employee involved. Only Red and Saul Greenspan would prove to be a source of concern for Tom and his staff. Nither was involved in anything illegal but both men were shady and had no problem operating on the edge. The problem was both were making the company more profitable and to tell the truth were probably two of Comp-Tech's more valuable employees. Boyd cared deeply about them both but each of them knew that if they went too far Boyd would do what ever he had to do to save his company. Tom was not yet completely aware of that fact.

Tom reorganized the legal department, instated security measures and updated the way that the legality of a proposed venture was determined. This process took several months as the company was growing all the time he had to insure that his security systems would not be outdated before installed. His trusted staff was spread out over the company so as to make sure everyone was on the same page. With everybody doing the same things the same way. Tom preached his philosophy daily to his staff "progress within the process makes everything easier". Comp-Tech was growing into new areas each day. Tom knew he had to stay on top of a fast growing ever-changing operation. Within a year of Tom's hiring, Red had built the international operation into a five hundred million-dollar operation in Europe and at least two hundred million in Asia and Africa. Everywhere Red went Tom followed with a legal team for what ever country Red had begun operation.

Tom's first real assignment was to find out what was going on in regards to the company's holdings in Savannah? Boyd felt that the property could be developed into a profitable venture. Nobody in their right mind would have paid him the amount of money he got for the land if they hadn't convinced someone of its value. When he saw the type of work that Odfus was doing in the community, Boyd got an idea that could potentially be a windfall for Comp-Tech. He also could improve the conditions for a number of the residents in the area.

The idea was simple, small businesses grouped together in an industrial park type setting as support for a large company. An update of the old company town, one large manufacturer and a group of smaller manufacturers, that would supply the big one with component parts. A small shopping on the adjacent property restaurants, beauty shops, a black owned bank and several clothing stores. Capital would be provided to new businesses or sufficient operating capital to existing businesses, to expand and make a profit. Everything right there, within the inner city. Located on the bus lines so many of those who couldn't get to work because of the lack of transportation when jobs were away from town. Odfus's ministry could be supported through these joint ventures.

Boyd knew the work ethic of most people of the area; they are hard working Southern folks, who if given a chance, would be extremely loyal. This loyal, inexpensive work force was the key. Finding a group of investors who shared his view of the community would prove to be difficult. Things had gone so well in recent years that Boyd had nearly forgotten how pervasive racism is in Savannah. The key to the whole thing was the industrial park. The creation of new jobs would make the entire plan viable. Prejudice and stereotyping were the biggest obstacles to the proposition working.

Red was in Europe doing business and finding some people who would prove to be invaluable in the future. He was still staying away from drugs and out of trouble. Red was still having a good time and European women were proving to be just as vulnerable to his charms as American women had been. Red was enjoying women more now that he was sober; at least he knew who he was with and if he had a good time or not. But he was developing a conscience slowly. Ever so slowly, when it came to women he still considered them a convenient pass time.

Work and money, had become the most important things in his life, he wasn't using drugs but he was just as ruthless in his dealings with people. The only difference was he wasn't enjoying his use of people quite as much. Red's self-esteem unfortunately was being tied more and more to his business successes, his self worth was measured in making deals and earning money. People were still pawns in the games he played. But somewhere deep in his being, he felt a longing that he couldn't explain. No matter how much money he earned, he was never satisfied.

Chapter 38

Macy and Tom had both been deeply hurt in bad marriages. They gravitated to one another because of the pain they both had experienced. Macy's former husband had been abusive and irresponsible. She had feared getting involved with anyone for the ten years she had been divorced. Macy hadn't allowed herself to even have a fling or one-night stand; even Elaine called her a nun. Her children had become her life but they were now finished college and on their own. Work was all she concentrated on since the divorce.

There was something about Tom, something in his eyes. The gentleness and honesty of a child she thought. She trusted him like she had no other man. Tom sensed something in Macy. A quality in her that made him, feel safe. Somehow these two practical people developed more trust in each other in fifteen minutes than most couples do in a lifetime. Neither ever expected to be involved in an interracial relationship, it seemed that neither saw the other's color.

The only major problem to their union was their children, they each had two from their previous marriages. Tom's son was very devoted to his mother, he could not see her as the manipulating gold digger she was. He blamed his father for the series of affairs his mother had been involved in since the divorce. Her latest backfired after she married this one, but soon found out he was broke. Young Jeff was more than a little embarrassed that his father had chosen a black woman. Julie (Tom's daughter) warmed to Macy slowly but they have developed a solid relationship. Tom's daughter saw her mother very clearly. She felt that her father was entitled to a little happiness after having been married to her mother. Macy's two daughters were surprised but Tom won them over quickly. His obvious affection for their mother was enough for them. Their father's endless battle with alcohol and gambling and the seemingly end string of illegitimate siblings made Tom an attractive alternative. Tom was a man of great integrity and he really had no racial prejudices. He was also kind and generous; the sort of human being that everyone, I think should try to be. He was a prefect fit in the Williams family. Tom's mother found a great deal of happiness knowing that her son was content with a woman he loved after his disastrous first marriage.

Mary and Judith graduated from high school and were quickly accepted at Harvard both went into pre-law. Their freshman year went just like it always had for them… right at the top of their class. Judith had been unaware of her mother being seriously ill. Ellen had breast cancer. She died a short time after Judith was told of Ellen's illness. The loss was devastating to a young person aspiring to be a super woman… everything had always gone Judith's way. She had never had a major disappointment other than her grandfather's death but he had prepared the whole family for his death. Ellen didn't want Judith to know how sick she was. Ellen thought Judith might not go to the school she had dreamed of attending if she knew what was going on. Judith would have stayed there with her mother. Judith had no confidence in Jack's ability to care for anyone. She resented not being told how sick Ellen had gotten she felt that Jack was much too self-centered to really be there for her mother to be truthful, she blamed Jack for Ellen's sudden (to her) demise.

Chapter 39

Mary continued school. She finished Harvard at the top of her class. Then went on to law school and graduated with honors. Mary knew what she wanted and felt justified in doing what ever she felt she had to get it. Her life experience included very few blacks. She did not relate to the so-called black experience. Mary loved her family, had a few close friends. She felt that she had accomplished things by working hard. She was young and didn't see the obvious advantages she had. She considered most blacks to be lazy or at the very least unmotivated. To her racism was an excuse for weakness of character...an alibi used by failures.

Mary seemed to live in a world of her own. She never thought that she had any personal imperfections. Mary denied her own circumstances; she didn't consider herself a product of a broken home. Elaine her mother, Boyd was her real father; she even conveniently forgot about his prison experience... never thought about it or mentioned it. She in no way thought of Red as anything more than the black sheep of the family. To Mary, Paula was just another of Red's victims...just like the other women he had gotten pregnant. In Mary's private world Red was no good, and she was holding her breath until he screwed up again. She had decided a long time ago not to allow herself to be hurt by Red and his lack of responsibility. She respected Elaine and Wilma and the Williams tradition of taking care of people and loving your family so she maintained contact with Red.

Red's other daughter Grace was different; she was very much a part of the black community. She chose to go to Paine College for her undergraduate studies because Elaine had gone there. Then she went to the University of Georgia School of Nursing... because it was convenient. Grace loved Red and thought of him as her 'daddy'. She loved Elaine but Paula was 'mom'. Grace felt deserted by Paula. To her, Red could do no wrong. Grace blamed Paula for having an affair and ruining the happy marriage between her parents.

Mary was nearly six feet tall, strikingly beautiful. Grace was just as pretty but short and a lot less intimidating. The sisters differed on just about everything. The sisters were not very close in many ways. With the prodding of the family they talked to each other every week though they didn't seem to understand each other. Mary was self-absorbed with little compassion for others. Grace on the other hand was always trying to please everyone.

Mary did not date much in college; she had unreasonable standards for men to live up to. She liked sex but didn't like commitment. Hence she dated either married men or the type that could be manipulated easily. Grace on the other hand was consistently looking for Mr. Right. She had a baby, as a result, at sixteen and more heartaches as she got older. But Grace was so loving and kind that she always bounced back. The one thing that was constant for them both was their love for their family.

Mary always said she didn't like very dark men. She had dated very few black men. The fact was Mary related better to whites, rich whites, she had no time for "losers". A loser was anyone who didn't have a million dollars. When she met Ronald Harris, she professed hatred of everything about him. He was Rudy's son just about as dark as his father and about as huge with a booming base voice that could be heard from a great distance. He and Mary had attended law school together; his grades were as good as hers much to her dismay. After graduation Ron had built quite a reputation for himself as a trail lawyer. But out of court he liked his music loud (rap) or gospel he even shouts and says amen in church. In short he could not have been blacker physically or socially the antithesis of everything Mary wanted in a man.

Mary was the woman of his dreams; he was something out of a nightmare to her. Mary made a point to act like she hated Ron; it seemed on the surface that she did hate him, she called him "Big Black Sambo". Judith had always teased Mary about Ron. Judith accused Mary of having a crush on Ron but never dreamed that she really did. Judith respects the huge and brilliant young man's considerable ability in the courtroom. Ron represents his clients like his life depended on the outcome of the trial…he leaves no stone unturned when defending even a penniless client. Ron loved to go before a jury and argue Ron was a great trail lawyer he seemed to thrive on difficult cases. His voice would boom or purr, like a kitten depending on the point he was trying to make. He could quite literally hold a jury in the palm of his hand; at time his hands seemed big enough.

One afternoon Ron and Mary were both working late in the building they shared. Mary went down the hall to his office to get him to turn his music down. They got into an argument she slapped him. He grabbed her and kissed her, she slapped him again, he kissed her once more. Then he picked her up and carried her over to the couch. Neither one of them knows how it happened but her panties and pantyhose were somehow removed. They made love on the couch, the floor and the conference table. When it was over she tried to act outraged. But it was difficult to take her seriously with her hair standing straight up on her head and her skirt caught up above her butt. Mary was a black woman when it came to her ghetto butt… her skirt got caught over it. The skirt had to be pulled down when Ron pulled it down and remarked about how much he liked her butt. He said she looked like an African goddess. She ran out of his office, she tried to avoid him for a couple of weeks. But she found that she could not run from her own feelings.

He was truly everything Mary had ever wanted in a man. She had plans for Ron she wanted him out of that courtroom with all those "broke ass crack heads for clients". He was brilliant and was wasting his talent on those folks. But Ron is his own man he loves helping those that no one else will touch and "I make money," he would say. Six figures a year is good money but Mary has her eye on running Boyd's company one day. She agreed, "six figures is good money but seven is better." Ron always retorted, "not if you aren't happy."

Mary couldn't stomach much of his family at first but she would learn to really love Ron's mother and tolerate Rudy. Their marriage is solid they love each other. Ron understood his wife's ambition but he felt called to do what he was doing. They have three children she is still trying to change him without success. Boyd wouldn't mind if the giant young man did come into the business if Ron could handle his overbearing grand daughter he could handle international finance. Boyd realizes that for anyone to be successful at the level of his business they have to have a very deep commitment to the Comp-Tech way of life.

Boyd has always felt that Mary would be the one to take over when he steps down almost by default. But, while he knows that she is smart enough she lacks compassion. Her concern is for money not people Boyd believed that people were the most important part of doing business… the people that work for you, the individuals that consumed your goods or services. Mary didn't perceive of business being done that way in a lot of ways she lacked the necessary imagination. Mary was a great deal like Red "take care of number one" was her motto.

Grace had gotten married after college but the attempt at matrimony didn't work out. The young man mistakenly thought his working days were behind him but he soon found out that life wasn't going to be a free lunch. There is something so innocent and sweet about Grace. She seems like the perfect victim because she isn't afraid to trust but she has an inner strength. Many men underestimate because of her petite size and famine demeanor. She has been hurt on several occasions over the years. But she has learned to take care of herself without losing her faith in human nature. In truth Red seemed so proud of Grace and the way that she has of taking care of herself. She was his favorite and you could sense it. I never exactly was quite able to visualize her face but it seems that I can sense her beauty both spiritual and physical. He said that he had this vision of her having only a thin space in time to find mister right. He could help her find that perfect man for her only if she didn't know he was helping.

Chapter 40

Red started having dreams while he was in Europe; he would have visions of every woman he had ever known falling off a clock into a pit. He would then be left all alone in a life of unhappiness. This was his first experience with visions, he thought he was having flash backs from his drug using days or missing his family. You know how a man feels about his girls. He told himself. In his mine Red thought he owed his daughters a debt that he could only pay by doing something that would have a life changing effect.

Among the first real friends that Red made was Amir Asif a young Arab, living in Europe, doing much the same thing that Red was doing finding investments for his rich father. They both were party animals… neither used alcohol. Both abused woman emotionally. Both were motivated, by wanting to change the “black sheep” image they had. The two men desperately wanted respect for themselves really. Both men had caused their families a great deal of concern and now they were trying to establish themselves succeeding in everyone else’s eyes. They were doing a good job and their fathers were very proud of both of them.

Early on in their friendship Amir introduced Red to his sister Jassimine. The young woman was very westernized; she had lived in the United States since she graduated high school. She was extremely beautiful and she and Red hit it off very nicely. Under different circumstances the brief affair that they had would have gone unnoticed. But her family wanted her to marry someone from her culture and she was in a constant state of rebellion toward her folks. Neither she nor Red gave any thought to marriage anyway. Amir was quite upset when he was told that his new best friend was carrying on with his sister. Amir respected the fact that his sister was not like the other women in his country so he did not blame Red. Jessie, as she liked to be called, had many affairs and was very seductive although Red didn’t take much seducing. When Jessie told Red that her family was upset, he stopped seeing her out of respect for his good friend he said. The truth was Red had grown tired of her…she was getting serious.

The two would be jet setters developed a great deal respect for each other. So when Red told Amir about the project that needed money in Savannah, he jumped at the chance to invest. They were able to get a friend from Germany to come in with them. This deal set in motion a relationship with a German automobile maker for Comp-Tech to build a plant in Germany and later one in the United States. It is difficult to believe that one deal would open a floodgate of economical prosperity for thousands of people…but it did. That one deal established Comp-Tech as a major player on the international financial landscape. The simplicity of the Savannah deal caught the attention of the practical Germans. Though the Savannah deal was relatively small, only six or seven million a twenty per-cent return on their investment on the construction with a piece of all future profits. The potential for more profitable returns on their investments loomed on the horizon. The efficient way that the construction of the manufacturing plant was carried out proved to the investors that Comp-Tech knew how to keep construction costs down.

In essence Red had put Comp-tech on a new level, it opened the way to real money. Red was much more than a pretty face he had finally won his battle for respect. Red is one hell of a salesman. Red still had that nagging feeling gnawed away at his soul. Deep inside he felt that he was not good enough for his success, especially at this level. Red and his new friends were building a financial network that stretched across Europe, North Africa and most of the Middle East.

These two men were so alike though born half way around the world from each other. The young Arab was nearly a match for Red when it came to getting woman. His being married didn't stop him from taking part in his favorite hobby. The two womanizers were building another reputation though out the Continent. The trouble with having too many of anything is that it's never enough. That empty feeling seemed to worsen with each new conquest with each new deal. Red was in the process of getting everything he ever wanted but he wasn't fulfilled on the inside. Red made a couple of half-hearted attempts at various religious conversions none had a lasting effects. Red was too caught up in chasing money to commit to, much of the spiritual at that time. Spirituality gained through his visions would later play a major roll in his decision making process.

Drugs didn't fascinate him anymore, he had seen too much of the "good life" to blow it on such foolishness. Red sat alone one day thinking about Odfus and his twelve different types of motherfucker's theory, he decided that he was becoming a commonsense motherfucker. That empty "Is this all there is" feeling of being a whorish motherfucker was there but was not overwhelming him like it did in the past. He assumed that the bad feelings were sort of a residue of the past. He figured he knew all about God; Red would pray, but he didn't have a concept of the God he was praying to. He was so self-centered that he didn't really know how to pray. Most of his prayers were petitions to God for some special favor. He and Amir both had a view that God was a method of making their wants more available to them. Amir expressed the idea of submission to God but practiced little of it; Red made no such claim. They felt that anything that they might really want must be the will of God.

The two egomaniacs convinced themselves that they had figured out the secrets of the universe. The more monetary success they achieved, the more they deluded themselves about their spirituality. Red even started to profess a strange form of Christianity that promised material success to the followers of the financial Messiah. Both men, however, operated within man's law, only if they had a great probability of getting caught. If they were caught it would adversely affect the new image they were trying to project. It was front-page news when either one of them would give a thought to others in an unselfish way. If someone got hurt in their dealings with the two self-appointed gods, their response would be, "that was just the chance that you took in doing business with us; even the Bible said watch yourself when doing business."

Boyd rarely visited Europe. He trusted Ambassador Smith and the original English investors to do the right things for the company. His trust was not misplaced; plus Tom was watching everyone, especially Red. Boyd always says, "when it comes to money keep an eye on your friends so they can stay your friends. Keep your eye on your family so you'll stay in business." Tom agreed with that theory wholeheartedly. Boyd was aware that Red was doing something outside of Comp-Tech. Boyd didn't know the details but anything Red did would bear watching. Tom hadn't brought anything to his attention so Boyd wasn't alarmed about Red's business dealings at least not at that time. Tom had standing, but unspoken orders, to watch Red closely.

The first year brought nothing out of the ordinary to Tom's attention. Red's outside interests were actually helping him to learn more about investing. For a time Red was the fair-haired boy of Comp-Tech everybody was getting rich and everybody was happy. Europe suited Red. The social morays of Europeans allowed him to feel a part of "polite society." Red worked harder, studied longer and prepared himself better than his competition. The company grew from a net worth of a little over twenty million dollars to in excess of three hundred million in five years. Red got them in the door of the big time and Boyd made the most of it. While Amir operated as Red's chief backer in his private enterprise everything went well. The two of them became like brothers; Amir had access to a lot of oil money. Amir reminded Red of his childhood friend Bobby; the two of them had a similar temperament, Amir blindly went along with whatever Red did.

Chapter 41

Odfus' New Life Ministries leased their land to the German car manufacturer. They were paid with stock options and used this money to endow their plans for many years to come. They enlarged their feeding of the poor programs, opened a Christian based drug program, created a temporary employment agency for day laborer and subsidized several other small businesses. The Ministry's use of volunteers kept their expenses at a minimum, the people that they were helping became their staff in most instances.

Odfus started getting speaking engagements all over the country. The fees from his appearances went back into New Life. He lived modestly. The former hustler waged his own private battle against promoting himself. The reborn pimp sometimes longed to dress in fancy suits and let everybody know that he was the world's greatest preacher. Many people considered the Reverend a near saint but he knew that he was a crook that God had saved he prayed daily not to give in to his selfish desires. He trained Bobby Dykes and Eric, his son, to be humble and put their good work ahead of individual wants. Odfus wanted the two young men to replace him one day. Eric had the education to run the business while Bobby has the street smarts and charisma to attract people to join.

Several times, local leaders tried to get the Rev. to run for political office. Odfus always refused the limelight of politics. Odfus felt that light would blind him to the spiritual objectives he had set out to accomplish. Doing God's work, as he saw it, was all that Odfus allowed himself to think about. Peeler remained the Rev.'s chief source of spiritual advice. The jailhouse prophet only asked that no one tried to get him out of prison. Even after he became ill, he refused to allow Boyd to get him out to get the best medical attention available in the world. Doctors could not have helped Virgil that much anyway but his old friends wanted to try.

Though Peeler had inoperable cancer and endured excruciating pain he never lost control of his mental faculties. The old convict advised his star pupils to the end. Peeler even welcomed the pain saying that God was perfecting his soul. It was the least God could ask of him, to endure some pain, considering all the heartaches he had caused people. After years of suffering Peeler died. Boyd and Odfus buried their old friend in the Graveyard behind New Life's recently built Church about five miles outside Savannah. The congregation had grown so large that they needed the space to accommodate everyone. Odfus said in Peeler's eulogy. "I couldn't get him here while he lived, but, if I could have, that would have been temporary. This way he will be here with us always."

Boyd has an extremely simple way of looking at things "Know the difference between right and wrong and don't compromise what you believe in. It doesn't make any difference what the steaks are some things don't change. Your word has no price. Money isn't worth much if you are greedy because you will never have enough." Boyd has enough and everyday he gets more, each day he is more grateful for his success than the day before. This gratitude translates into generous giving to the less fortunate, to other worthy causes. His giving may have begun as a way of trying to make up for the harm he caused in his youth but the giving has transformed into simply a decent man trying to do the right thing. His foundation donates millions each year; Boyd has a personal say over where this money goes.

Boyd's welcome to the Williams Family humbled him with a sense of belonging and purpose. The Williams family was unique in that this family was all the type that loved to give a home to strays, any kind of stray. Being a part of this family wasn't based on material possessions. Just act like a human being with a need for human kindness and the capacity to return the love you were given was all they asked. Wilma was the matriarch of the family. At that time she was in her eighties. The lovely old woman exuded energy and caring that infected the whole family. The love and acceptance she showed Boyd that day when they met while he was in prison did much to open his heart to the possibility that he could change.

Wilma lived to be one hundred two years old. She had a love for her extended family and made an attempt to touch their lives in positive ways. She kept in touch with everyone of her relatives no matter where they were. The successful ones, the ones in jail the relatives that were rich and the penniless ones as well. She remembered something special about each of them that she met...she tried to meet them all. Grandma Lillie had passed those duties on to Wilma. Wilma selected Elaine to take over the job of keeping up with the family. Boyd hired her a staff. Keeping up with the Williams' had become a full time job. Elaine hoped Grace would one day take over for her.

The kindness of the Williams family began a long time ago. The family adopted inter-racial babies in the twenties. Everyone that knew where the Williams farm was and knew that they could get something to eat there if they were hungry. Their kindness extended to any homeless child who was lucky enough to come in contact with one of them, to this very day they are a haven for stray people. No one is completely sure of who is a blood relative or an adopted family member. The family is spread out from Augusta to the far corners of the earth. Long before Boyd's enormous wealth his family did things for people regardless of race or personal circumstances.

Chapter 42

Judith missed her mother; the two them had been almost too close. Ellen had so many disappointing things happen in her life. Jack had been unfaithful so many times with so many of her friends that as time passed Ellen's circle of friends grew smaller. I guess she wanted to do like Julia Roberts did in that movie; ask that all of the women that had sex with her husband to stand up at one of those luncheons Junior League type love to have. She didn't. Therefore, Judith was in many ways Ellen's best friend since none of her friends at the club or in church were off limits to Jack for a long time. Judith trusted only a few people and her mother along with Mary were her only confidants. The grief Judith felt for her mother's lost was unimaginable. Mary and Judith's family did what they could to help but Judith had to find her own answers.

Her second year at Harvard was very uncharacteristic of Judith the standards she normally set for herself were near perfection; she got two C's and wasn't at all concerned…the first time she had ever gotten anything below an A minus. Mary nearly had a stroke, she let Judith know that she was letting herself down. But, Judith knew she couldn't make the kind of commitment she always made to everything that she wanted to accomplish. She had to admit to herself that she really didn't want to go to school; not now, she didn't care enough, right now she couldn't do her best. With her mind as confused, grief stricken and unable to focus as it was. Judith seemed to be searching for something, in general acted like she was a thousand miles away and nothing mattered. All the things she thought were important had lost their meaning. Judith finally had to admit that she was overwhelmed with grief, she dropped out of college. For the first time in her life she didn't know what to do. Jack had finally grown up, he taken care of his wife and provided as much emotional support as any human being could have. Good time Jack had finally taken some responsibility. He didn't run away and get his daughter to fill in for him…like he had done in the past. Though mature beyond her years, Judith couldn't handle her own grief. In her heart she felt that Jack would return to his old ways. For a long time Jack had been the type of man that would develop a dependence on anyone who tried to help him. Judith still had a lot of resentments. Jack and Ellen had been happy in Ellen's last few years… Ellen was able to see her husband finally grow up. But throughout her life Judith blamed Jack for anything that went wrong whether or not he was to blame. Most of the time he had caused whatever it was to go haywire. Judith even held Jack responsible for her mother's death. She was too resentful to take her own time to grieve, refocus and start her life over without Ellen Judith's world was torn apart, in time she would grow to respect her father again but she had to finish grieving first.

Judith's Uncle Jim suggested that she come to Europe for a while, relax and try to find a reason to go on without her mother. Judith gladly accepted his invitation. At the end of the second semester she excitedly departed for London. The days between her mother's funeral and the end of the school year dragged slowly and monotonously like water dripping from a cactus. Judith was over loading herself with too much of what she considered her duty. Jack had not completely fallen to pieces after Ellen's death. Judith and Ellen had been Jack's backbone, what little he had. In a strange way Judith missed the weak dependent Jack.

Judith was very angry with Jack she couldn't believe that he had changed. Judith wanted to get as far away from her father as possible.

After Ellen's death, Jack went to work even harder at Comp-Tech; the company was developing and he had promised his wife that he would continue to work hard. The job that Boyd gave him had been more than a way to make a living it turned out to be a way to make his life mean something. Jack had found the thing that everyone seeks, peace. Before becoming a part of Comp-Tech there was no way that Jack could have survived the pain of losing his wife. He not only survived, he helped his daughter get through the ordeal by leaving her alone. He helped her by giving her space to find her own answers and not troubling her with his grief. Judith still thought of her father as a selfish, childish womanizer. He had changed though she couldn't see it. Judith felt that Jack was going to try to dump his grief off on her. She knew that she was not equipped to have a parent dump their troubles on her. In a very real sense she had lost both parents her father wasn't the man she knew anymore. Jack simply told Judith he loved her and left the door open for her to come to him if she needed him. Judith had never been abroad and was looking forward to the experience. Maybe when the time was right she could finish school in Europe. Judith still had the whole world open to her. Judith's uncle had mentioned she might even go to work with him in the diplomatic service. He thought that at the very least travel would broaden her outlook and relax his brilliant but temporarily without direction young niece. Ellen had been the order in Judith's universe; life had a pattern with the dependable and steady Ellen to guide her. Now somehow Judith would have to find her own way.

Jay Smith, Furman's grandson and Judith were kind of a match created by their families. In truth they were fond of each other. Everyone expected the two ideally suited young people to be married one day. To many old Southern families doing what's expected is still very important. A political family that had politics deep in their blood doing what is expected is the only accepted behavior. From a political point of view they were the perfect couple. Jay was likely to become governor one day. Many believed he could be senator or maybe even President, who knows. The granddaughter of a former Governor and the golden boy of Georgia politics a political marriage made in heaven both of them always thought it was their duty to do what their families expected of them. Circumstances would delay this politically perfect marriage if those two words can be used together. In this case these two people were honest and committed to the highest ideals of public service. They were both too young to be jaded. Judith had a way about her that seemed to make others around her better because of her honesty, compassion, and concern. Judith radiated love and she got love in return, though she was comfortable with just a few really close friends.

Jay had seen much of the joy that was so much a part of Judith's appeal taken from her by the death of her mother. And Jay felt so powerless to help her. He was all for Judith going to Europe. He felt unable to do anything but hurt with her in this situation which only made her feel worst so he told her "Just don't forget me." Sensing the pain he was in she promised " I won't. How could I?" Judith felt committed to a relationship she did not know if she wanted to be in. Though the two of them loved each other, in a way each wanted some kind of young romance that sweeps one off their feet the kind of love that very few of us are fortunate enough to find but at some time we all have thought about and wanted it.

Chapter 43

Red arrived in London on a sunny day in April. It was a slight chill in the air, but the sun was shining. He went straight to his hotel. Most Londoners were amazed at the sunny day, not Red, sunny days in Georgia came a dime a dozen. Red spent the next several years in Europe, at least a couple of days a month in London. He would learn to appreciate sunny days in London before long. For now anyway each new day was an adventure, something exciting and different from sunny Georgia. Red for the first time in his life felt free and alive. Imagine just a short time ago he had lost everything now he had it all. Red had the freedom to explore his talents, expand his limits and grow as a businessman. He could grow as a human being too if he chose. Red had everything the material world had to offer. He visited the all centers of financial power. The capitols of Europe, had become his playground.

Red's role in the company was to find investments and employees and put the right people in the right positions. He assembled a top notched construction company; Red staffed it with individuals who were experienced. Red also got an aggressive staff that went after construction jobs with much more energy than most European companies. His American style of doing business was taking Europe by storm. With a United Europe just over the horizon, the sky was the limit, Red was cashing in on things that his competitors, who had nationalistic views, were missing out on.

Red fell in love with Zurich, the money Mecca totally captured Red's imagination. He based his operation there. Red studied the Swiss system of banking and tried to understand the way that Swiss people think. He even tried to adopt some of their conservative ways. Money, money and more money dominated Red's thinking; even his legendary womanizing was taking a back seat to his new obsession. The Swiss liked stability even more than the conservative businessmen in Georgia, no fooling around became Red's new motto. And he made an effort to become a lot more discreet. He could have fun when he went to France…he projected a corporate image from head to toe during business hours.

Comp-Tech was quietly becoming a huge international conglomerate. By doing business outside the United States provided two very important benefits. First the rest of the world is in more of a developmental phase than the industrialized and intensely competitive United States. The second benefit is, not having to deal with the racism that black companies encounter, particularly technological companies. Boyd believed in doing business, not trying to prove a point or make some kind of a statement. The best way to prove something is to do a good job was his motto. In most countries good work is rewarded with more work, regardless of the race of the owners of the company.

One of Boyd's long-term plans had been to purchase a bank either in the Cayman Islands or the Bahamas or maybe both. Boyd had a great vision for the future but his plans had turned out to be just a start. Capital is the most important asset any company can have. Comp-Tech was not burdened down with debt most of their net worth was in cash, having enough money makes expansion possible. Red learned very quickly, so instead of trying to reinvent the wheel, he followed established success procedures. The Swiss are still the world's bankers, he did what they did. Comp-tech was therefore able to have a very large cash flow. Most of the corporation's assets were liquid and easily moved, allowing the company to invest quickly in high profit ventures. Comp-Tech made a fortune on the early growth of computers; at one juncture they owned ten per-cent of all the computers companies in the world... without holding a majority interest in any of them. Computers and construction were just the tip of the iceberg just the beginning. At a quick glance Comp-Tech didn't seem so big, with their money from European investments, they bought or took over American companies. Boyd made money in the U.S. companies and diversifying his company's holdings. Comp-Tech became very adept at the art of the take over. They were so diversified that nobody paid much attention, as they became a worldwide financial power. Comp-Tech is into everything from fast food to producing music. Over two hundred successful companies, several Banks and holding companies are now wholly or partly owned by Comp-Tech.

Money and power brings responsibility and Boyd understood that in a way that few men have ever understood their position in life. He seemed to know how to care for the individual needs of each stockholder, employee and the company's best interests...a difficult balancing act that most executives can't do. Red showed no evidence of having such abilities...his only concern was money. Red soon developed a new distorted view of life that had money as a Deity. The depth of Red's commitment to and fascination with money was deeply imbedded into his soul. Red's dedication, discipline and fervor can only be described as a conversion religious in nature.

He studied and immersed himself in all the information available on banking; money transfers and stock markets in Europe, Asia and the United

States. He and his partner developed ways that they could make money appear to be in two places at one time. This could be done in places that were not yet computerized, they could play a lot of games in the time that money showed up from an underdeveloped country. They could make a company appear a lot more profitable, thus more valuable to purchase than it really was. It was first just an experiment, just fooling around with his computer. But, Red saw it actually could be done so he started his own company.

Amir was the first man that Red had been close to since he and his childhood buddy, Bobby's friendship came to its disastrous end. Amir's family had money and he was a big help in getting some investors. The two prodigal sons were happily passing money around the world as quickly and casually as diners passing rolls at the dinner table...they reached for the money like starving men would reach for food. They then invested that money back into numbered accounts and to the Caymans and then the money was sent though the same process all over again. Amir was an unofficial partner but for the first time in his life he was making his own way. However, he refused to be too visible because he didn't want to incur the anger of his father. Amir provided valuable help but the operation was Red's baby.

Red also knew not to even give the impression his business had anything to do with Boyd's. He knew Boyd would not like this or any fast money scheme especially if it was questionable as to its legality or morality. But Red figured that he could separate the two enterprises. With the speed of computers Red was able to pull it off. He was using his own money and figured what harm would it do, making a lot of money is fun he thought. Comp-Tech is first. This investment thing is nothing more than a very profitable hobby, Red told himself in his usual self-serving rationalizing way.

Judith quickly became bored with shopping and sightseeing. She was not a person given to frivolous pursuits; she wanted and needed something to do. So on Red's trip to London in July; it was suggested that she go to work as Red's Administrative Assistant. No one really remembers who made the suggestion, but everyone agreed that she'd be great. Judith's youth gave her an idealistic view of the world of money and the good that it could do, if directed properly. She had a deep appreciation for its power to better conditions for people by creating jobs, business opportunities to make life easier and cures for diseases, everything for the good of mankind. She coveted very little for herself. She had everything, just being a part of this force for good. Youth, with its naiveté, can be a form of insanity or at least confusion caused by faulty perceptions. Let's just say she was a little naive about the greed factor in business. Whether a little crazy or a lot naive, she entered into her job with a great deal of enthusiasm. Judith's attention to detail, her thoroughness and just plain common sense approach to dealing with people soon made her an invaluable part of Red's staff. Diversity was what Boyd called for. Red was to hire staffs, invested in companies, start new companies and buy old companies. All of these transactions were made, at Boyd's directions. One third of the High tech industries in the developing countries of Africa were built by Comp tech and some of them are owned by Comp Tech. Red and Judith worked together very well. They seemed to have similar temperaments and motivations. Judith was different from any woman Red had ever known...he actually respected her.

Judith learned her common sense approach from her grandfather. He had spent long hours lecturing her father on responsibility, how to do business and how to influence people. Unfortunately, Jack never took any of it in. But, Jack's little daughter hiding behind the couch or sitting on the stairs was taking in every word. Governor Smith, although educated at the University of Georgia Harvard Law School, used southern colloquialisms like nervous as a cat in a room full of rocking chairs, don't drive your best mule to church or don't chew tobacco unless you've got a place to spit. These things drove Judith's grandmother almost to distraction. She would cringe every time he would say them, but he would say them anyway. He always seemed to make a point. Most people knew how intelligent Governor Smith was and respected his intelligence. But with him, talking that way was just of part of his charm. He knew how to get things done.

After serving two terms as governor, he retired to teach law at the University of Georgia and spent his remaining time doing that and playing with his grandchildren. While working at the University of Georgia, a group of last year law students challenged him saying he didn't know what went on in courtrooms. He put together a staff of first year law students and prepared his case. The one thing they didn't count on was Governor Smith's ability to communicate. Judith was about twelve years old at the time. As she sat there listening to her grandfather make a fool out of the students and win his case, she became or should I say she decided to become a lawyer. She admired her grandfather. Even today when she thinks of her grandfather, she smiles.

Chapter 44

Judith and Red traveled throughout the world together. They were together everyday. They went sometimes from Switzerland, maybe to Japan or would be in Egypt or Italy. Every beautiful romantic place in the world, they saw together. As time went by, something happened. Red had never thought of Judith as being the beautiful woman that she had become even at nineteen. Red thought of her always as his daughter's little friend the little girl that was always around like a member of the family. Amir was the first to notice the beautiful young woman that Judith had become. Amir asked her out she declined. Red still became incensed at Amir. Red had to be restrained from hitting his friend. In a moment of candor he later said that he had never been that angry with anyone. Amir was aware of Red's affair with his sister and was surprised by his friend's attitude about his attraction to the young woman. And suggested Red had an interest in Judith that wasn't fatherly. Red even more angry at the suggestion that he was interested in this child. But inside he knew that she wasn't a child to him anymore.

For several weeks, for the most part anyway, Red suppressed his feelings for Judith or at least successfully hid them from those around him. Red and Judith had villas across from one another in Zurich. Red found some southern fried chicken in a small restaurant on the out skirts of Zurich. It seems that the owners had visited America and like most people quickly developed a taste for that Southern delight. Red and Judith loved fried chicken, many nights when Judith was a kid and stayed over with Mary, they would all get some fried chicken. It's funny but it seemed like that was the only time that Red and Mary enjoyed each other's company. Red, Mary and Judith would look at television or just sit and talk for hours. These were happy times, great memories the only times when Red seemed like he was Mary's father. Red was feeling a little melancholy, so; he got some and figured he would give Judith a nice surprise and bring her some chicken, they could eat it and talk about old times. He figured that they had spent enough time talking about what they would be doing on a new deal they were working on. It would be just like old times. But, when he got there and rang the bell, Judith was just getting out of the shower. She was wearing a tank top and cut-off Jeans and her hair still wet. As Red entered her villa, he saw her in a different way. For the first time he had to admit to himself that he did desire her. At first Red couldn't believe he was standing there staring at his daughter's best friend's breast as they gently pushed against the tank top. Her skin still moist from the shower and her nipples, starring him in the face, calling him. Crying out for him might be a better way of putting it. He became even more confused as his eyes drifted down. He stood there looking at her stomach as the tank top rose and exposed her navel, as the cutoffs clung between her well-formed thighs and her shapely legs induced excitement almost causing him to lose control. Then as he regained his senses, he really felt ashamed. "What am I thinking about? I just haven't been going out much lately." He told himself. Then he said, "Judith, um aah, I just got you some chicken and ah here. I'll see you tomorrow." And then he left. The abruptness of him leaving worried Judith. She wondered if something had happened and if he was upset with her. She tried to stop him and he said, "no, I will talk with you tomorrow". She could tell that he was upset, so she went back to doing what she was doing and eating her chicken. She couldn't get Red off her mind so she went across to his villa and knocked on his door. He was still there. He hadn't gone anywhere. But, he called and made a last minute date. The date that he had made wasn't the date he wanted. Judith had gotten under his skin. Red tried to tell her was going to leave in a few minutes and they could get together tomorrow. He'd talk with her later. Now she felt a little hurt wondering, is there something I've done? Why is he so uncomfortable? She went back to her villa and within thirty minutes she heard a knock on her door. It was Red again. He said, can I come in? She said, sure have a seat. She was thinking he would tell her why he was upset with her. They sat there and talked about what happened during the day and just silly small talk. Red seemed to be afraid to talk to her about why he was acting so strangely. Then somehow they wound up in each other's arms.

Of all the women that Red had been with and there were a heck of a lot of them, there was something different about Judith. He'd been with models, actresses and beautiful women all over the world, but this was the first time that he'd ever given himself totally to another human being. It was something he really enjoyed and cherished. It was a strange feeling for Red. Sex was new to Judith. There had been an encounter with her and Jay. Now that seemed like something that happened in the back seat of his car. She thought she loved Jay at the time. But, she never had feelings as intense as her feelings for Red. She felt that magic that she never felt with Jay… that magic that I believe that we all dreamed of as youth. She guessed they had always been there. She remembered one night telling Mary, God your dad is so fine! She had a crush on Red from the time she was about twelve years old. As they worked together, that crush grew into something very deep and very meaningful for her. Though until tonight, she did not know what she really was feeling. Judith didn't know quite what to do. Things were happening so quickly; her thoughts were spinning around in her head like tiny sparkles of light from the source all the fire in her being.

However, both Judith and Red quickly decided to keep their affair secret for now. Both of them knew how Mary would react. She had an under the surface near hatred for Red anyway and how he'd been a womanizer and neglected her. Mary resented her mother for putting up with Red because in truth, Mary never did. There were a lot of things Mary hadn't dealt with concerning how she felt about her parents. She respected neither. This could definitely ruin Judith's friendship with Mary. "Any woman who would go to bed with my father must be a fool." Mary confided in Judith one day when the two of them were in high school.

As the months passed, Red's other business was profiting even more than he had imagined. Red's relationship with Amir was becoming strained. Although Amir had never asked Judith out again: He never even showed the slightest interest in Judith but Red always managed to keep them apart. Red let his memories of Bobby and how he blindly gave him his first wife, an unwanted wife but his just the same. Now after all these years those events were causing distrust to creep it's way into Red's mind. Red had not yet come to grips with the fact that he had ruined his own marriage but for now it was easier to blame Bobby. Red had never felt much of anything for Paula but he, in his own way, loved Judith. Now Red started to avoid his new best friend. Partly because he had lost interest in the party life but mostly because he didn't trust anybody with Judith his feelings were too intense. Red began to look for new investors. Amir sensed Red's lost of trust and confidence in him and figured that Red was planning to double-cross him. The two men drifted apart. Amir resented the way his former friend had treated him, he felt betrayed.

Then Red got his not so unexpected visit from Tom. Boyd had no idea at the time what was going on and that Red's business had attracted certain unsavory characters. The speed with which money traveled around the world, the great number of dishonest or greedy people who were trying to launder money, became an irresistible combination for speculators of all sorts and those with money to hide. Red could care less about how his investors got their money. Where the money came from was quickly lost in the maze of transfers from bank to bank anyway. Only the odor of dirty money was left behind. But Tom had a nose that sniffed out anything rotten.

Tom told Red he felt it would be better, particularly now that there was an attempt by some Amir's father's people. The English management team that Judith's uncle had assembled was more loyal to him than Boyd. Business in Europe depended on good relations between Judith's uncle and Boyd. Amir had convinced his father that the people at Comp Tech couldn't be trusted.

There were a lot of things hanging in the balance. Red wasn't exactly what every father would want for his daughter. The race issue, though never a problem before might be the straw that broke the camel's back. Comp-Tech might have been lost. Judith had a mind of her own it didn't take her long to come out from Red's spell. She had been thinking for sometime that maybe what attracted to her about Red was the fact that he was so much like her father. She loved him but the devil may care attitude of always being willing to take a chance wasn't exciting to her. She felt that Red, was not really ever going to be too stable. Red never would want to stay in one place too long. Mary also felt that Red's days as a womanizer weren't over and might not ever be completely over. Judith saw how miserable her mother had been for much of her life. She was having second thoughts about rushing into anything with Red anyway. Mary had been Judith's best friend her hole life and she didn't want to lose Mary's friendship.

When Tom came and talked with Red about what was going on with his business, Judith saw the entire picture she saw that Boyd didn't need anything that might be a source of concern until this mess was over. Judith didn't like the people that Red had been doing business with so she asked Red to get out of it and he refused. He figured it wasn't his business where the people were getting the money. He was making money and wasn't doing anything wrong, as he could see it anyway. Then Judith dropped the bombshell on him and told him she was pregnant. Being a good southern Baptist girl, she had no intention of having an abortion. This really complicated things, as Red didn't want her to have an abortion either. He loved her and wanted to have a life with her, but there was too much at stake for everyone concerned for them to have a life together now. Judith's family was key to keeping things together, a baby might bring everyone together or it might and probably would drive a wedge between all of Comp Tech important players. Tom helped them to make arrangements to have the baby adopted by a family in Sicily that worked for Comp Tech. Red decided that he would leave Comp-Tech and work at his money exchanging system full time in his own business and made it clear that the two were two separate organizations. Red had accumulated assets of over $5,000,000 and felt that it was too much for him to give up. He was earning much more than the $350,000 salary a year that Boyd was paying him and he didn't want to wait on somebody's death to be in charge. So, he went out on his own. Judith discreetly had her baby and returned to the United States. The baby went to Sicily.

Chapter 45

Red continued his travels throughout the world, but made what would prove to be a big mistake. He based his operations in Miami, Florida. That gave the DEA a chance to investigate what he was doing. They were actually after Edmund Scallia, a Colombian who was reputed to have control over most of the world's supply of cocaine. Scallia was one of Red's biggest investors. He laundered millions of dollars for Scallia. The DEA approached Red and told him who Scallia was, what he was involved in. For the first time Red realized what Tom had tried to tell him a couple of years before. He agreed that he would testify against Scallia, but the only thing that he could really testify to was that Scallia had a lot of money and where he had invested the money. They were in all legitimate businesses.

Red remembered his vow that afternoon in the small cell that he and Slick had shared never to go to prison again. He really wasn't thinking logically the fear of jail and the guilt of being involved with drug dealers had him at the mercy of the DEA. All the evidence they had on Scallia had to come from some other place, but Red didn't realize it. The truth was the DEA had played a game the old shell game. While they focused the attention toward Red. The actual damning evidence came from Carmen Espinosa, Scallia's girlfriend. They had made a secret deal with her. The young woman had family in Columbia, she didn't want them to be hurt, she had seen first hand how Scillia corrupted everyone around him. Carmen, like so many other women had fallen in love with Red. They had an affair, she saw that she could still have a deceit life. She was a country girl, good at heart just caught up with one of the evilest men on earth.

Red thought he had testified against her as well. He had tried to warn her, but he thought his warning went unheeded. She had already cut her deal long before Red even got into the situation, she knew that if Red got more involved with Scallia he would be completely corrupted. By him getting involved it gave her a way out, a cover, because the DEA faked the whole big trial for her as one of the defendants.

Red was the father of her baby and she loved them both. Somehow Scallia found out about it and was very angry his ego was hurt because he considered Carmen one of his possessions. Scallia's temper troubled his superiors quite a bit. He took too many chances and went on too many person vendettas. They didn't have the time, or the money to spend on any kind of personal vendetta about a woman, or any other personal issue that someone had created themselves wasn't the kind of thing they got involved in. They certainly didn't need the attention of killing a prominent person would surely bring. Scallia considered his superiors cowards, he thought they were easily intimidated. He was a bully really who had been a street thug that had work himself into big money. But at heart he was still that street punk. Scllia's threats had frightened Carmen and she'd reached the point where she felt she had to do something. She wanted to come to America and the DEA was snooping around so she made a deal. When all was said and done the real bosses of the cartel regretted not getting rid of Scallia when they first heard of trouble in Florida.

Red's oldest daughter Mary decided that maybe they should take action against Scallia so she discussed that with Boyd. In the meantime Red went to visit Peeler in prison and Peeler told him about what Mary was trying to talk Boyd into. He knew that Boyd was capable of murder, but on the other hand, he knew the agony Boyd felt when he had to kill the guy in prison. Red definitely didn't want to put his family through anymore pain. His daughter had no conception of what she was actually getting herself into. Mary had put some of past behind her when it came to her father she also didn't want her own children hurt. Red knew she wasn't thinking so he decided to talk them out of it. He told Boyd he would handle his own difficulties, he'd made his own bed hard and was going to sleep in it for the first time in his life. He told Mary to stay out of it because she didn't know what she was getting into and he wouldn't be gone forever. Boyd could take care of things if they didn't start some kind of war. Little did they know that if they killed Scillia nothing would have been done about it, Boyd did let it be known that anything happened to his family there would be hell to pay. Boyd wasn't in favor of killing Scallia but Tom had heard the rumbling of the dissatisfaction within the cartel about the hot head they had for a front man. Tom felt that a few dollars in the right places would bring this entire matter with out any danger to the family. Somehow Tom had found out the identities of a several members of the cartel who he had done legitimate business with in South America. Tom didn't let on that he had knowledge of their illegal activities. They played a game with each other but each got the message.

After the baby was born, Carmen took him to Boyd's mansion outside Augusta and left him with family...literally on the doorstep. One thing about Red's family, there was always room for one more so they decided to keep the baby. No one knew where the baby came from or whose baby it was until Mary suggested having a paternity test done. Mary committed on how much the child looked like Red but nobody knew whose baby it was at the time. Fortunately it was about two weeks before Red's trial so he got a chance to see the baby before he left for his witness protection stay. During the time leading up to the trial, Scallia had made a lot of threats about killing Red and also other threats about harming the family. The results of the test didn't get back until after Red left. Everybody had their minds on the trial; all the younger men in the family submitted to the test but all the samples didn't get tested right away. When the test result came back Mary's only comment was, "that dog." Then strangely enough she insisted on adopting the child.

When it came time for Red to face the music, he had made his own decision and had prepared himself for it. Tom gave his assurance that the family would be OK. Red accepted his fate, he seemed to be changing his values from just being concerned about himself to thinking about how his decisions might affect others. A peace came over Red that he had never enjoyed before the whole family noticed it. Red's transformation into the person that I knew had begun.

His trial was going to be held in the shiny new Federal Courthouse building. A fitting but austere place, that justice is supposed to be fairly and blindly melded out. The room was stark and a little cold, though well lighted, the benches were hard and unforgiving to the seat. The flags and seals of the republic hung like intimidating reminders of how unjust the criminal justice system can be. The invisible noise that the silent cries of the innocent wrongly imprisoned lost souls make saddens your dreams. As the laughter of the guilty set free make an eloquent cry for the hypocrisy of the system. The inaudible blood stained cries of the walls with their terrible knowledge all the heinous crimes for which no human punishment would be just corrupts even the injustice of the imperfections of the system and all that goes with it.

Red sat quietly on a seat on an otherwise empty row, thinking that he had never he felt so alone. He realized that he had driven everyone that he ever loved out of his life at least for a while. This was the day he was to testify. He had been over his testimony a thousand times. He was ready. The ten minutes crept by until the judge entered. The prisoners were lead to the tables along with their lawyers. Carmen Espinosa glared at Red with her eyes glassy, full of hurt and anger, Red thought as she walked pass him. She was his only regret in the whole thing. He hadn't realized the depth of the feelings that he had for her and really regretted what he thought he was doing to her. He had tried talk to her but she would not listen to him. She didn't want Scallia to know that she rolled over on him. The irony of this whole farce was that the only thing that Scallia ever found out was that Red and Carmen were more than just friends, his ego was hurt.

Red had planted a bug in Scallia's hotel room in Mexico and thought that Carmen had condemned herself out of her own mouth. But, she hadn't it was all a part of the plan to set Scallia up to take a fall. He didn't know it but the love that she felt for Red made Carmen want out for both of them. When Red's name was called, Carmen whispered "fagot" in Spanish and made a gesture towards some ancient South American god to put a curse on Red.

Maybe I should have listened to Mary, he thought, when she had suggested to he and Boyd that they kill Scallia. But, he was glad that he didn't listen to that, but he would miss his family. He would be back with them one day. Red was selfish, more than a little crooked, but not really a criminal. He certainly wasn't violent unless he was directly threatened. Red always wanted to be some that that thought others wanted him to be Boyd wanted riches and power. The difference between Red and his father were now apparent to Red for the first time in his life and was the first indication that fate had something else in store for Red than being an international tycoon.

Red testified for two days and had to undergo quite a bit of hard cross-examination from the six attorneys. They wanted to know how he had gained so much of Scallia's confidence without knowing of being involved in the dope smuggling. Scallia's lawyer tried to make it appear that Red was the guilty party. The desperation of this tactic became very obvious
When there was no evidence to support this claim. One of the other attorneys tried to deny that Red even knew his client and in fact Red had never met the man in person but phone records sufficiently proved a connection to the jury the Carmen testified that they went places together, quite by accident naturally. Each of the others lawyers took their turn at trying to discredit Red or the evidence none were able to do that with any real degree of success. The lawyers did their best but in the end Red did just fine. He kept very exact records and left nothing to chance that good old Swiss training.

At the end of the two days of grilling by some of the best lawyers money can buy, the life of George Tillman began. His years as Redmond Perry, Jr. were over at least for a few years Red said to himself. As he reflected on the past years since he was released from prison. Peeler had told him that everything was going to be all right at the end of the day. Then the man he thought was so craze; told him that he would have to be gone from his family more than five years after that everything was going to be alright. Scallia, wouldn't try doing anything stupid to his family, Boyd could handle things. Red followed the mad man's advice. With his new identity in tact George left with the confidence that he would see his family again and that he would take the pressure off of them by not being around to remind them of his selfish thoughtlessness.

Chapter 45

George was relocated in a small town in Washington State and that's where I met him. Throughout all of George's turmoil, he still attended NA meetings regularly. We met on a Tuesday night during a regularly scheduled NA meeting. We were really an odd collection of folks. George didn't seem to fit in with us. He seemed too sensible, too self-assured. We all gravitated to him because there seemed to be something special about him. He had a sense of humor whenever you talked to him you would either leave laughing or thinking about what he had said to you. It seemed that only the most and I mean the most confused sought him out for advice. He was there when you needed him; that was the promise he said he made to himself.

In all my years of knowing him, George never lied to me nor did I hear of him lying to others. He was generous with his time and material possessions. He often said I couldn't say no to any one in need. He said that his duty was to serve his fellow man. He did that with a passion that consumed everyone around him. You became better just by knowing him. I had a lot of problems when we first met. I still do today but I know that he helped me to come to grips with a lot of them.

George's sense of humor got him into trouble at times, maybe I should say got me into trouble, he liked to play practical jokes like putting shaving cream in your shoes... that type of thing. Once he had me go some forty miles into Spokane looking for some grunion traps. I know what's a grunion? He got a good laugh out of that one. Telling me that this beautiful woman wanted to talk to me, and she had asked to have me come over to her table where she and some other women were sitting. I thought he was pulling my chain but I went anyway. She nearly had me thrown out of the place but I wound up taking her out once or twice, thanks to George, after he worked his magic charm on her. I had never seen anyone as able to get his way with people as George. After that incident in the restaurant, I tried to listen to every word that George said to me at first to get pointers on how to win friends and influence people mostly woman. But as our relationship grew I found that he had many things to teach me.

Chapter 46

George welcomed our family of misfits with open arms. For a long time I thought that I was one of the least needy. I did everything I could to deny my true nature. He was there for all of us; where he got the patience to deal with us is anybody's guess. The guys that chose him as a sponsor varied in every conceivable way, there were twelve of us at the end. Some black, some white, one Korean, two native Americans and me mister in between so I thought. My identity crisis as I called it; came more from the weird thinking process in my head than from my experience. I was looking to let others define who I am and letting their opinions form my self-image. Today I can say I know who I am without qualifying it. The race of my parents no longer defines my identity nor makes me long to be one or the other, I am both. Though I have sense enough to know that I'm black socially and practically speaking, you know that drop of black blood theory, but the most important thing I've learned is that I'm me and that's OK.

I was born in a small town in Washington State about 40 miles south of Spokane. My parents were as odd a couple as you might imagine. Not because she was white and he was black that was only the beginning. Through it all we were a happy family. Not many blacks lived in the area where we lived. The most overt racism that I encountered was the prejudice shown by blacks toward my mother, mostly from dad's family. The only white racism to speak of, I faced was from mom's family. It was directed toward dad and me, I guess that is why it hurt so much.

I was a good athlete and kind of a novelty to my classmates and their parents. Thanks to my father, we were happy because we had each other and that was enough. My father was so strong and caring that he never allowed me to hate anybody. Mom on the other hand was so naive, into her artwork, child-like and self-centeredness that she didn't seem to notice the reactions of other people. If she had noticed things like that, I probably would have been even more messed up. No matter what, my mom always let me know that I was loved. Loved by everybody but me, I guess because I never showed much love to myself.

Dad was a big dark brown man with a smile that could melt the coldest heart. I guess it was because he was such a truly good and decent man that mom's artist temperament and lack of responsibility didn't drive him crazy or for that matter bother him much at all. She was a very gifted artist but a very needy human being. Dad in all honesty loved being needed. That was much of what appealed to him about mom. She needed so much from every one who was close to her.

Mom was born and raised in Forsyth Georgia. Her father was the unquestioned king of his castle. My father was much the same way but you could talk to him good luck at changing his mind though. Both men were the man of the house both of them without a doubt. I guess by marrying a black man she could have a man like her father and still rebel against him. Mom wanted someone that made all the major decisions, earned the money and ran the show. Mom's mother did as she was bided. She passed that along to my mom and as long as mom could paint and sculpt everything was all right with her. Underneath mom's hippie facade was a southern belle. The helpless female who needed that strong man to protect her and take care of her. Dad was the good black knight on the big black horse there just to ride to her rescue. Her father was a white knight, he loved her but he couldn't get pass the disappointment he felt when she married my dad. I can't get myself to call mom's parents my grand's because in reality they aren't. Walter and Lilly Anne McClelland were born at the wrong time and place for that to be.

Robert William Fairfax (my father) was born in the Watts section of Los Angeles. He was an only child, both of his parents came from large families so he had lots of cousins. His father worked in the construction business. My grandmother was in housekeeping at one of the major studios. But when dad was about eight or nine years old his mother became ill. Either he or his father would take care of her for the remainder of her life.

My father was a good football player (offensive tackle). However he was an even better student, he had a capacity to work hard at an early age. He always knew what was important and that he wanted to succeed. He got a scholarship to Stanford, started three years on the football team, got pro offers but he was not quite big enough for the NFL at two hundred forty five pounds. He had made the dean's list all four years and had a great job offered him in Washington. It was very important to my father that he succeeded in his chosen field, chemical engineering.

Mom and dad met while dad was at Stanford. At the time mom was in full-blown rebellion against her father, Old Walt, as I like to call him. She had left college and moved into a commune near San Francisco. She and a few friends went over to Stanford to demonstrate against the lack of black students in the California College system. Mom and dad fell in love at first sight, I really believe that dad was the first black that she had known personally. Other than Mamie the housekeeper that worked for her family while she was growing up she had never interacted with a black person her own age. But Mom wasn't prejudice, she was an artist caught up in her own selfishness and cared little about the world around her. If you did her bidding she cared about you, if you didn't, you weren't part of her world.

I think she saw how similar dad was to old Walt. Mr. Responsible and the hippie, dad the caregiver mom the needy. Three months later they were married. OLE Walt was never the same after he disowned mom, something that I think was in all likelihood more painful for him than mom. His stubbornness caused him not to speak to her again. Her sister, Amy, has kept in contact and has done her best to accept dad and me. Aunt Amy told mom that their father's last words were " tell your sister I love her" stubborn to the end the old man had promised to never utter mom's name again.

Grandfather Fairfax died suddenly less than a year after mom and dad married; he had a heart attack. My granddad's death left dad with the responsibility of taking care of his mother. Fortunately, both my grand parents had insurance that covered the nursing home expenses incurred for the two years grand mother Fairfax lived after my grandfather's death. Dad somehow commuted back and forth between the Bay Area and Los Angeles. Dad's relatives helped a great deal during that time and he remained close to his aunts throughout his life.

It was a very proud day for the entire Fairfax family when Dad graduated. He got his dream job in Washington, sold the house his parents left him and started a new life. My father always told me that he was the most blessed man alive because of mom and me. Dad advanced quickly and soon became the head of research and development. Dad wasn't much for causes or demonstrations, but he believed that if a black man got a chance he had better make the most of it. Dad's motto was "I can show you better than I can tell you."

My earliest memories of my childhood were happy ones. Mom and dad loved each other and each loved me in their own way. Mom was an artist she showed little interest in much else. She painted, made sculptures and did her best at being a mother and wife. She taught dad and I to draw, make pottery and sculpt. Dad knew that if we were to be happy he and I would have to enter her world. I was a really bad sculptor, dad got to be pretty good though. She took us to art galleries, museums and exhibits. I knew the difference between expressionism and non-expressionism before I could spell either. Abstract was my favorite; I really liked it, I could paint something and no one could say it wasn't good. Dad found that he had some talent at painting and used it as a way to relax. We enjoyed our times together painting of making pottery, but, mostly it was our family time.

My pop was the kind of man everybody loved. To me he could do anything. He had a good voice and sang in church solos even. The preacher was always getting him to speak he headed the deacon board. He could out run any of my friend's fathers, hit a baseball further than any of them. I was the fastest kid in my class and I couldn't beat him even when he ran backwards until I was fourteen. Dad and I would talk he taught me to play football he even tried to talk to me about sex and drugs. Then one afternoon I was all set to tease him about beating him in a race the day before. We got a call to come to the hospital. He was gone, killed in a fire at the chemical plant trying to save four other people. They survived but he didn't.

I was left with the responsibility of taking care of my mother. Dad like his parents, believed in insurance, he had enough to take care of mom and me. His company provided for us as well. Dad was a hero to the employees at the plant they raised money for me to go to college. It was put in a trust for me. Mom didn't have to work but she didn't have a clue about running a house either. I wrote the checks bought the food ran the house. To be honest I enjoyed being in charge, it made me feel like I was dad but I wasn't ready for all that responsibility. Dad was my hero and I did well in school and better at football and track. I was pretty much left to fend for myself. George always told me, "You did a pretty good job."

Many people considered me to be the best football player in the class of 1983, in the state of Washington. I won the state track champion in the high hurdle. I had the third fastest time on the West Coast. I had a lot of college offers and as it turned out, I didn't need to use my trust fund for college. I choose to stay home, Washington State, they paid for everything. We weren't very good until my senior year. I made all-conference at wide receiver and was chosen to play in the Blue-Gray Game. I used to say that I started using after I got hurt in that all-star game. I really felt sorry for myself, until one day George and I, were playing touch football. He was a nearly twenty years older than I, he was faster, stronger and a better athlete. He was almost as good as I was when I thought I was such a hotshot. I asked him if he played in college he said "Yes but it was too much like work and I didn't like being second string." I couldn't imagine him not being the star. He told me about the team that he was on at Florida A and M. Bob Hayes and Robert Paramour were both faster than he was. They went undefeated the year he played and were among the first Black College teams to play on television. George told me one day, "I started at cornerback and played some running back but I got into the fast lane, if you know what I mean."

I know now that I was obsessed with the dream of being a famous football player. I never tried really to fit in anywhere else throughout my young life. When I started using drugs, it made feel that I belonged. But when I didn't have drugs, I felt more out of place than ever. My problem was me I feared rejection so much that I felt rejected by people even before I met who ever I might have encountered. I was estranged from my relatives both the black one and white ones, I thought that my relatives gave both black and white people a bad name. The reality was that I was both and wanted to be neither. I built a wall to keep everybody out. The black side of my family, were militants, and separatists while the white ones were old-line southerners. Each side would have accepted either my mother or me but not both. All I had to do was renounce my mother and my black relatives would accept me. No chance of my being accepted in Forsyth no matter what I did. That was their problem, not something wrong with me, but I made it my problem.

Self-pity, uniqueness, isolation, and drugs drove me deeper into myself and deeper into drugs in my own private hell. Fortunately for me, I had a high bottom at least as far as material things were concerned, (that's what we say in recovery when you've reached the point where you've had enough). That's when I met George. That's the baggage I brought with me into his life. George was the first person who really understood that the things I felt were painful to me. The others that he befriended were just as sick as I was, we clung to one another like our lives depended on it and they did.

Chapter 47

Boy, we really were a strange collection of walking human problems. George seemed to know what each of us needed. We could talk to him about anything. He'd listen because he cared and above all, he was patient. How he put up with me alone was a mystery; but eleven of twelve just like me is incredible. He helped each of us work through our many problems. All of us wanted to change and we worked at it to the best of our capabilities. At least that's what George told us.

Not long after I met George, one of the other guys George sponsored suggested that we go on a camping trip. His was named Charlie Switzer a strange acidhead who loved to camp in the woods. Charlie was a born con artist; he like to call himself "a born again con artist." Somehow he talked us all into going on a camping trip to Montana in the winter. Late March is winter in Montana; I don't care what Charlie says. Only Charlie could have gotten all twelve of us to go on that trip. Strangely enough, in many ways that trip changed all our lives.

We each took a week, off from work those of us who were working. George had just come into some money and said he would pay the expenses of the ones who didn't have any. We had gone to conventions and out of town meetings and always had a great time. We had been to a N.A, camp out but it wasn't like this adventure. Charlie was so excited he almost got me in the sprit of camping. Since we were from so many backgrounds, we made a decision to let each of us plan something we really liked and the rest of us join in.

George rented a couple of large vans with the racks on top; we all had gotten camping equipment. Too much equipment, and like all inexperienced want to bees or would be campers we bought stuff that was too fancy and unnecessary. George was the worst, he had the money and could afford it. When I asked him why he got so much stuff he said, "I want to be comfortable Soul Brother". George always called me some kind of black term, he teased me about my identity crisis. He would call me brother, soul brother, my Nig, my Nigger, spook, coon or something all the time. He taught me that I was a unique person that words couldn't define or destroy. He also pointed out that most of the Western Hemisphere was made up of people like me. Mixed and mixed again, except most of them don't think about it. I looked at and saw he was right.

We loaded the vans, piled into them and started our journey. The drive across Idaho on I90 didn't take long. We decided to stop in a small town near the Flathead Indian Reservation. This part of Montana is known as Glacier Country. We set up camp at one of the public campgrounds. I had never seen water as clear as the lakes. The name of the camping area escapes me but all the scenery is breath taking, it's a part of America that everybody should see, at least once. The scenic and historic sights ranging from churches old mansions to golf courses. The way that the sky looks early in the morning is worth a trip to Montana.

To say that I never had much appreciation for the outdoors would be the understatement of a lifetime. The first week we split up into two groups the "indoors-man" like myself and outdoorsman, like Charlie, George and a couple of others claimed to be. Want to bees that's what I called them, they hired an outfitter named Michael Bear. He nearly choked when he saw all the equipment we had he laughed until he nearly couldn't catch his breath. Michael Bear at one time or the other claimed to be a member of at least six different native-American nations. You never quite knew when he was pulling your leg or giving you an education on Native-American customs, religions or folklore.

My group, seven of us, went sightseeing each day while the others went into the wilderness. We set up camp and went our separate ways. Something happened when they went into the wild. A peace seemed to come over all the guys who went. George seemed the most profoundly effected by the experience. As for me my spiritual condition was greatly improved. I got in touch with something that had been missing. My previous attempts at spirituality were feeble at best, I guess was trying to force things. But when I woke up one morning and looked up at the sunrise in the sky. I had to admit that it's very easy to believe that only God could make something that beautiful. I had spent most of my life cooped up inside never paying any attention to the beauty around me. I found out on later camping trips that Washington is just as beautiful as anywhere is on earth. For the first time I think I communed with nature, it was like I met God. The way that the morning smelled, the campfire, the coffee and the feel of the morning air against my face. A peace came over me that I had never experienced before in my life.

George and Michael Bear quickly developed a bond, I guess it began when Michael saw the amulet that George wore. Michael Bear had one like it, he has told me at least twenty different stories about what it meant. Neither George nor any of the others would discuss what they did when they went into wilderness. Well, Michael Bear did but I doubt if they changed forms or climbed trees and fucked squirrels. These were Michael's stories depending on the day of the week or his mood. George told me that if I wanted to know I could come along. I almost went once but I saw him pick up a snake so I change my mine about going. I have a thing about snakes and rats.

George stopped eating meat and when we camped out, he always marked off a perimeter and no animal would enter. At least that's what Michael Bear told me. But, thinking back I never saw even a bird in our camp, after a large mountain lion came into camp one night. George calmly walked up to the huge cat and asked him to leave or so it seemed. The cat ran away, thereafter not a single stray animal entered the camp that I remember seeing.

Our first camping trip wet our appetite for more of the outdoors. I loved every minute I spent camping. I have never been so wrong about anything. Michael Bear returned to Washington with us. He, Jerome one of the guys George sponsored, and George went camping almost every month, spiritual retreats George called them. They would go to nearby places where Native Americans lived. Have sweats that are when they would go into a tent and smoke tobacco and have visions. Of course Michael said they would form change to maybe a bird and fly to Canada.

Chapter 48

George lost about fifteen pounds and seemingly gained stamina, he could run miles without getting tired. The no meat diet agreed with him or maybe it was all that flying, according to Michael. His love of animals became almost an obsession I thought. He collected strays on the farm like crazy. Birds, farm animals, deer, he stocked his pond with fish and ducks took up there by the hundreds. Chickens, peacocks, dogs, cats, wild and domestic animals made the farm one the liveliest, nosiest places you could imagine. Any stray person or animal could just come there and live. One day George came to me and said " I want to set up a foundation to keep the farm going even after I'm gone." He had bought several hundred acres some of it undeveloped even for farming. He said he wanted to turn it into something like a reserve and the farm into a place that people could get help from addiction. I would say that it was more of a commune, than a treatment center. There were neither time limits nor formal group sessions. Just people with the same problem trying to help one another. We developed a plan to fund the farm through investments and cottage industries.

George's money had been held in trust; at the time I didn't know the details of where his money came from. The government had released it after two years of his being in the witness protection program. George wanted his money put to good use. He had a very genuine respect for business and knew how to invest money. I'm an accountant and a pretty good one but George knew the stock market better than anyone I had ever seen, we set up trust accounts, made investments and solicited donations; we bought a restaurant, a giant chicken coop, chickens, apple orchard, vehicles and farm equipment. We provided jobs for the guys on the farm, built four buildings as barracks, sixty people could live there. George's little cottage was the first building built by the guys on the farm, they did a great job. George loved his little domain. He spent over two million dollars. When we finished the farm was beautiful, energy efficient and a place for reflection and growth of the human sprit.

I refused pay for what I did on the farm, George said I was foolish to do that; you should be compensated for work you do. He said, "look soul brother you are very good at what you do, by not being paid, you cheapen your profession." He set up a trust for me, said I could save it for retirement. I was compensated by profits from our enterprises, George said if I had a personal stake in the businesses they would be run well. George was very generous with money, he would help whenever there was a need or money would solve the problem. His generosity would prove to be his undoing or should I say the jealousy of someone George thought was his friend, would be.

The years on the farm were happy ones. Our sponsorship family grew as each of us took on the responsibility of sponsoring new people. The way that the farm trusts were setup there was always going to be enough of everything to run the farm very comfortably. George was the glue that held everything together, everybody loved and respected him and we had few problems. Our unofficial treatment plans were working better than most places that cost a lot of money. We mixed some hard work with a lot of love and acceptance. George used to say, "the only way to grow is to stretch your limits".

George's little group of hard core outdoorsmen grew slowly. They all seemed happy and at peace, George seemed to have a special glow about him, nothing seemed to get under his skin. Most of my curiosity had been forgotten; the whole thing seemed harmless enough and I didn't have to listen to anymore of Michael Bear's stories if I didn't ask. The spiritual path that a man chooses is his business. I really started to be open-minded about that sort of thing. Sometimes when they were nearby we could hear them chanting, the beads rattling and the drums beating and see the smoke rising from the sweat tents. I never saw any huge birds or strange half man half animal creatures, just regular people worshipping in their own way.

More people came to the farm each week we had to get several trailers, about ten in all. We put them in any spare spot we could find. George's sponsor's (sponsor) started coming to the farm and he fell in love with it. Frank was in his early seventies and loved to fish and talk with young people in recovery. He was like a grandfather to all of us. His trailer was a special place; he and his wife would feed us and pamper us like proud grandparents. Never having had grandparents made them all the more special to me. Frank and George were the only two people on earth that could stand George's sponsor. Ray Kelly, an obnoxious little man who seemingly had a fantasy of being a human. The more people looked up to George the more jealous he became. Ray, did work hard at times and was helpful because he knew plumbing and something about electricity. We all tried to like or at least understand him, but his attitude prevented any real chance of building any kind of lasting relationship with him. His petty resentments, jealousies, and his obvious ill feelings toward George alienated us from him.

Michael Bear and Jerome were probably closest to George; at least they spent the most time with him. Jerome seemed to depend on George for almost everything. It appeared that George couldn't make a move without Jerome… we all teased him about George being his father. George seemed to be a father figure to him and everybody else except Frank. We really were like family; Michael Bear even claimed to be a relative, a distant cousin. He said that their grandmothers were sisters and he stuck pretty much to that story. That amulet was a family heirloom, most of the time. For sure both of them prized it greatly and kept it with them all the time. They went to Florida just the two of them and Jerome of course, but they were closed-mouthed about what they went to do. George discussed his trips less and less as time went on; or maybe I wasn't as curious as I had been.

My mother was stricken with breast cancer and was hospitalized for six months. She came to live on the farm in one of the trailers; she had developed a drinking problem. I really think she didn't even know she was out of control. The farm was an ideal place for her, she could paint and sculpt and be free. We developed more of a relationship than we had, since dad died. She stopped drinking and looking for Mister Good bar and seemed to be growing up. Those last few years with her are very special to me; we really got to know each other.

Chapter 49

About a month before George's death, he did his fifth step with Ray. Frank had expressed some misgivings about Ray and George's relationship. Frank told me he felt that Ray's jealousy was getting the better of him. He felt that George could no longer trust Ray. I'm pretty sure that Frank passed these feelings on to George, they were very close. I think that George did the fifth step (that's when you tell someone all about yourself) to try to save the relationship. One afternoon Ray and I were looking at the news on television and a report about a South American drug dealer came on, I've never seen him show that much interest in anything. He wrote down the name of the lawyer that was defending the drug lord. I regret not saying anything about this to anyone, but Ray was always trying to seem important. I didn't want to hear the bull that Ray would have told me if I asked him about it either, so I didn't question it.

George and his crew were on a camping trip; they had gone to the mountains this time. When they came back; for the first time in a couple of years George seemed upset. He told me that he was confused and wanted some time to be alone. He wanted some answers to some questions, then he joked, "I just don't know what the questions are." I guess he didn't know what to think. He had a vision when he was in the mountains. George told me "I couldn't quite figure out what it was about" then George said, "I think I'm going somewhere. Promise me you will take care of things". George went on to say "a lot things are happening I can't tell you about yet." Looking back on it; it seemed that we were all caught up in events beyond our control.

I found out later George's family was trying to find him, Boyd was attempting to broker a deal that would allow for George's safe return home. Comp-Tech was doing some business in South America. Tom had found out Scillia was a front man, some government officials controlled the cartel. The real bosses of the cartel were upset at Scillia because they knew the truth about Carmen providing the damaging evidence. Scillia had talked too much. They also knew of the personal grudge he had about George and Carmen's affair. Boyd had offered a million dollars for George safe return and safety thereafter. The only problem was Scillia had other plans. His pride had been hurt and Scillia wanted to get even. Carmen had a brother who had a bad temper and an overly protective attitude about his sister's honor. The ironic thing was that Carmen got pregnant on purpose; if she couldn't be with Red she would have a part of him with her. Carmen's brother hadn't seen her or talked to her for two years and Scillia had lied about what happened between Red and Carmon. If Manuel had known, of the times Scillia had beaten his sister and forced her to prostitute herself. Manuel had no idea that Red had been a ray of hope for her. Her first real chance to get out of the life of fear and brutality she had with Scillia.

Ray contacted the lawyer he had seen on the news report with George's whereabouts and new identity. Scillia thought if he got to George before he was given specific instructions not to hit him no one would dare do any thing about it. What this basically ignorant man could not understand was that his backers were sick of him, and they had a billion-dollar legal project hanging in the balance. He just wasn't that important to them. They wouldn't forgive and forget this silly little personal vendetta of his, he didn't know how much money was riding on the deals with Boyd. As soon as Scillia found out where George was, he sent Manuel Esponnsa to kill George. Scillia told one of his henchmen, "I'll just tell them somebody picked up the contract."

Scillia had an exulted view of his importance to the operation and underestimated the nerve and resolve of his superiors. These people didn't like him much; they considered him dangerous. He was a gangster, plain and simple they were business people. Scillia liked to take chances, live on the edge but his conservative bosses liked money and power. They knew that Scillia had out lived his usefulness.

Boyd had sent a group of detectives out looking for George; in fact they were getting pretty close. George had told the government he didn't want to be found. And they had done a pretty good job of seeing to that. The last couple of places George went, the Agents handing the case didn't know George's real name. But Tom's people had narrowed it down to a small town on the West Coast. George told me he felt he was going to move to a new place. He also felt he was being hunted for the first time since he had been at the farm. Jerome grabbed him and nearly pulled him out of the room bodily when he told me that.

To be honest, that week went pretty much like any other week. Everybody was wondering where Ray was, that was the only thing really out of the ordinary. Ray had skipped taking about two thousand dollars with him out of the farm's checking account. His wife was both upset and relieved at the same time. They were living on the farm and George told her not to worry, she and the three kids could stay there as long as they wanted or needed to.

We had planned to have a big open house that Saturday and everyone was busy sprucing up the farm. We put up flyers all over town. This was the biggest flea we had ever planned. Mom put the finishing touches on a couple of her sculptures; she was gaining some renown, as an artist. Some collectors and museum people were coming to look at her work. She was very excited so was I we hadn't worked on her sculptures since dad died.

Michael Bear, Jerome and a few others of the hard core campers had left early that morning to go hunting. A lot of our visitors like fresh wild game, pheasant and that type of thing. George didn't hunt so he stayed behind. He loved his yard especially his flowers. George cut the grass around his cottage. He took a shower then sat down to relaxed. George had a thing about his flowers, he would sit and look at them for hours. We would tease him about talking to the flowers, we all thought that for him to sit there that long; the plants had to be talking back to him. Of course, Michael Bear said that they were and that George had powers to have all things communicate with him. Michael Bear even started calling George some name I can't pronounce that meant Gentle Breeze. Michael said that the wind blows over everything and is kind when it blows softly. Pollen is spread from flowers and other plants. Some of God's creatures eat or hide in foliage. Soft winds blow the scent of prey to hunting animals. George did try to help everybody; that's true.

It was not at all unusual for people to just walk on to the farm. New tenants came in by just walking up, all the time; so when this short, very slim man, with dark hair appeared behind George, no one thought anything about it.

Then everything went crazy, I mean really crazy, nobody can agree as to what happened next. I heard the shot and I guess I saw what happened. I know I saw it, George, being shot that is but... I blacked out. Others say they saw a hawk crash into the shooter head seemingly clawing the man's eyes out. Everyone agrees about this part of the story. But a few of the witnesses say that the hawk was trying to stop the man from shooting George, but; got there too late. A huge bear came running out of the woods and grabbed the man pulling his head off. Snakes appeared out of thin air and started biting the man. A dove flew in, out of nowhere and seemed to stop the bear from further mutilating the man. Then the dove led the bear, back into the woods. The huge black creature didn't look at anyone else, it just ran away making some kind of horrible baleful sound. A high pitched crying, mournful, frightening wailing that I will never forget. I heard that sound even though nothing else registered. The hawk flew away, one of his wings seemed to be injured and the snakes disappeared as quickly as they had appeared. We all felt an eerie stillness; it was as if the wind had stopped blowing. Those of us who remained at the farm in the moments after the shooting were left in shock, with that horrible sound ringing in our ears.

Someone called the police, it must have been Frank, he was the only one of us who might have had their wits about them at a time like that; but I really don't know who called. The police arrived after some time. I can't say how long it took for them to get there. Everybody was running around crying, screaming, or in a daze, too shocked and confused to speak. The cops tried to question us but we; most of us didn't believe what we saw…I don't know what I saw. The police were a little dubious of our accounts of what happened. But the facts pretty much substantiated what we told them. The man's eyes were on the ground near his headless body… he had been bitten by different types of snakes several times. All I could do was stand there too shocked to speak…people tell me that the snakes crawled over my feet to get to the killer.

After several minutes Michael Bear and Jerome came running out of the woods. Both were naked from the waist up and Jerome was badly bruised and his arm seemed to be broken. He said that a bear throw him against a tree. Michael somehow had frightened the bear off. Both Michael and Jerome were soaking wet with blood dripping from their body and hands when they came out of the woods. They both took showers and changed clothes. When the police got there, Jerome called one of the cops to the side and they talked a few seconds. Then the two walked over to Jerome's trailer. They went inside for a few seconds. Then they got into a police car and drove off nobody had any idea where he was going or why. Jerome still had blood all over him. When he left was carrying a small leather attaché case. Within an hour all the police were gone and have not been back. They took George's body and refused to tell us where. When we inquired, we were told that they didn't know what we were talking about.

After about a week we searched Jerome's trailer and all of his belongings were there but no personal papers were left behind. We found one scrap of paper with a number on it. We called the number and it had been disconnected. The lawyer that handled George's affairs called and told us that we could stay on at the farm the foundations were legal. He said that FBI types had been by his office and had advised him to tell us to leave things alone. We of course had a board and we met and decided to remain open with me as director. We decided to hire a couple of councilors and make the farm an addiction treatment center. It was very rough for a while, fortunately we didn't need contributions to stay open… but for a time we just got by. The neighbors have slowly warmed back up to us we haven't had any more open houses though.

The years without George have been lonely for all of us at the farm. All of the unanswered questions about George what happened to his body, who was he, why did he do the thing he did. I went over these questions over and over. I spent many a sleepless night trying to piece things together. We hired detectives but they were always unable to find out anything the never got any further than the police station. I don't think the local cops had the answers anyway. We all had to guess about who George was and where he came from but no one knew. Our question persisted; what governmental agency was involved and who was Jerome and how did he fit into all this?

Chapter 49

Fortunately I stayed busy, I had two full-time jobs: my comptroller at the chemical company and the Director of the farm. I worked eighteen hours a day so I didn't have much time to think. But at night I would dream of George lying on the floor dying. With his eyes wide open with a lifeless unblinking stare that ripped through my soul like that sound that haunted me. I would wake up in a cold sweat, as time passed, I was the nightmares persisted. He was gone and there was nothing I could do about it. Just knowing that made me relive the events of that horrible day over and over trying to make some sense of the whole thing.

"I told you I was going away but, my spirit was coming back to be with you homeboy." That was the way my first encounter with George, being somehow present with me at the lake began. I couldn't see him or touch him but he was there. I heard him without him speaking. He was there without being there, you know like that feeling you get, when you first come into a statistics class. It takes a while but sooner or later you start to get something out of the class but you don't quite know how. I didn't believe that I had just had a vision, well I didn't see him but I felt him there with me. I had to admit I felt better the next day. I really felt George's presence all that next day and for several weeks thereafter but, different more like a memory. The night at the lake, in my mind he wasn't really dead. How could he be, if I could talk to him? George was there, of that I'm sure. Maybe, if I had been satisfied with just feeling his presence I might have found peace but I fought the visions thinking that I was going insane. The visions persisted; I couldn't get any peace. It was like George was inside my thoughts talking inside my brain. I would be awake and functioning during some of the times he would advise me on something at work or tell me what to say to someone. Then he wouldn't be there with me for a while. When he was there I thought I was nuts but when he wasn't I wanted him to be; I was confused to say the least.

For a few months he made his presence known in much the same way, he told me some things, nothing specific. I guess it was like having an extra voice in my head: somebody else's voice. I still wasn't buying that communicating with the dead stuff… the spirit world, yea right. Nope not me, I have enough trouble with the living. Don't need any with the dead. The visions were getting more realistic the information was getting more tangible. I still wasn't buying it though. The more the sessions seemed to be real the more I thought I was losing my mind. George seemed to get a little annoyed after a while. So one night he said to me" you are so full of it that I have to give you some kind of sign." He told me where to go to find Jerome.

He said, "this should prove that there are forces at work in the universe you don't understand." I guess the only reason I went was because he appealed to the accountant in me. George asked me, "do you want to spend a lot of money on shrinks? You've got a small car. How much gas would it take to go to Seattle? Use your head brother-man."

He told me to go to the tenth floor of the Federal Building in Seattle...I went. I saw Jerome I don't think he saw me though. I knew he wouldn't tell me anything at work. Jerome was coming out of the FBI field office when I saw him. I went back to the farm and told Frank about it. He suggested that we wait a while before we try to contact Jerome. Frank asked me to tell him more about the visions. I began by telling Frank "It's real difficult to explain the way that we communicated I would hear George talk but it was like he was on the inside of my head. Not just his voice, he was there. But it wasn't like I was possessed he didn't control me. We talked though through my thoughts or some sense. I know I'm sounding nuts but it happened." Frank is just about the most open-minded person I know, but even he suggested I get some professional help. I took him to Seattle he was nearly convinced but I could have seen Jerome by accident.

The next time George allows me to feel his presence he is in a much better mood, in fact he asked me jokingly "do you know the secrets of the universe?" I had to confess that I didn't. Well he said, "I'll tell you something else. Ray K's body is going to is going to wash ashore in Miami at least enough of it to identify him through finger prints." It seem that when his body was thrown from the ship it some how got trapped between some rocks and covered up. The salt acted as a preservative, there was a slight earthquake that freed his body and the current washed it ashore. George went on to tell me how Ray was killed and that Scillia was killed with him. Sure enough that very day the police came and told Ray's wife that they had found his body. And of course it was on the news and in the newspaper. I woke Frank up and told him about what George had told me.

George explained that the first couple of years he had to check on his youngest daughter. He said she ran away from everything and was making some poor decisions. She had been a nurse and quit to be an airline stewardess just so she could travel and party and forget. She did just that for a year George said "I didn't do much as a father while I was alive I helped her more like this I'm glad she is OK now." We laughed when he told me how he first made his presence known. Grace had a gentleman friend in her bed when he spoke to her she sit straight up in bed and screamed. Her companion was asked to leave without an explanation. Her love life changed drastically with her father going everywhere she went. She started reading spiritual books, meditating and George even got her communing with nature. Grace began attending church again. George proudly told me, "she is living a decent life and found herself by believing in something she didn't understand."

After I got use to the idea of having George around, it wasn't that bad, really. We made decisions together just like old times. Really, I guess I needed someone or something at that time my mother was getting worst. The cancer was spreading and she was spending more time in the hospital. Her mother came to visit a couple of times so did her sisters. I took care of whatever arrangements had to be made for them to visit. It wasn't the time to try to force a relationship. Mom's father never did come just when I was about to judge him harshly he died. He had been sick and; he had not told anyone not even his wife. He kept it a secret so mom's mother would feel free to visit. OLE Walt was hard to figure, somewhere deep down he still loved mom, but he chose not to let anybody know. Mom lived another year it was a difficult time for me. Thank God, she seemed happier that year than I had seen her for a long time, happier than any time except for her time with dad.

Chapter 50

George and I would talk about a lot of things; we both loved the farm and the work that was being done there. He helped me raise funds, we bought more land and helped more people. It was very rewarding but still I thought about Jerome a great deal. George told me that Jerome had grown very fond of us. Each month we would get an anonymous donation from Seattle. One day George told me to get Frank and Michael Bear and go to Seattle. We went to a bar around the corner from the Federal Building. Jerome was there about to take a drink for the first time in twenty years. We had been his only real friends, the life of undercover assignments and assumed identities had finally gotten to him. He was burned out, he didn't want to go on his next assignment. When he saw us he cried, so did we. He resigned and returned to the farm with us. I really needed an assistant and he was more than able to do the job. Our little family was reunited, only Frank knew about George being inside my head.

George revealed his life to me little by little, it seemed like he was implanting his memories into my mine. I knew things that happened before I was born…before he was born for that matter. I knew all about his family even little things like the birthday of his grandchildren or other relatives. I wasn't becoming him, all of my memories were there and I had become a zombie or anything like that… I just had his memories. That's why I say it was more like you would download a computer. Then George suggested something to me that I thought was crazy. Well if I had the right to call anything crazy after this experience.

He said why don't you move to Georgia. I had just stopped working at the chemical plant. They were downsizing and I didn't want to move; I got a nice severance package and along with what I inherited from mom I was in pretty good shape. George said I could put any demons from the past to rest. Find out who I was and know what the black experience is for other blacks. I was always talking about what I had missed out on. Mom's artwork was very good and I wanted to exhibit her work. My Aunt Amy wanted to as well so I decided to move east.

This was the most difficult decision of my life I really did not want to leave my friends. The work at the farm was very satisfying. But this was all I had ever known. I wanted to venture out, maybe it was the memories George had implanted of Paris and all those places. None of us at the farm could stand to say goodbye, so we called it a leave of absence. I guess people at the airport must have thought we were a gay football team or something.

Three rather large men crying and hugging, as an older man tried to comfort the younger ones. I loved those men more than I think I could ever love anyone.

When I got on the plane I felt George's presence leave, not the memories just the presence. I was on my own I guess for the first time in my life. I was so excited, I felt like a kid in a candy store, all these choices. The stewards directed me to my seat. I sat down and began reading a book after I fastened my seat belt. I dozed off, I think before we took off. The next thing I remember is looking up into the most beautiful eyes I had ever seen. I was paralyzed for a second and couldn't speak. She said, "are you all right, sir?" After a few seconds I regained my ability to speak and mumbled, "yea fine."

She looked at me like OK I hope so. She was the most indescribable woman I had ever seen. Not the prettiest but real pretty. Not the sexiest, but close real close. What ever you look for in a woman wasn't missing, in just one look at her I was in love for the first time in my life. I sat there thinking about the house with the white picket fence; the two point seven kids, the whole nine yards. I needed George's help; he would know what to tell her. He would say just the right things to make her melt in my arms. I remembered the line he used on a woman we met in a restaurant. I rehearsed it at least a thousand times.

She came back and I braced myself just to talk to her, I knew would get her. I had just the right line. "Are you all right sir?" she asked. Her voice sounded like something out of a dream or heaven… more like a dream from heaven. "Yes I am," I said with surprising confidence. "It's just that your eyes are so beautiful that when I looked into them I couldn't think." OK she said with a laugh that sent chills through me. What was that perfume she was wearing? "What's your name?" I asked? She said "Hope," I said "Hope I love you." She patted me on my hand and said, "I love you too" and walked away. About twenty minutes later she came back wearing sunglasses. We both laughed, but I was a little relieved not to have to look into her eyes. She said, "I thought I needed to put these on. I don't want you to get out of control." We talked for another moment or two she said she'd be back she had to see to the other passengers. When she got back I asked if she could have dinner with me when we got to Atlanta, she said she would. The flight seemed to take seventy hours after that and I was on the edge of my seat from then on. But eventually we got there and got off the plane. It took seemingly twelve more hours for the crew to deplane, but they did.

George had told me about the Georgia Terrence so I made a reservation there. Hope said she could have dinner, but would have to run after that, she was moving. Her apartment was nearly empty but there were a few more things to pack. We went directly to the hotel from the airport. I checked in and we went to dinner she wanted to go to a place not far from the hotel. We ate, the food was pretty good. She took me back to the hotel and went home. She called about twenty minutes later and we talked for three hours. She finished packing as we talked. We made a date for breakfast at the hotel. Sometime between two o'clock A.M. and nine o'clock A.M., I knew that I had to spend the rest of my life with her.

It was a scary feeling, to be that vulnerable to a stranger. I decided to tell her I was in love with her. Then I figured that the move had made me feel insecure. She was there and so much more beautiful than anybody I had ever seen. No that's not what I should tell her I thought. I finally decided that I didn't know what to say. Then the knock on my door when I opened the door, she looked better than yesterday … I said, "Damn" when I saw her. How could one woman make me feel so helpless? " I want to talk to you" came out of my mouth without me saying it. She gave me that out of the corner of her eye look that women do when they are sure that you have lost your mind. She said, "what, OK I'm hungry so don't take long''. "I love you" appeared on the sound waves it was my voice but I don't know who said it. She said "I love you too now let's go eat." " I said, " I'm serious." She said laughingly "so am I, I'm hungry as hell. I said "I love you really,". She looked me right in the eye and said "I said I love you too what more is it to say?" "I'm hungry I guess" I said with a silly grin on my face.

At breakfast we talked about her two children, her failed marriages and her quest to find herself. She told me everything about herself and I did the same. I didn't tell her about the computer download of another man's memories though. About an hour and a half into our breakfast I got a call from my Aunt Amy. She asked if she could come see me the next day and get started on mom's exhibit. I said fine, we could talk about it over lunch, she agreed and we set a time. Hope and I spent the rest of the day sightseeing.

She showed me the whole city from Turner Field to the church she attended; we stayed busy. It was almost like we didn't trust ourselves at the hotel or stop to think about the fact that we were stranger. We had a lot of fun. We ate at Sylvia's soul food in downtown Atlanta, I had heard about it. The food was as good, as I heard it was, we both ate too much and had to go back to the hotel after along walk. At breakfast we had decided that Hope would spend the night at the hotel in the bedroom. I was to sleep on the couch. That arrangement was my idea because she seemed so nervous when she came to the room that morning. She had a frightened look on her face almost like she was afraid of being caught.

To say we felt like we had known each other for a long time would be an understatement. But we wanted to move slowly on the sex thing or I should say she did, I was OK with it. Her company was nice, she made me laugh, not just the kind of laughter you laugh when somebody tells a joke. The kind of laughter that comes from a soul at peace, I found everything I had ever searched for in my life in her eyes.

She asked if I wanted her to have lunch with my Aunt and I the next day. I said yes it probably wouldn't take that long I told her. We talked a long time about how she should be introduced she decided that Hope Johnson would do. That next day was full of surprises. Aunt Amy didn't come alone. Mom's entire family came with her. She bought her three children, grandmother Lilly, her older sister Jenny and her children. They came to welcome me to the family. I was completely taken by surprise I didn't know what to say it was so unexpected. I had gotten used to suppressing my feelings for them. Now I had new feeling to deal with, some of them were a surprise to me. I was a little bitter that they had waited so long and that mom didn't live to see this. I understood why they had waited; that made me wonder about myself did I feel inferior to them? Hope cried with happiness for me. I put on what I thought was a good front but I had to think about all this. I had given up on ever being a part of mom's family. But now they assured me that to them anyway I was a McClelland, as much, as any of them.

Lilly Anne McClelland saying to a black man "call me grandmother" took a lot then she said that losing mom before they could straighten things out made her realize that family was the only important thing and asked me to forgive her. Then I cried; she had to mean what she said and it was difficult for the both of us I thought. She kissed me and told me she loved me, that really blew me away. I wondered if my Aunt Kwinta would have been as warm to mom? We spent the day talking about mom. We had all had missed out on so much they invited me to come visit, I said I would just as soon as I got settled. They fell in love with Hope just like I did and told me to bring her with me when I came to visit.

I have never had a better day, I knew all my past demons weren't dead, but I felt a lot better and a real connection to my family for the first time. But time would tell how close we would become. Hope and I talked about it and she told me to take it easy and let things happen. We looked at television and talked. We decided that I would go home with her to Augusta after she tied up all of her loose ends in Atlanta. We went to our rooms and went to sleep or tried to anyway. The way she looked, the way she smelled everything about her made it hard to sleep. The next morning we had room service for breakfast.

"How did you rest?" she asked. "OK'' I lied "I didn't I don't like this sleeping arrangement" she said. I laughed and said "I don't either I didn't sleep a wink." Hope looked at me with a softness in her eyes and said, "I know what we feel for each other is real. But I promised myself; well I know that it's silly. I am a thirty-two-year-old woman with two children. But I can't help it I haven't had sex in two years. We can work it out; I know you care and it's not fair to you" I suddenly became possessed again by George's spirit full of disapproval and anger. He said in my voice "Let's go to South Carolina and get married. I brought my birth certificate with me. Do you have yours?" She answered "Yeah but that's no reason to get married" I retorted completely on my own "We love each other", I looked at her sitting there and said "I know I love you want us to be together the right way forever." But the way she looked that morning I might have married her for sex alone. At that exact second George's spirit called me an asshole.

Things were happening so fast but I started to feel like I was trapped by my own desires. I felt free, responsible and happy I felt or I should say I knew all about her. So we finished getting her stuff in the moving van the movers went to Augusta we drove to South Carolina. Straight down I20, all the way to Aiken SC, I didn't have the slightest doubt that marrying her was doing the right thing. We had a simple ceremony just us, the justice of the peace, that performed the ceremony and a witness, his wife.

As crazy as it sounds I didn't know her full name until she signed the marriage license. Grace Hope Johnson "by the way what is your maiden name" I asked with a straight face. I didn't know her name but I knew she loved me more than anyone I had ever known. Maybe by knowing so little about her I wasn't bogged down in some past indiscretion. Yet I was surer of her and her love for me than anything else on earth. She looked at me and answered, "it's a long story I'm not exactly sure what it was myself." I didn't question that either, looking back I think she had worked some kind of magic on me; maybe it was that she was so right for me. It was as if she stepped out of a dream and into my arms. It was like I was under the influence of something.

Chapter 51

Well we decided to go on our two-day honeymoon in Aiken. What a place to have a honeymoon, downtown Aiken South Carolina; I think I was too anxious to finally make love to her go to Hilton Head or Myrtle Beach. We found a motel near I-20 it wasn't bad it had a pool, however, we didn't go swimming. We watched television for a short time went out and got take out food. But mostly we stayed in bed, we talked, made love and talked some more, made love again and repeated the process. She was everything I ever dreamed of as lover, woman and companion. I teased her about being over-sexed but every time we make love, it gets better and it was better than any other lover, the first time was better than anybody before. I guess she has an effect on me that nobody else has. I have never been in love before. She is different from any woman on earth, the one made exactly right for me.

As she talked about herself, I realized that I did know all about her. I was not at all surprised to find out who she is. She is George's Grace and I had loved her ever since he told me about her. As unbelievable as this whole thing is, I knew it was right. I guess love is the greatest mystical force in the universe, all my fears were vanished. I some how realized that George wanted us to be together. The word fear best describes what I feel when I meet someone that gets under my skin, although no one had ever gotten to me the way she had. I guess the only way to explain how I felt when I looked at Grace was the feeling of the loss of control. The instant after you do something and you get that "Oh shit what have I done" feeling. Wanting to change what I've done with ever fiber of my being, crying out not to change anything. The improbability of it all let me know that this whole thing was somehow spiritual or totally insane. All of this had happened to us for a reason I think. Everything can't be explained but there is a reason to life itself, maybe life just isn't always reasonable or simple. Grace said that every time something happens in her family it happens in some improbable fashion. Though the family is very successful they do things a little differently.

Grace said that her family lives by faith, but not conventional beliefs or even explainable beliefs. She went on to say that her family all believed in signs and direct contact with a loving spirit... that guild the universe. This drove her sister up the wall being that she is so modern and pragmatic. For years Boyd seldom made a move without consulting Peeler. Without exception, the advice he got from old convict would prove to be the right thing to do. Boyd would do the necessary research, get all the background information but he never went against Peeler's advice. After Peeler's death, he would go and meditate for hours out at the lake and look for a sign. That is what Peeler told him to do before he died again Boyd made very few bad decisions. Every time this process would drive Mary crazy, but she never missed a chance to go to the bank.

George then seemed to say farewell to us, we each sensed a new peace inside us, it was like his work was done. He seemed happier since we got together, he knew that we were the missing pieces that our lives needed to be complete. That restlessness that we both felt inside was gone and a new feeling of closure to his death entered our lives. He was there for me but more than just as a memory. He was gone to us as the force that held us together as struggling people though. The love Hope and I had for each other seemed to grow when I could no longer feel his presence. But for me everything brought us closer to each other. We now could talk about any subject and not fear that we were not going to understand what we might say to each other. I felt my thoughts about my wife were private. We have to find our own way to stay together. I now knew the destiny that George said awaited me. Grace and I were meant to be together. I decided to continue calling her Hope. She was Grace to Red but she is my Hope for happiness and I love her. Now that I am a member of the family I am going to call my father in-law by his real name.

Hope told me about the conflicted feelings her sister had about Red, of course I knew all about it. She went on to explain that her great grandmother (Paula's grand mother) had named Mary and her, I didn't know that. The old lady felt that a name should mean something. Mary Faith after the mother of Jesus and Faith because everyone needs faith to make it through. Grace, because we are saved by grace. Hope because you have to have hope to face tomorrow. Hope said that granny probably came up with the names because she distrusted Red so much. "Those children gonna need all the help they can get with a father like that" granny would always say. But the old woman loved and respected Elaine and was happy that Elaine was in the girl's life. But deep down the lovable old girl cared deeply about the carefree and irresponsible Red.

The next thing we did was go to meet the rest of her family or should I say our family. By this time I didn't know what to call most things or what was real and what wasn't. The trip from Aiken to Augusta is short, but I think my mind ran through every possible turn of events. By the time we got there I had thought about being shot, rejected, accepted, welcomed with open arms and put in an institution when I told them this story.

We drove down I20 pass the city of Augusta then to an exit about ten miles south. Then we took a state highway for probably five or six more miles. Then we turned onto another road, it was paved but narrow we went down it for about half a mile until we got to a gate with a guardhouse. The guard spoke politely as he opened the gate and let us in. What we saw next was the most breath-taking estate I have ever seen. The tree-lined road curved around a wooded area and exposed a lake with clear water that shinned in the sun. On the other side of the lake were three large houses each as beautiful as the other but each different in their style. The houses were spaced one at each end of the lake, the other in the middle about five hundred yards from the lake with a circular driveway in front of the houses. The smell of the spring flowers along with the beautiful colors of the dogwood trees seemed to creep into my soul. The old south seemed to come to life for a boy from the West Coast. The whole scene is like going back in time. A time when cotton was king but these blacks were no slaves.

The plantation like atmosphere belied the fact that this money came from hi-tech industries throughout the world. When I looked around, I could see that this was where George (oops Red) came from and belonged; all the time he took mowing his lawn and pruning his flowers and the pride he took in the way they looked when he finished. I could see him working long hours on all these plants happily clipping, nourishing and talking to his flowers and trees. This whole place looked more like a park or plantation set out of a movie not at all like somewhere that I would call home.

We drove up to the house. The one on the far left as you entered looking across the lake. Hope pushed button for the garage door opener. We entered the garage she was home at last I was lost inside my mind scared as hell of what might be in store for me. Where are you when I need you George I mean Red, pop whatever your name is? Help! What would the family be like would they accept me? Would I accept them? I felt like a kid you know like a cat in a room full of rocking chairs. I'm a southerner now I can say things like that. I didn't think about it but I had the advantage over these people I knew them all. Red had told me about them. I even knew what some of them looked like. None of them had a clue about me.

I couldn't think anything positive. I was trapped in those feelings of being an outsider, a half-bread, not belonging. My old bugaboos slapped me in the face harder than any time since I went with my mother to my aunt's house in South Central LA. Even then every one had been nice to me. My aunt was a racist but she loved me. It was mom she wasn't too thrilled about. I had married this sweet, kind trusting woman and I knew that there was no way that I could pass inspection.

Hope entered the kitchen and began to busily look around and moving things exactly where she wanted them to be. All the furniture was there but not quite arranged in the way that she would have decorated her home. She didn't want the plates in the cabinet that someone put them in she moved them immediately. I felt a little neglected playing second fettle to some plates. Here I was feeling like running all the way back to the farm in Washington State. Why couldn't she see or sense the way I was feeling? Then she turned to me and asked. "Are you all right?" "Yes I am fine." I answered still standing by the door with a lost look on my face holding a suitcase. "Well put the suitcase down you're home." She said trying not to laugh. "What's the matter baby." She asked like she was talking to a baby. That really ticked me off. "What do you mean, baby." Then she couldn't hold her laughter any longer I got madder for an instant but then I started to laugh too. I told her how I felt and she really started to laugh. Then she kissed me and said the whole family was going to love me as much as she does.

We spent the rest of the morning unpacking clothes and rearranging furniture. We ate lunch and to tell the truth I felt a lot better. At about three thirty we walked over the middle house. Hope held my hand as we walked I guess I might have run away if she hadn't. As we approached the back door. An aging casually dressed man whom I recognized immediately as Boyd warmly greeted us. He extended his hand greeting me with a smile, a huge hand and a firm grip. "Hi I'm Boyd Tillman."

It seemed like her entire family was there, her kids ran up and hugged their mom and pretty much ignored me the other children tired to ignore us both. Their parents of course made them greet us both The women in the family question me about everything about myself from where I was born questioned me about my parentage and so on. Rosette now in her eighties listens and seemed to approve of me at least as a first impression. Elaine through aging was still a very pretty woman; Mary through not the friendliest gave me the impression that she would wait and see maybe her little sister hadn't messed again. She wasn't convinced one way or the other but I would regret it if I hurt Hope she would see to that. The men in the family were very cordial. I enjoyed the afternoon and felt a part of the family. We had a great dinner the woman all brought something they were all great cooks even Mary. To my surprise had taken time off from work to cook something. I was warned not to eat Hope's cooking and everyone was relived to know I could cook and enjoyed cooking. The joke was that since the Wilma death Grace had taken the title of worst cook in the family. She had even taken her in abilities to new heights they didn't allow her to make coffee she might burn the water.

Naturally, there were questions about how we met and how long we had known each other I kind of ducked those but Hope didn't. That made for a little nervousness on my part and a few curious looks from Mary but not much else. Somehow, I mustered the courage to tell Hope's family the story I just told you they believed it. That's when I got the surprise of my life. The entire family then welcomed me on a whole new level. It seems that Mary of all people had a dream that she had related to Elaine. A particularly vivid dream, where someone from out west came into the family. This person would be the one that would take the business over when Boyd retired and he would lead the family business into even greater successes.

Mary dream included a few details about my private life. She asked if I had recently lost my mother and was she an artist? She then told me about my relatives in Georgia. The dream gave few other details but Boyd had also had a dream that someone that knew Red was coming. He asked me to show him the amulet that Red had given me. When they all saw it everyone stood in shocked silence. It was like the Messiah had finally arrived. Boyd told me to be at work that coming Monday. No not to take over the business but to learn and grow into the job ...he isn't ready to go anywhere just yet.

I got into the swing of things slowly I'm a very good accountant and I listened to Red when he was trying to teach me about business. But Red couldn't hold a candle to Boyd. This nearly illiterate or should I say this man that no little formal education knew his way around the world of high finance. I had sense enough to watch his every movement. Mary cooperated mostly because Ron had no interest in taking over the business. The rest of the family viewed me as the rightful heir because of the amulet. Anything Boyd believed the rest of them including Judith's family went along with, without questioning. He had made them all rich and they had faith in him and I am beginning to see why. Each month it seemed that Boyd would give me more authority and responsibility. I loved the job. I can make decisions and not worry about being questioned Boyd took all the flack.

Two years into my new way of life, Boyd had a mild stroke. He subsequently retired. The board voted me the new CEO. I can say for now is so far so good we are still in business and in fact still growing. Maybe there is something to this fate thing.

Who knows, we all might be crazy, but for sure we are happy.

THE END

ABOUT THE AUTHOR

I was born in the height of the baby boom. At a very early age my favorite actor was James Dean. I liked being a tortured outsider. Being black in the south in the fifties also shaped my thinking. My first political idol was Malcolm X. I went through the sixties getting trapped in all its vices. You might say that I was a casually of that period.

My rebirth in the early eighties I would consider to be miraculous. My involvement with twelve-step program has been the happiest time of my life. During this periods of time I have learn that there is hope and God is a reality and a necessity for most of us. I hope that my writing puts someone in touch with these facts of life.